Ageing with a Lifelong Disability

of related interest

Integrating Care for Older People
New Care for Old – A Systems Approach
Christopher Foote and Christine Stanners
Foreword by Bob Kane
ISBN 1 84310 010 X

Care Services for Later Life
Transformations and Critiques
Edited by Tony Warnes, Mike Nolan and Lorna Warren
ISBN 1 85302 852 5

Choosing Assistive Devices
A Guide for Users and Professionals
Helen Pain, Lindsay McLellan and Sally Gore
ISBN 1 85302 985 8

Quality of Life and Disability
An Approach for Community Practitioners
Ivan Brown and Roy I. Brown
Foreword by Ann Turnball and Rud Turnball
ISBN 1 84310 005 3

The Psychology of Ageing
An Introduction, 3rd Edition
Ian Stuart-Hamilton
ISBN 1 85302 771 5

Ageing with a Lifelong Disability

A Guide to Practice, Program and Policy Issues for Human Services Professionals

Christine Bigby

Foreword by Gordon Grant

Jessica Kingsley Publishers
London and New York

First published in the United Kingdom in 2004
by Jessica Kingsley Publishers Ltd
116 Pentonville Road
London N1 9JB, England
and
29 West 35th Street, 10th fl.
New York, NY 10001-2299, USA
www.jkp.com

Copyright © Christine Bigby 2004
Foreword copyright © Gordon Grant 2004

Library of Congress Cataloging in Publication Data
A CIP catalog record for this book is available from the Library of Congress

British Library Cataloguing in Publication Data
A CIP catalogue record for this book is available from the British Library

ISBN 1 84310 077 0

Printed and Bound in Great Britain by
Athenaeum Press, Gateshead, Tyne and Wear

Contents

List of Figures and Tables

Figures

Tables

Foreword

This book addresses an important and often overlooked subject, ageing with a lifelong disability. It deals with an area of major tension for policy, namely how best to plan for the lives of people whose needs and circumstances commonly fall into the interstices separating disability services and services for older citizens. It is a dilemma that has not yet been satisfactorily resolved, not least because the challenges involved have been far from adequately deconstructed. This book makes a commendable contribution in tackling this problem through introducing theoretical perspectives that may help in uniting thinking and strategic planning, and also through providing empirical evidence to illustrate ways forward that have meaning for older people with disabilities, their families and front-line professionals. The book's virtues are strengthened by the author's ability to draw upon experiences in countries at the forefront of development work and research in this field, particularly the USA, the UK and Australia, but also other European countries like the Netherlands. Christine Bigby has spent many years researching the lives of older people with intellectual disabilities and their families so she is uniquely placed to produce a volume of this kind.

A book on the subject of ageing with a lifelong disability is also very timely for reasons beyond important questions about the coordinating responsibilities of services. In developed countries people with lifelong disabilities are living much longer, and therefore able to experience the joys and tribulations of all the life cycle demands like everyone else. This therefore puts a premium on supports being available to help people to anticipate and plan to realize their hopes and dreams throughout the life span. Besides having considerable resource implications, it also suggests the importance of understanding ways in which the expertise of informal as well as formal support can be harnessed in ways that serve people's interests as they age. Experience also demonstrates that people with lifelong disabilities aspire like everyone else to be contributing members of society so that they can realize their talents, confirm their status as citizens and receive proper acknowledgements of their efforts. This book contributes evidence about how such issues can be addressed, yet it also details how social, economic and institutional barriers created by society can still impede progress. In so doing it throws down the gauntlet to all of us.

The book is organized in five sections dealing with, in turn, theoretical perspectives, physical and psychological needs for older people, social dimensions of ageing, older family carers, and finally policy directions. The first four sections are complemented by a series of vignettes about the lives of older people and their families that help to 'bring to life' the more abstract and conceptual issues introduced elsewhere. The over-arching theoretical issues serve well their intended function in bringing some synthesis to diverse literatures and experiences. Readers will therefore find *Ageing with a Lifelong Disability* engaging for the way it seeks to anchor grand theorizing with biographical and life history material about the everyday lives of individuals and their families.

A strong emphasis is placed on the role that person-centred planning (PCP) should have in supporting continuity in people's lives and as a vehicle for integrating support to enable them to age in place as far as possible. This appears to be a central commitment of policy initiatives in many countries. As the author demonstrates, whilst there are many PCP models with good descriptions of their application and how they are experienced, there is as yet little in the way of robust outcome data about their effectiveness from systematic evaluation studies. Evidence is in this way usefully dissected to help the reader to question the status of knowledge and the assumptions upon which policy and practice is based.

One of the strengths of this book is the way it has managed to synthesize diverse literatures on health and social dimensions of ageing. This will make it particularly relevant to those who are responsible for devising ways to help people to age in place, to lead a healthy and socially included life, to be a contributing member of society, to have opportunities to realize dreams, and to maintain control of important domains of their lives. In so doing it reinforces the importance of rights-based discourses and of perspectives that acknowledge the role of (personal) agency and the recognition of individual capacity in enabling people's visions to be achieved. This prompts some fundamental thinking about changes required of present-day services and how they might work better together in people's best interests.

Students of social work and social care, nursing, medicine and professions allied to medicine will find something of value and importance in this book; so too will planners and front-line professionals struggling to find useful models about how best to support people with disabilities as they age. Those who shape policy should also be influenced by what they read in these pages. Let us hope that the result is a more responsive society that values people with lifelong disabilities and makes a proper financial commitment towards helping them to lead an enriched and fulfilling life.

Gordon Grant
Professor of Cognitive Disability
School of Nursing and Midwifery
University of Sheffield
UK

Acknowledgements

This book is based on work I have undertaken over several years. I am indebted to the individuals with intellectual disabilities, their families, the staff and organizations involved in the various studies without whom it would not have been possible. I would also like to thank colleagues involved in this work, in particular, Chris Fyffe, Jeffery McCubbery, Patise Frawley and Elizabeth Ozanne.

Writing the book was made possible by six months study leave from the School of Social Work and Social Policy at LaTrobe University and the generous provision of working space and quiet support from colleagues in the School of Social Work at the University of Melbourne.

I would like to thank Professor Gordon Grant for his critical comments on the manuscript and for his work on the Foreword. Finally, the support and forbearance of my partner John and daughters Jessie and Jacquie, who have lived through this task, must be acknowledged.

PART 1

Perspectives on Ageing

Chapter 1

Successful Ageing

Continuity and Adaptation

A new phenomenon

Ageing with a lifelong disability is a relatively new phenomenon which is illustrated by the dramatic changes in life expectancy for people with intellectual disabilities from about 20 years in 1930 to 70 years in 1993 (Carter and Jancar 1983; Strauss and Eyman 1996). The current cohort of older people with lifelong disabilities is the first sizeable group to have survived into later life. Ageing throws up new opportunities and challenges not for only individuals and their families but also for the helping professions and human service systems. Research on the characteristics, needs and aspirations of older people with a lifelong disability and related policy and service developments are of recent origin. Prior to the 1980s there was little debate about this matter. In the context of ageing populations in Australia, Europe and the USA, people with a lifelong disability are one of the fastest growing but smallest groups of older people.

Responding effectively to ageing with a lifelong disability is very much uncharted territory for human services. Neither Disability nor Aged and Community Care service systems have significant experience, knowledge or expertise around the issues it presents, nor of strategies for tackling these. Evidence suggests that many older people with lifelong disabilities are not ageing successfully. They have high rates of unmet health needs, and, as an extensive UK project concluded, many potential cliffs exist for older people with disabilities to fall from. These include being 'retired' from day programs and inappropriately placed in aged care accommodation (Thompson 2002, p.24). A comprehensive policy framework for ageing with a lifelong disability does not exist in either the UK or Australia. While general policies such as Valuing People (DH 2001) in the

UK and the Victorian State Disability Plan (DHS 2002a) can be applied to older people, the translation of these to specific policies and programs is often deficient and leaves grey areas of unclaimed responsibility for service provision.

The ageing of people with a lifelong disability raises two distinct but interrelated sets of issues: those around the inevitable loss of parental support for adults living with elderly parents; and the achievement of successful ageing for all people with lifelong disabilities regardless of where their earlier years have been spent. The first set of issues revolve around the agonizing question asked by the parents who have provided lifelong care for their adult child: 'What will happen when I die?' How will the tasks fulfilled by parents be replaced? Associated issues are how best to assist elderly parents to continue care and plan with their adult child for the transition from parental care. Finally, how should middle-aged adults with lifelong disabilities be supported to prepare for the post-parental phase of their lives. The second set of issues is concerned with ensuring that ageing people with lifelong disabilities, wherever they have spent their earlier years, have opportunities to age successfully. Challenges here centre on devising and implementing policies that assemble the most appropriate array of supports to address their needs. A central question often posed is what respective roles should aged care and disability programs play in the provision of support services. The complexity of these issues is magnified by the diversity of the population of people with a lifelong disability in terms of ethnicity, culture, gender, capacity, class and their life experiences.

People with lifelong disabilities include those with a range of physical, cognitive or developmental impairment. Also included are people who acquire a brain injury in early adulthood or suffer from a chronic illness. The largest and most well researched group is people with intellectual disability. Many issues associated with ageing are similar to all groups. However working with people with cognitive limitations has particular challenges: for example, to ensure their voices are heard, wishes respected, and opportunities for choice, engagement and inclusion are maximized. These are complex challenges as, for example, choice for people with intellectual disabilities often requires both the existence of opportunity as well as effective support. The main focus of this book is people with intellectual disability although the issues presented also exemplify those encountered by other groups of people with lifelong disabilities.

Change and continuity

Ageing is a process, not an event. Ageing occurs at a different rate with diverse manifestations for each individual and is strongly connected to earlier parts of the life course. Health, lifestyle, informal and formal supports from earlier years combined with genetic dispositions all influence the processes of ageing for an individual, its challenges and accompanying opportunities or vulnerabilities. In general people with a lifelong disability age in a similar manner to the general community, but as a group they experience some unique and distinctive challenges.

The ageing process has many dimensions of change at an individual level – physical, psychological and social. These occur in a context of changes in attitudes, expectations, policies and available support systems. Adaptation to change is the overriding challenge of the ageing process for individuals, families, professional and service systems. Professionals must acquire knowledge of age-related individual and contextual changes. They will need to understand, navigate and negotiate new partnerships or different aspects of service systems than those relevant in earlier parts of the life course. New ethical dilemmas may arise, particularly in relation to health issues or death and dying.

Yet the individual ageing process is also characterized by consistency. Atchey's continuity theory suggests that 'despite significant changes in health, functioning, and social circumstances, a large proportion of older adults show considerable consistency over time in their patterns of thinking, activity profiles, living arrangements, and social relationships' (1999, p.1). This theory reinforces the significance of the earlier life experiences of people with lifelong disabilities to the ageing process. A person's quality of life and adequacy of support networks in their younger years will impact on their experience of ageing. Significant continuity with earlier years also exists from a contextual perspective. The same principles – equity, choice and self-determination, participation and inclusion, and human rights – form the foundation for supporting people with a lifelong disability to achieve an optimal quality of life irrespective of their age. Many of the same tools, such as individualized programs/funding, person-centred lifestyle planning and a family-focused approach provide the foundations for good practice. Professionals working with older people confront similar issues to those encountered in earlier parts of the life course, although situational details may differ. For example, discriminatory attitudes, inadequate resources for support, the necessity to negotiate sometimes conflicting interests of the person with a disability and their carers, identify the wishes of the person with a disability, weigh up individual choice against notions of best interest and decide when formal mechanisms for decision making are necessary. Essentially, whilst professionals require new knowledge about individual and contextual changes associated with ageing, work with older people is informed by the same values and principles of good practice that apply across all stages of the life course. Indeed all the good practice imperatives that apply to successful transition from youth to adulthood – communication, coordination, comprehensiveness, continuity and choice – are equally applicable to the transition to later life (Heslop *et al.* 2002). In this sense many professionals from the disability field already have a framework and professional tools to apply to working with older people.

Theoretical perspectives on ageing

Approaches, perspectives and models provide schema or frameworks to assist in organizing thoughts and in seeing phenomena in particular ways. Perspectives suggest ways of thinking and understanding the world, but unlike theories do not seek to provide comprehensive causal explanations of the how and why of actions and consequences. Ageing can be viewed from many different perspectives, each of which magnify and bring to the fore particular aspects. Awareness of multiple perspectives increases the chances of gaining a fuller picture of ageing, its meaning and implications for people with lifelong disabilities.

An illustration of the value of different perspectives is the idea that the ageing process can be viewed from, biological, psychological or social perspectives each emphasizing different associated changes. The biological perspective draws attention to the physical changes that occur with old age, that affect health and reduce physical functioning; the psychological perspective, changes that occur in mental functioning such as memory, learning, personality and emotional coping; and the social perspective, the changing roles and relationships experienced by older individuals both at the level of relationships with family and friends and in broader social structures such as the world of work and social organizations. Flowing from these different perspectives is a 'biopyschosocial' approach that suggests complex interactions between biological, psychological and social factors determine and modify the ageing experience (Minichiello, Browning and Aroni 1992). This approach is primarily grounded in health-related concerns and argues that the processes of health and illness can be better understood by incorporating psychological and social explanations in considering the nature, causes and treatment of disease. For example, recovery from physical illness in older people is not only dependent on biomedical factors, but is also influenced by psychosocial factors such as the nature of persons' social support and relationships.

Person in environment perspective

This book has a greater emphasis on the social rather than the biological aspects of ageing, acknowledging the tremendous impact that social processes have on the lives of people with disabilities. Very broadly the book adopts a 'person in environment approach' that recognizes the multi-layered social contexts in which people age, ranging from immediate micro worlds of family and friends, the meso level of organizations and service systems to the macro social structural aspects of the society (Hooyman and Kiyak 1999). Each level of the social context impacts directly or indirectly on the development and opportunities available to the person with a disability. Allied to this is a life course perspective that sees the pattern of an individual's life and their social support networks developing over time, with earlier parts influencing later stages. Thus, each individual's life course occurs in a particular historic time, influenced by the macro social changes of that time (Hareven 2001). The temporal and social contextual nature of the ageing process is summed up simply by Hagestad and Dannefer who suggest that 'old age is part of lifelong journey, of individual lives embedded in changing social contexts hence of complex interplay between biographic time and historic time' (2001, p.7).

The significance of historic time and changing social context is highlighted in relation to the current cohort of ageing people with intellectual disabilities. This cohort has lived through a period during which policies have shifted from a focus on segregation and institutional care to inclusion and community support. Some of this cohort have spent much of their lives in large-scale congregate living, only moving out in mid and later life as institutions have been closed. Indeed much of their earlier life and family history may have been left behind, lost in boxes or destroyed, creating particular challenges for them with tasks of life review and reminiscence. In contrast the majority of people in future cohorts born in the 1970s and beyond will have lived all their lives in family homes or smaller community settings.

The person in environment perspective draws attention to the importance of both the immediate social environment and larger social context in which people with disabilities live and age. This perspective emphasizes the interrelationship of different layers of social context, family, friends, acquaintances, communities, services, policies, attitudes, values, ideologies and structural factors associated with organization of political and social processes of society. A useful way of thinking about this perspective is Cantor and Little's (1985) ecological model of ageing that uses concentric circles to illustrate the social contextual layers in which each individual is embedded (Figure 1.1).

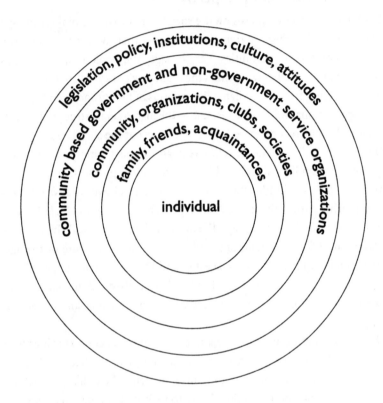

Figure 1.1 Social contextual layers in which individuals are embedded

An examination of this model and its application to people with an intellectual disability illustrates some of the unique aspects of their ageing experiences and the different factors that impact on it compared to people without disability. At the core is the person with a disability whose biological ageing process may be influenced by disability related genetic, health or physical factors. For example, some people with Down's syndrome, show premature physical signs of ageing and have much higher risk of early onset Alzheimer's disease compared to the general population (Evenhuis *et al.* 2001).

In the second layer is family who provide the bulk of support for older people. People with intellectual disability, however, often lack key family relationships that provide support in later life, including children or spouses. Their closest family are likely to be siblings, and more distant relatives and as they age they are less likely to live with family members than older people in general.

In the second layer are also friends, neighbours and acquaintances and in the next quasi formal community based organizations such as sporting clubs or community choirs. Despite the current emphasis on community inclusion, such relationships or memberships are often missing from the lives of many older people with intellectual disability who may be present in the community but seldom actively participate in community activities or organizations. Rather it is paid staff and formal services from the fourth layer of service provision that often dominate their lives.

As people with intellectual disabilities age, support from family tends to decline and formal services play a more significant role in their lives than is the case for older people in general. In the areas of accommodation, lifestyle planning and support, maintenance of relationships with family and friends and health promotion, older people with intellectual disability are particularly dependent on support from formal services. Not surprisingly, formal service provision organizations have a significant influence on their lives. Such organizations will be drawn from the different sectors of disability and ageing rather than just ageing, and contentious issues will include which sector, if any, takes responsibility and has expertise with this group. Organizational policies on issues such as 'ageing in place' or 'retirement' will have a major impact on the transitions an older person may face.

The next layer is that of policy and legislation and clearly influences will come from not only the aged care and health sectors but also those of disability and human rights. The nature of legislation will be reflective of the dominant philosophy, political ideology and cultural values. Older people with lifelong disabilities may be subjected to a double jeopardy resulting from negative stereotypical images of both the old and disabled. Changes in role expectations for older people such as that from worker to retiree may pose particular challenges for older people with intellectual disabilities, many of whom will not have participated in the workforce in their younger years. These later layers should remind professionals, however, that the cultural context of ageing might be that which is dominant in a society or one that is specific to a particular minority group within it. As the different layers are considered it is evident how the experience of people with lifelong disabilities might be different from other groups, and, why, due to their high reliance on formal supports, it is important to focus on how service systems consider and respond to people ageing with a disability.

A particular emphasis in this book is informal social networks that are made up of family, friends and acquaintance, the inner layers of Cantor and Little's model. Informal support not only provides the bulk of care for older people but is also fundamental to physical and emotional well-being and quality of life (Bigby 2002a). Because of their life experiences, as suggested above people with an intellectual disability often have quite different informal support networks from other older people. An emphasis on informal networks draws attention to the coexistence and complementarity of informal and formal sources of support, and the roles that formal support can play in nurturing, building or strengthening the informal.

Theories of successful ageing

Across cultures and history, different perspectives, theories and values have informed the outcomes sought for older people and constructed diverse notions of what constitutes successful ageing. For example, Erikson's (1973) theory of life cycle development suggests successful completion of old age involves the attainment of psychological peace and ego integrity, review and acceptance of the life course. From the perspective of Cummings and Henry (1961) successful ageing involves disengagement and withdrawal from the social life of the community. In contrast, Lawton and Nahemow (1973) propose an activity theory of ageing that emphasizes the importance of maintaining activity in later life, replacing lost roles with new ones and continuing involvement in society and interpersonal relationships. Nahemow's (1990) approach is one of ecological theory, utilizing the concept of environmental press suggesting the vulnerability of older people to the nature of their social and physical environment and the importance of ensuring that the environment is neither too demanding nor too devoid of stimulation. Laslett conceptualizes later life as two distinct life periods each with its own challenges. The Third Age, as a time when older people are still healthy and maintain functional skills, involves a refocusing of the life activities from work to avocational endeavours and friendships. The Fourth Age, in comparison, is typified by increasing infirmity, frailty and decreasing ability for self-care (Laslett 1989). The value of these theories is the focus on different aspect of the ageing process, the breadth of thinking about older people they represent and the challenge they present to professionals to consider older people from quite distinct perspectives.

Various indicators of successful ageing are identified in the literature. For example, Hawkins (1999) suggests that material security, strong family and kin networks, sociability, good health and physical functioning are consistently associated with a 'good old age'. In her view indicators of successful ageing for people with developmental disabilities include good health, perceived satisfaction and the opportunity to be a contributing member of the community. Janicki defines successful ageing for all people including those with intellectual disability as:

> an individual retaining his or her capacities to function as independently as possible into old age and promoting the belief that persons who age successfully are able to remain out of institutions, maintain their autonomy and competence in all activities of daily living, and continue to engage in productive endeavors of their own choosing. (Janicki 1994, p.146)

Some theories however make it very difficult for people with lifelong disabilities to aspire to successful ageing. For example, Jorm and his colleagues (1998) define successful ageing as the absence of disability, high cognitive skills, excellent or good self-rated health and living in the community. High levels of education, high income, non-smoking, regular exercise, and good mental health are all associated with achievement of this definition of successful ageing. It seems too that successful ageing is associated with chronological age, as 44 per cent of those in their early seventies met the criteria compared to only 6 per cent in their late eighties. Rowe and Kahn (1998) suggest that successful ageing has three main components, absence of disease and disability, high cognitive and physical capacity and active engagement with life, including both productive capacity and interpersonal relationships.

Conceptualizations of successful ageing such as those of Jorm *et al.* (1998) and Rowe and Kahn (1998) are based on outcomes measured against a set of criteria that reflect dominant norms and values. Most commonly the criteria are: good physical and mental health, cognitive efficacy, social competence and productivity, personal control and subjective life satisfaction (Baltes and Baltes 1990) which are associated with high income and high cognitive functioning. People with intellectual disability, young or old, have difficulties on many of these dimensions. This approach tends to exclude them from possibilities of successful ageing, highlighting the difficulty of judging success by generic criteria that reflect predominant social norms. This approach also fails to take into account the heterogeneity of individuals and the very different individual and social contexts from which they embark on the ageing process.

Continuities of success across the life course

Guiding principles

As suggested earlier ageing is characterized by continuity. The principles that underpin disability policies and the provision of formal support services are equally applicable to those who are older. One way to think broadly about what successful ageing means is to consider the visions that these principles encapsulate for older people with intellectual disabilities and the suggested outcomes or aspirations people may hold for themselves or others seek for them.

The 1990s saw the emergence of a new paradigm regarding policy and service provision for people with an intellectual disability, variously referred to as one of rights, community membership or inclusion (Bigby 1999a; Mansell and Ericsson 1996). Though articulated differently across jurisdictions, this paradigm represents a common thrust towards implementing policies based on the principles of equity, choice and self-determination, participation and inclusion, and human rights for people with intellectual disability. For example, Valuing People (DH 2001) in the UK is underpinned by the principles of rights, independence, choice and inclusion and the Australian Victoria State Disability Plan by the principles of equality, dignity and self-determination, diversity and non-discrimination (DHS 2002a).

These principles emphasize the personhood of people with intellectual disabilities, whereby, regardless of age, they are individual citizens who should have the same and equal rights in society as all other citizens. They should not be discriminated against because of age or disability; nor should these characteristics be used to deny them opportunities to exercise self-determination and choice or to be included in the community. Hughes (1995) suggests that one way of countering the age discrimination that is rampant in society is the additional value of celebration, which celebrates old age as a valid and noteworthy achievement. This highlights and affirms the diversity that comes with old age and its importance as part of the life course.

These principles suggest that older people with intellectual disabilities should have the opportunity to mix with people of all ages, use generally available community facilities, and be included in the broader community, groups, activities, organizations and the social milieu that is made up of people of all abilities and not be segregated on the basis of age and/or disability. However, the principles of inclusion and equity do not mean differences should be ignored and that specialist supports are not necessary; nor do they negate the legitimacy of age or disability based groups or friendships. Rather they emphasize that grouping people with similar characteristics must be based on choice and common interests rather than with respect to age or disability. They also acknowledge that because of their disability some individuals do have different needs and may require different or additional types of support to meet their needs. Hughes interprets equity and the idea of normalization as making available to older people whatever is necessary for them to live their life with same or a better quality as others in society. The comparison here is with others in society and not just other older people. This approach solves some of the difficulties of applying more narrow conventional interpretations of normalization to older people with intellectual disabilities that questions the value of trying to replicate for them the devalued status of older people in general (Wolfensberger 1985). Thus, one marker of successful ageing may be progress towards the implementation of principles of equal rights, citizenship, community inclusion, participation, dignity and self-determination for an older person with intellectual disability.

Aspirations and outcomes

The concept of quality of life is increasingly used to pinpoint outcomes sought for people with intellectual disabilities and measure quality of services. Quality of life is a multidimensional concept that seeks to identify and measure both objective aspects such as income, health status or accommodation and subjective aspects such as personal satisfaction with relationships or extent to which activities are meaningful and provide a sense of personal fulfilment. It is based on common human needs and unique individual life experiences (Schalock and Alonso 2002). The emerging consensus is that eight key life domains contribute to a person's overall quality of life. The indicators of these are relevant across all ages, although a focus on older people would perhaps emphasize some of the following aspects:

- *physical well-being:* physical health, healthcare, nutrition, exercise, mobility and the absence of pain and discomfort

- *emotional well-being:* mental health, happiness and the absence of stress and anxiety

- *interpersonal relations:* maintenance of social relationships with family, friends, acquaintances, strength and importance of ties

- *material well-being:* housing, productive meaningful activities, income

- *personal development:* maintenance and development of cognitive and adaptive functioning

- *self-determination:* identification of personal goals and aspirations, control and choice over lifestyle

- *social inclusion:* social roles, activities, acceptance in the community

- *rights:* legal rights, protection and advocacy, avenues for decision making, equal opportunities, access, safety.

Quality of life is however still a contested concept surrounded by considerable critique and debate in relation to its conceptualization and measurement. For example, Hatton (1998) critiques the validity of using measures of subjective well-being and life satisfaction as life indicators. He also discusses the potential for the scientific status sought by a quality of life approach to shift the focus from individual identities, experiences and aspirations and extend the dominance of professional frameworks and power. Michael Bach (1994) suggests a social well-being approach grounded in an ethical stance to conceptualizing quality of life. Adopting this approach, quality of life lies in presence in a person's life of a set of conditions for developing and realizing an authentic life plan based on their own narrative, and depends on the degree to which the conditions necessary to develop and realize a life plan are distributed to individuals or groups in ways that accord with principles of social justice and just distribution. This perspective shifts the focus from the individual to public policy and the ways in which society organizes and distributes the conditions for people to lead authentic lives (Bach 1994, p.147).

Nolan's work on achieving a 'sense of' security, continuity, belonging, purpose, achievement and significance aims to provide directions for care staff and inform service development across a range settings for older people and pays perhaps greater attention to the subjective and perceptual nature of what constitutes a good life for an older person (Nolan, Davies and Grant 2001). Although framed around older people and caring relationships, the senses framework reflects the principles of disability policies discussed above and encapsulates a much more person-centred approach to realizing the outcomes of these principles and what they may mean for older people with intellectual disabilities. The framework proposes work towards achievement of six senses:

- *a sense of security:* attention to physical and psychological needs, to feel safe from pain or discomfort and receive competent sensitive care

- *a sense of continuity:* recognition of the individual's biography and connection with their past

- *a sense of belonging:* opportunities to maintain or develop meaningful relationships with family and friends and to be part of a chosen community or group

- *a sense of purpose:* opportunities to engage in purposeful activity, identify and pursue goals and exercise choice

- *a sense of achievement:* opportunities to meet meaningful goals and make a recognized and valued contribution

- *a sense of significance:* to feel recognized and valued as a person of worth, that you matter as a person. (Nolan *et al.* 2001, p.175)

This approach positions outcomes in relation to the subjective views and perceptions of the individual rather than externally imposed subjective criteria and sensitizes professionals to key dimensions of importance in older person's lives.

Guides to action and charters

The principles discussed in the preceding section, the six senses and the concept of quality of life, provide not only important indicators of the directions for successful ageing and what it may look like for an individual, but also guides to action. Interventions to realize principles or improve the quality of life of an individual can occur at various levels, at the micro individual system, the meso organizational and service system level or the macro societal level of attitudes and structures. For example, achieving physical well-being will depend at the micro level on the health status of the individual in their younger years, their current lifestyle, including diet and exercise as well as genetic predispositions and access to healthcare. At the meso level it will depend on the training and skills that support staff have in nutrition, identification indicators of health problems, acting as health advocates within the medical system. At the macro level it will depend on policies that promote notions of active healthy ageing for all members of the community and funding available for both generic and specialist health services.

A much more prescriptive approach towards achieving successful ageing was adopted by the report of the UK Foundation for People with Learning Disabilities on the Growing Older with Learning Disabilities project, which proposed the following charter of rights for older people with intellectual disabilities.

The Foundation for People with Learning Disabilities calls for older people with learning disabilities to have the right to be supported to:

- ◦ develop person centered plans to meet their current and future needs.
- ◦ develop and maintain new friendships.
- ◦ maintain links with their families when they have left home.
- ◦ lead full lives with activities of their choice both during the day and also at evenings and weekends.
- ◦ have choices about where they live and with whom.
- ◦ have access to services which can adapt to their predictable age-related needs, both with respect to staffing and to their environment.
- ◦ have access to independent advocacy.
- ◦ have their physical and mental health needs met.

They should

- ◦ have access to regular health check-ups, screening (including screening for the early onset of dementia if they have Down's syndrome) and to prompt treatment if they become ill.
- ◦ have their religious, cultural and ethnic needs respected.
- ◦ be cared for in terminal illness, as far as possible in a familiar environment, in a way that respects their wishes. (Foundation for People with Learning Disabilities 2002)

Charters of this kind, whilst providing a clear set of messages and directions forward for policymakers, cannot hope to cover the diverse situations of all older people with intellectual disabilities or all the eventualities and decisions that professionals confront. A more general set of principles and processes that can be applied to any situation is also necessary.

Processes of successful ageing from diverse starting points

Baltes and Baltes suggest an approach to successful ageing that shifts from a focus on meeting specific criteria to one of process – how do people age successfully? Refocusing on processes allows individual and contextual diversity as well as choice to be incorporated (Baltes and Baltes 1990; Baltes and Carstensen 1996). The theory of 'selective optimisation with compensation' proposed by these writers is concerned with the process of adapting to ageing, the minimization of losses and maximization of gains. The focus is on the selection and achievement of individual goals in the context of losses or change, physical, social and psychological, associated with the ageing process. The theory locates the process of ageing in the context of an individual's pre-existing levels of functioning and emphasizes the relationship between notions of success and the achievement of goals that are meaningful to that individual. It suggests that successful adaptation involved three core processes: greater selection of activity and function as physical capacity reduces; compensation for loss of either skill or function by internal and external adjustments; optimization, making the most of what you have, by engaging in behaviours and activities that maximize reserves and enrich life choices. For example, an older person with reduced stamina due to a heart problem may decide not to attend a day centre all day, every day, doing a range of activities with various groups of acquaintances, but select three or four activities they find most enjoyable and organize to participate in them on specific days during the week with a group of chosen friends, in the mornings, when they tend to have most energy and feel at their best. In relation to an older parent an example would be the replacement by formal services of the out-of-home recreational tasks previously undertaken by an older parent for her middle-aged son with intellectual disability (selection with compensation) whilst she tries to spend as much time with him as possible on the evenings when he is at home (optimization).

One of the most useful aspects of this theory is its emphasis on the many ways in which change or loss associated with ageing may be compensated for, by altering individual behaviour, or adapting the external social or physical environment, by increasing opportunities, changing support offered, or introducing supportive technological mechanisms. As in the example of the older parent, increased reliance can be placed on external supports rather than solely relying on the capacity of the ageing person. It also draws attention to individual choice and the ability of an older person to focus their capacity on the pursuit of specific goals rather than, as often occurs, adopting a more global approach that reduces or limits all opportunities or activities. This approach reinforces the importance of individuality or the sense of significance of each person; that each individual has their own characteristics, needs, wishes and aspirations and it is these which should be at the fore in supporting their adaptation to changes associated with ageing. In relation to older people with intellectual disability, it highlights the importance of an individualized planning approach, whereby plans are constructed with an individual in conjunction with those who know them well. It reinforces the view that plans should reflect the individual's own aspirations, and are firmly connected to and incorporate their social context, networks and previous life experiences. It emphasizes that older as well as younger people have personal goals, and require support to explore, decide and put in place opportunities and support to realize goals. The theory can also be used to inform planning processes by a putting a focus on external as well as individual adaptations to changes that may be necessary to support individuals to realize goals.

Continuity and person-centred adaptation to change

This book adopts a simple framework to successful ageing that emphasizes continuity and a person-centred approach to adapting to changes associated with ageing. This emphasizes continuities across the life course; connections between lifestyle and experiences in younger years with experiences of ageing; the importance of continuing into later life connections between family, friends and acquaintances and familiar social contexts; and the continuing applicability of the guiding principles of equity, choice and self-determination, participation and inclusion, and human rights as the foundation for supporting older people with an intellectual disability to achieve an optimal quality of life. This approach recognizes the myriad changes that occur as people age and the impact of multiple levels of the social context on people's lives. It suggests that a central feature of successful ageing is adaptation to change that reflects individual choices and goals. This process rests on the use of individualized planning processes that firmly connect the individual in their context and relationships and assists in the identification and selection of individual goals and formulation of plans for adaptation of individual behaviour, physical and social environments and support in line with these. The approach recognizes the value and complementarity of both formal and informal sources of support, and the imperative that policies are in place which reflect the guiding principles and can accommodate the flexible adaptation of formal supports to reflect individual goals.

Plan of the book

This book explores a dual set of issues, supporting older parental carers and middle-aged adults with an intellectual disability to care, plan and prepare for the transition from parental care and ensuring people with a lifelong disability can age successfully. It aims to increase professionals' understanding of the social phenomenon of ageing and the challenges and opportunities posed by ageing for individuals with a lifelong disability and their families. This will equip professionals to act at all levels, individual, program, service or policy, to support appropriate adaptation and adjustment to age-related changes. The quality of life of older people with lifelong disabilities is particularly compromised by unhealthy lifestyles and negative stereotypical images associated with both the disabled and older people. These will only be confronted and overcome by knowledgeable professionals in the health, aged and disability sectors forming alliances and working together.

This chapter has set the scene by discussing the perspective of the person in the environment and processes of successful ageing that provide a framework for the rest of the book. The book is divided into five parts. Part 1, comprising Chapters 1 and 2, has a primary focus on theoretical perspectives. Chapter 1 provides a framework based on continuity and adaptation as the basis to consider aims and processes of successful ageing for people with a lifelong disability. Chapter 2 outlines the diverse groups of people ageing with a disability and provides a profile of the group on which the book is focused, people with an intellectual disability. The chapter considers the lack of knowledge about this group's own perspectives on ageing and highlights the negative impact that ageism and negative stereotypical views of ageing have on older people with intellectual disability. The last section discusses individualized planning as a mechanism to counter stereotypical views, ascertain aspirations, organize supports and assist each older person to achieve a sense of significance.

Chapters 3 and 4 make up Part 2 of the book and have as their focus achieving a sense of security, by understanding, responding and adapting to the physical and psychological needs of older people with intellectual disability. Chapter 3 discusses the high risk of poor health faced by older people with intellectual disability as a group and the specific issues that affect particular sub-groups. The focus then turns to strategies for health promotion and to ensure optimal healthcare. Chapter 4 considers psychological and emotional aspects of ageing for people with intellectual disability, an area about which there is little research or understanding. Grief and loss are used as examples to illustrate some of the obstacles to coping experienced by older people with intellectual disability and their high risk of mental health problems and possible supportive strategies. The chapter concludes with an overview of Alzheimer's disease and ways of adapting support as it progresses.

Part 3 includes Chapters 5, 6 and 7 and highlights the social aspects of ageing, relationships, lifestyle and a place to live. Its overarching theme is the issues to consider in supporting a sense of continuity, belonging, purpose and achievement for older people with intellectual disability. Conceptualizations of informal support networks and the importance of family, friends and acquaintances to the well-being of older people with intellectual disability form the core of Chapter 5. The chapter considers the dynamic nature of social networks as people age and strategies to support build new or maintain existing relationships. The starting point for Chapter 6 is the social expectations associated with retirement and a consideration of how older people in the general community spend their time. The debates about retirement and the types of day programs most suited to older people with intellectual disability are examined and the conclusion reached that the notion of lifestyle is more appropriate in thinking about how people make choices and organize their time. Finally processes to optimize lifestyle choices and provision of support are considered. Chapter 7 is concerned with where people live and ensuring a sense of continuity in people's lives as they age. The central concept is that of ageing in place; adapting a person's home and support to their changing needs as they age rather than having to move house to achieve a different type of support. The breadth of possible housing and support options for older people with intellectual disability with a particular focus on two subgroups: middle-aged people living with parents who have to make the transition from parental support and possibly also the family home when parents die; and ageing people living in shared, supported accommodation whose need for help with tasks of everyday living and healthcare may increase with age.

A switch to the other set of issues dealt with in the book occurs in Part 4, which is concerned with older parental carers who will be outlived by their middle-aged adult children with intellectual disability who reside with them. Chapter 8 explores the relationships between older parents and their adult children with whom they live and examines the issues they confront in regard to continuing the current situation and thinking about the future. This provides the background to Chapter 9, which is concerned with provision of additional support to older parents. This chapter considers the rationale for reaching out to offer quality support to parents. It also suggests strategies for working with older parents.

Part 5 comprises Chapter 10, which considers the type of policies required to foster successful ageing for people with lifelong disability and to develop and support the diverse range of strategies for adapting support to optimize the well-being of people ageing with a lifelong disability. The chapter includes specific examples of developmental iniatiatives applicable at a local or regional level.

Each chapter concludes with recommendations for further reading and where appropriate a guide to useful resources. Each part concludes with a set of vignettes and questions for discussion to help illustrate some of the major issues covered. The vignettes are all based on older people and their families encountered in various research projects. However, all names and identifying features have been changed and names used are pseudonyms.

The Appendix provides a background to Chapter 3 for readers without a basic knowledge of the key biological changes associated with ageing and particular health risks that affect all older people. It also draws attention to the variability of the ageing process, the significant impact of past and present lifestyle and environmental factors on health and the extent to which individual adaptations and those to the social and physical environment can compensate for or manage age-related changes.

Further reading

Ageing and Intellectual Disability: Improving Longevity and Promoting Healthy Ageing – Summative Report and other reports produced by the Special Interest Research Group on Aging and Intellectual Disability, Inclusion International in collaboration with the World Health organization. Available to download from www.iassid.org or in special issue of the *Journal of Applied Research in Intellectual Disabilities* (2001) vol. 14, no. 3, pp.171–275.

Foundation for People with Learning Disabilities (2002) *Today and Tomorrow. The Report of the Growing Older with Learning Disabilities Programme.* London: Foundation for People with Learning Disabilities. www.learningdisabilities. org.uk

Nolan, M., Davies, S. and Grant, G. (2001) 'Integrating perspectives.' In M. Nolan, S. Davies and G. Grant *Working with Older People and Their Families.* Buckingham: Open University Press.

Useful organizations

Rehabilitation and Research Training Centre on Ageing and Developmental Disabilities at the University of Illinois in Chicago. www.uic.edu/orgs/ rrtcamr/

Special Interest Research Group on Ageing and Intellectual Disability (SIRG/AID) of the International Association for the Scientific Study of Intellectual. www.iassid.org

Chapter 2

Older People
with Lifelong Disability

Strategies to Counter Age Discrimination

The populations of developed countries have aged over the last 25 years, as the proportion of older people has steadily increased, due to increased life expectancy and falling fertility rates. For example, in the UK from 1951 to 2000 those aged over 65 years increased from 16 per cent to 21 per cent of the population, and, for the first time exceeded the under 16-year-old age group (www.statistics.gov.uk). In the last decade Australia has had a 22 per cent growth rate of older people with their proportion increasing from 11 per cent in 1991 to 12.5 per cent in 2001. The post-war bulge in fertility that occurred between 1955 and 1970, known as the baby boom, means the proportion of older people will continue to increase until at least 2021, when in Australia it is projected to reach 18 per cent of the population. The oldest old, those aged 85 years and over, have been the fastest growing group of older people, increasing from 0.4 per cent of the UK population in 1951 to 1.9 per cent in 2001 (AIHW 2002a; www.statistics.gov.uk).

In keeping with general population trends in developed countries, populations of people with lifelong disabilities are also ageing. For them, however, increases in life expectancy have been more dramatic than for the general population, although in comparison their life expectancy is still reduced. For example, across the life course people with intellectual disability have a higher age specific mortality rate than the general population (Eyman and Borthwick-Duffy 1994). Nevertheless, the changes in life expectancy are significant. For example, a study of residents in a UK institution found that between 1930 and 1955 just under 10 per cent of residents survived to age 50 compared to just over 50 per cent between 1955 and 1980 (Carter and Jancar 1983). More recently, a US study of people with Down's syndrome found their average life expectancy to be 25 years in 1983 compared to 49 years in 1997, demonstrating almost a doubling of life expectancy during this period (Yang, Rasmussen and Friedman 2002).

With the exception of people with Down's syndrome and those with profound and multiple disabilities, the life expectancy of people with intellectual disability is now more similar to that of the general population. Janicki *et al.* (1999) estimate that people with a mild intellectual disability have a life expectancy of 2 per cent less than for the general population, whilst those with a moderate or severe disability experience a 7 per cent reduction in life expectancy. Their US research suggests that the life expectancy from birth for the general population is 70.1 years compared to 66.1 years for all groups with intellectual disability except those with Down's syndrome for whom it is 55.8 years (Janicki *et al.* 1999). Unlike the general population, gender differences in life expectancy for people with intellectual disability have not been widely explored.

This chapter will briefly consider the diverse groups of people with disability who are likely to be ageing with a disability, and then focus particularly on the largest group about whom most is known, people with intellectual disability. The size and characteristics of this group will be considered and a brief profile painted that provides a foundation explored further in the chapters that follow. The second part of the chapter turns to a consideration of views about ageing held both by people with intellectual disabilities themselves and service providers. It illustrates the negative impact that ageism and replication of stereotypical views of older people have on people with intellectual disability. Finally, the approach of using individualized planning and case management to focus on the individual and combat negative stereotypical views is discussed.

Diverse groups ageing with a lifelong disability

Disability may be present at birth, acquired during childhood or adulthood, or associated with the ageing process. The proportion of the population that has a disability increases significantly with age, with the largest group being those with age-associated disabilities. Australian estimates suggest that the group with early onset disability account for 4 per cent and those with disability acquired between the ages of 45 and 65 for 11 per cent of the total population with disabilities (AIHW 2000). By definition intellectual disability is associated with early onset, whilst vision and physical disabilities have high rates of onset between the ages of

45 and 65 years, and disabilities that stem from psychiatric problems, hearing and acquired brain injury are more commonly associated with onset between the ages of 18 and 44 years (AIHW 2000). People with intellectual disabilities are the largest subgroup of people ageing with a lifelong disability, and those with severe physical disability acquired during adulthood are the other sizeable group ageing with a pre-existing disability (AIHW 2000).

Dedifferentiation

A shift away from the differentiation of people with disabilities by diagnostic grouping towards policies that encompass all people with disabilities has been evident in recent years (Bigby and Ozanne 2001; Ericsson and Mansell 1996). For example, the UN *Rules on the Equalization of Opportunities for People with Disabilities* (1994), UK and Australian anti-discrimination legislation do not differentiate between type of disability. This trend has been influenced by the social model of disability that distinguishes between impairment and disability. The model directs attention towards disabling social structures and processes, emphasizing the common social oppression experienced by people with impairments (Oliver 1996). Although not without its critics, it has sought to reduce the focus on the nature of impairment and medical or functional spheres (Crow 1996; French 1993). A parallel trend that has also reduced the emphasis on diagnostic grouping has been an increased focus on the individual and their unique needs and choices. This has its origins both in the disability movement (Bradley 1996) and in the very different perspective of the economic rationalists and the restructuring of welfare states this has set in train (Baldock and Evers 1991).

The trend away from diagnostic groupings towards generic disability policies is termed dedifferentiation by Scandinavian writers (Sandvin and Soder 1996) and has the advantage of drawing attention to the collective disadvantage and discrimination experienced by people with disabilities. It also has the potential to remove stigmatizing labels. However, for policy implementation at program and service development level, recognition of differences between groups of people with disabilities, particularly those with and without cognitive impairment can be critical to identification of barriers to inclusion and provision of support that reflects and accommodates their needs. Whilst the outcomes sought for people with disabilities may not differ between groups, the support necessary to achieve these may well do so. For example, the support required to exercise choice or participation in the community for an articulate person with a mobility impairment might be quite different from that required by someone with intellectual disability and severe communication impairment. Failure to differentiate the impact of specific impairments and the disadvantages that stem from the interaction of these with social structures, at the level of policy implementation may lead to neglect and loss of expertise and commitment to meeting specific needs. For example, Felce (1996) suggests that as people with intellectual disability become just one of many groups for whom managers are responsible, recognition of the challenges presented by this group in regard to choice, decision making, communication, engagement and inclusion may be lost. Achieving equity of outcomes for people with disabilities, Rioux (1994) suggests, will not be achieved by invisibility and it may be necessary to differentiate between groups to ensure their differences are accepted and accommodated by society.

The rationale for distinguishing between people with disability on the basis of age of onset and nature of disability is the impact that living with disability, specific impairments and the life course stage of onset have on the ageing process itself, social and economic circumstances and the type of support required to achieve quality of life outcomes. Drawing these distinctions is a helpful way of organizing knowledge or thinking through issues that affect people with disabilities, but should not become an end in itself. It is both impossible and senseless to draw hard and fast lines of demarcation between groups. Grey areas will always exist, such as when age-associated disability starts and that acquired during adulthood finishes.

People with severe physical disability

Severe physical disability may be present from birth, such as cerebral palsy, and in some instances is also associated with intellectual disability, or may be acquired during child or adulthood as a result of trauma, such as spinal cord injury. This group includes people who had polio in childhood and experience post-polio syndrome in later life. Many people with severe physical disability will not have cognitive impairments but require high levels of support with self-care, mobility and activities of everyday living. Evidence suggests that people with severe physical disabilities experience changes associated with ageing at an earlier age than the general population (Balandin and Morgan 1997; M. Cooper 1998). They may also experience secondary disabilities or health complications associated with long-term changes in their physical functioning (Gething 1999). As early as their thirties and forties this group may require increased levels of personal support, health and other services to facilitate their continued ability to remain in the community and minimize the progressive impact of disability.

Other groups ageing with a disability

A small subgroup ageing with a pre-existing disability is people with neurological diseases that are acquired in mid-life and are degenerative. These include
multiple sclerosis, Parkinson's disease and Huntington's disease. Due to associated health issues and the disabling nature of these diseases, people in this group
may experience high levels of dependency at an early stage in the ageing process
and the requirement for specialized medical support may dominate provision of
services. Another small group are those with lifelong sensory disability, who have
often led very independent lives and developed an identity and culture associated
with their disability. People with acquired brain injury from traumatic accidents
form a relatively new group; that is comparatively young at this point in time, but
who are likely to form an important subgroup in the future. Other disability
groups, such as people with psychiatric disabilities or drug and alcohol problems,
also have increasing numbers who are ageing. However, they are more often
included in mental health rather than disability service systems, although there is
clearly overlap and shared interests between the two systems as between 25 per
cent and 40 per cent of people with intellectual disability also have mental health
problems (Emerson *et al.* 2001).

Unbalanced research focus on intellectual disability

The results of an extensive international literature search show quite clearly that
research, policy and service developments for older people with disabilities focus
on those with intellectual or developmental disabilities (Bigby *et al.* 2001).
Studies identified that do involve people ageing with a physical disability are primarily concerned with health and residential support needs (Balandin and
Morgan 1997; M. Cooper 1998; Gething 1999). This finding reflects the results
of a Canadian review of all literature published between 1989 and 1995 on the
topic of ageing with a pre-existing disability (Tremblay *et al.* 1997), which found
that 44 per cent focused on people with intellectual disability, 11 per cent people
with spinal cord injury, 7 per cent people with post-polio syndrome and 2 per
cent people with cerebral palsy. Absent from the literature were studies that considered other groups such as people with spina bifida, visual and hearing impairment, juvenile rheumatoid arthritis, autism or cystic fibrosis.

The unbalanced nature of the literature may be accounted for by people with
intellectual disability being the largest subgroup ageing with a lifelong disability
and other groups being even newer to survive to old age. While this book focuses
on older people with intellectual disability, many of the issues that confront them
may be illustrative of those that affect other groups.

Defining ageing and estimating numbers ageing with intellectual disability

Although ageing is a process, being an older person and old age is most commonly defined by attainment of a particular chronological age that in the past was sex differentiated as 60 years for women and 65 years for men. Differentiations are often made between the 'young old', aged 65 to 75 years, the 'old old' aged over 75 to 85 years and the 'oldest old' aged over 85 years. It has also been suggested that the term ageing should apply to the 55 to 65-year age group and aged or old to those over 65 years (Janicki *et al.* 1985).

Whatever age is used, demarcation of people into a group on the basis of one dimension alone, chronological age and use of terms such as 'the old' or 'old age' conveys strong messages of difference, and suggests that at a certain age people acquire a set of characteristics that makes them different from younger people. Inevitably, as discussed later in this chapter, stereotypical views emerge about groups who are differentiated in this way. One of the aims of this book is to demonstrate the continuity across people's lives; that 'being old' is not a fixed static state identical for all people but rather an evolving process affecting each person differently. Nor does being old necessarily change aspirations for a fulfilling life, the need for support to pursue one's dreams or the principles that should guide the provision of support.

When is a person old

One stereotypical view is that people with intellectual disability age prematurely and thus a younger definition of an older person is warranted for them. Explanations for the evolution of this view are the widely acknowledged premature ageing processes experienced by people with Down's syndrome and the use by researchers of younger definitions of an older person to ensure this group are not excluded from studies of ageing. Early research on ageing people with intellectual disability used ages as young as 40 years to define entry into old age, although more generally the age of 55 years has been used. However, a trend is emerging, particularly in the UK literature, to counter the stereotype of premature ageing and adopt in relation to people with intellectual disability the more conventional age of 60 years used for the rest of the population (Grant 2001; Hogg and Lambe 2000). An offshoot of this may be the increased recognition and exploration of middle age as a life phase for people with intellectual disability.

A more flexible approach than strict chronological age is frequently suggested by service providers to accommodate premature age-related changes, although Australian research suggests that such an approach can result in much younger people with high support needs being classified amongst those who are ageing (Bigby *et al.* 2001). Seltzer, Seltzer and Sherwood (1982) suggest that a definition of older should rest on three criteria as well as chronological ages:

- whether in the absence of illness or physical trauma a person displays greater physical disability and lessened physical resources

- whether in the absence of illness or physical trauma a person displays diminishing levels of functional skills especially in relation to self-care, personal hygiene and activities or daily living

- whether the person or familiar others see him or her as an older person and as preferring to shift to different and age-appropriate activities.

How many older people

Issues of definition result in inconsistency across studies which adds to the complexity of estimating the numbers who are ageing with an intellectual disability by hampering the comparability of data. Further complications are the dearth of accurate data on the population of people with intellectual disability, and the bias of research towards older people who are in touch with disability service systems. Although most people with more severe levels of disability are in touch with services, those with milder disabilities are less likely to be. Research that has utilized vigorous outreach and case finding strategies suggests that as many as 25 per cent of the older people with intellectual disability are unknown to disability service systems and thus not included in samples that only draw on service populations (Bigby 1995; Hand 1993; Moss, Hogg and Horne 1989).

Varying figures have been used to estimate numbers of older people with intellectual disability. The most commonly used figure in relation to the US population is 0.4 per cent, of the population aged over 55 years (Le Pore and Janicki 1997), which is similar to the figure of between 0.4 and 0.5 per cent for the UK suggested by Hogg and Moss (1993). In relation to Australia, Wen (1997) suggests a figure of 0.13 per cent of the population aged over 55 years and for New Zealand Hand (1993) suggests 1.43 per cent of the population aged over 51 years.

In the UK estimates fairly consistently suggest that older people make up about 12 per cent of the population with severe intellectual disability (DH 2001; Hogg and Lambe 2000), whilst in Australia, the proportion is generally smaller at around 6 per cent (Bigby 1999b). Thus in the UK the number of older people with intellectual disability was estimated to be 25,000 (DH 2001). In Australia, a national survey conducted in the early 1990s located 2543 people (Ashman, Suttie and Bramley 1993). Despite the variation in figures several trends are evident:

- the number and proportion of older people with intellectual disability is increasing and will continue to do so until after the baby boom generation moves into later life in 2021

- the absolute numbers of older people with intellectual disability are small and form a very small proportion of the general older population and of the population with intellectual disability

- unlike the general population there has not been a high rate growth in the 80-plus age group amongst people with intellectual disability.

These trends are illustrated by figures from the database of clients registered with an intellectual disability in Victoria. In 1982, 321 (3%) clients were aged over 60 years, the number increased to 559 (4%) in 1990 and again to 1327 (6.7%) in 2000 (Bigby *et al.* 2001). Ninety per cent of older people with intellectual disability are aged between 55 and 75 years, 50 per cent between 55 and 65 and only 7.6 per cent aged over 80 years (Ashman *et al.* 1993).

Using Australian Bureau of Statistics projections of the aged population for June 2000 and Wen's estimated prevalence of people with an intellectual disability aged 55 years at 0.13 per cent, the estimated number of people aged 55 years and over with an intellectual disability in Australia in 2000 is 5323.

Figure 2.1 summarizes these projections for Australia and Table 2.1 does so for each of the states. These figures demonstrate a steadily increasing number of older people with intellectual disability with a 68 per cent growth in numbers from 2000 to 2020. The largest rates of growth, though from a very small base number, will occur in the Northern Territory and Australian Capital Territory. They illustrate a continuing steady growth in future years as the size of aged population increases, but that despite a high rate of growth older people with an intellectual disability will remain a very small subgroup of older people.

The implications of these demographics are that the growth of older people with intellectual disability and their demands on support services are likely to be gradual and manageable rather than overwhelming. The opportunity exists for a planned approach to developing policy and adapting service systems to enable flexible responses to the changing needs of increasing numbers of older people with intellectual disability. However, the small numbers also mean the potential exists for their specific needs to be neglected amid demands of larger groups such as young adults making the transition from school. It also means that mainstream and disability services will have limited exposure to older people with intellectual disability and therefore are likely to require proactive pushing to develop expertise and support tailored to this group.

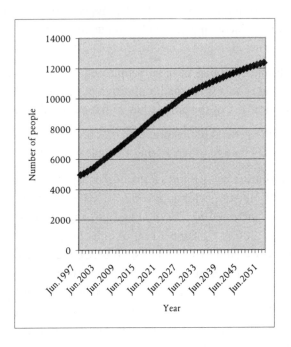

Figure 2.1 Projected number of people with intellectual disability aged 55 years and over in Australia

Population characteristics

Older people with an intellectual disability are a diverse group, in terms of ability, life history and experiences, connections with family and friends, culture, service use patterns and the individual impact of the ageing process. Attitudes towards them, the availability and nature of formal supports will vary considerably by state and country. In spite of this diversity however, some commonality and trends are evident across jurisdictions in terms of the personal characteristics, socio-economic circumstances and access to support. Drawing on key research findings these are sketched out below. The chapters that follow will further explore the meaning, significance and implications of these characteristics.

Table 2.1 Projected number of people with intellectual disability aged 55 years in each Australian state from 2000 to 2020 and percentage change for five-year periods

Year	No 2000	No 2005	% change 5 years	No 2010	% change 5 years	No 2015	% change 5 years	No 2020	% change 5 years	% change 2000–2020
South Australia	467	528	14	588	11	650	11	707	9	51
Victoria	1348	1533	14	1719	12	1910	11	2090	9	55
New South Wales	1858	2122	14	2401	13	2703	13	3008	11	62
Western Australia	472	567	20	671	18	781	16	891	14	89
Northern Territory	23	31	35	39	26	48	23	57	19	148
Australian Capital Territory	66	83	26	99	19	113	14	127	12	92
Tasmania	140	156	11	171	10	184	8	194	5	39
Australia	5323	6161	16	7046	14	7984	13	8921	12	68

Rates of ageing and life expectancy

- As a group people with intellectual disability age at a similar rate to the general population, and have a slightly reduced life span compared to the general population. There are however, some notable exceptional subgroups such as people with Down's syndrome.

  - People with intellectual disability do not age more rapidly than the rest of the population (Moss, Lambe and Hogg 1998, p.5).

  - More than half of all people with intellectual disability can expect to live as long as the general population (Hogg and Lambe 2000).

  - People with Down's syndrome and those with severe and multiple disabilities have a lower than average life expectancy (Hogg and Lambe 2000).

  - Many people with Down's syndrome experience premature ageing (Evenhuis *et al.* 2001).

  - At all ages people with intellectual disability have a higher age specific mortality rate (Evenhuis *et al.* 2001).

Health status and skills

- As a group older people with intellectual disabilities have less severe disabilities than their younger counterparts and are more skilled in relation to adaptive behaviour and functional skills (Moss 1991).

  - Older people with intellectual disability are more competent than at any other stage of their lives (Edgerton 1994).

- As a group older adults with intellectual disability have rates of aged related conditions comparable or higher than the general population (Evenuhuis *et al.* 2001).

  - Older people with intellectual disability are at risk of aged related conditions such as sensory loss, reduced mobility and increased falls and accidents (Day and Jancar 1994).

  - Older people with intellectual disability have high rates of untreated health conditions (Beange, McElduff and Baker 1995).

  - As a group older adults with intellectual disability have poorer health than their younger peers (Cooper 1997a).

- ○ Older people with intellectual disability have lower levels of epilepsy than their younger counterparts and lower levels of incontinence, until the age of 80 years (Evenhuis *et al.* 2001).

- As a group people with intellectual disability have high risk factors for ill health, particularly lifestyle related factors such as exercise and diet and socio-economic status (Rimmer 1997).

Psychological and mental health

- As a group older people with intellectual disability have high rates of psychological disturbance, largely accounted for by a high rate of Alzheimer's disease among people with Down's syndrome (Cooper 1997b).

  - ○ People with Down's syndrome have a high risk of early onset Alzheimer's disease, 30–39 years a 2.0 per cent risk, 40–49 years a 9.4 per cent risk, 50–59 years a 36.1 per cent risk and 60–69 years a 54.5 per cent risk compared to a 5 per cent risk for the general population 65 years plus (Prasher 1995).

  - ○ People with Down's syndrome have a greater overall risk of being affected by Alzheimer's type dementia, they are often affected at an earlier age, and may experience a steeper decline in functional ability and loss of skills in a shorter period (Wilkinson and Janicki 2002).

  - ○ Among individuals with intellectual disability, with the exception of people with Down's syndrome, the age of onset, symptoms and duration of Alzheimer's disease are comparable to that of the general population (Janicki and Dalton 2000).

  - ○ It is not clear whether rates of Alzheimer's disease among people with intellectual disability other than Down's syndrome are comparable to that of the general population. Janicki and Dalton (2000) report a rate of 5 to 10 per cent for those over aged over 60 years, whilst Cooper (1997c) reports a higher rate of 21.6 per cent compared to 5.7 per cent among the general population.

- Older people with intellectual disability have a continuing ability to learn (Lifshitz 1998).

Lifestyle and accommodation support

- As a group older people with intellectual disability are less likely to be employed or attend a day program than their younger counterparts (Walker, Walker and Ryan 1996).

  o Older people with intellectual disability are less likely to have opportunities for meaningful leisure activities than their younger counterparts (Walker *et al.* 1996).

  o A high proportion of older people with intellectual disability who attend day programs attend age integrated segregated specialist disability programs (Ashman *et al.* 1993).

- As a group older people with intellectual disability are much more likely to live in shared supported accommodation than in a private home with family members or friends (Emerson *et al.* 2001).

  o Older people with intellectual disabilities are likely to be relocated to mainstream aged care facilities as they age, but still be substantially younger than other residents (Bigby 2000).

  o Families and other advocates are often not satisfied with the responsiveness of mainstream aged care facilities, where the emphasis is on care rather than support. They are also often dissatisfied with the quality of care provided (Bigby 2000; Thompson and Wright 2001).

- As people with intellectual disabilities age their access to specialist disability services is likely to be reduced and restricted (Bigby 2000; Thompson and Wright 2001).

Social relationships and inclusion

- As a group older people with intellectual disabilities are less likely to have strong advocates and robust informal social networks than their younger counterparts (Bigby 2000).

  o In the post parental care phase, parental support is likely to be partially replaced by a key informal network member, but the chances of having such a key person reduces as people age (Bigby 2000).

  o Residential mobility and retirement from formal day programs characteristic of older adult's lives are likely to result in disruption of relationships and loss of contact with long term friends (Bigby 2000).

- ○ Older adults with intellectual disabilities are more likely to have acquaintances than close friends (Grant, McGrath and Ramcharan 1995).

- ○ Older adults with intellectual disability live on the margins of communities rather than being active participants (Grant *et al.* 1995).

Disadvantage and discrimination

- Older people with intellectual disabilities experience substantial discrimination on the basis of age (Walker and Walker 1998).

  - ○ Older people with intellectual disability are less likely to be resettled from institutions than their younger counterparts (Walker and Walker 1998).

  - ○ Staff have lower expectations of the potential for growth, development acquisition of skills and greater levels of independence of older people with intellectual disability compared to their younger counterparts (Walker and Walker 1998).

  - ○ Compared to younger people staff have more limited views regarding older people's needs for skill development and a meaningful lifestyle (Bigby *et al.* 2001).

  - ○ Older people with intellectual disability have fewer choices and opportunities for active programming than their younger peers (Moss and Hogg 1989).

Stereotypical attitudes and discrimination

The foregoing profile does not paint a positive picture of the potential for older adults with intellectual disabilities to have a high quality of life. It demonstrates, however, that this bleakness is not an inevitable part of ageing. Many of the more negative aspects of their lives do not stem from their inherent characteristics or the process of ageing per se but from age-related discriminatory societal attitudes and structures endemic in service systems. These result in systematically low expectations, limited opportunities and poor access to support for older people with intellectual disability (Bigby *et al.* 2001; Moss and Hogg 1989; Thompson and Wright 2001; Walker and Walker 1998). For example, research reveals:

considerable disparities between older and younger people with intellectual disabilities in the opportunities they are offered for participation in the everyday life of the community in which they live…many care workers assumed that older people led sedentary lives, went out less than younger people, had fewer friends and that therefore less effort needed to be made to develop activities and foster integration. (Walker and Walker 1998, p.37)

Such views become self-fulfilling prophecies and contrast sharply with evidence that older people with intellectual disability can adapt to community living, become more independent, learn new skills, acquire new interests and want to lead active lives.

From early research on ageing with an intellectual disability, the multiple jeopardies they confront have been identified. As members of multiple disadvantaged groups in society – 'the aged', 'the disabled', 'the poor', 'women' – they are likely to be subjected to dual, triple or even deca jeopardy of discrimination (MacDonald and Tyson 1988). Australian research as well as that conducted in the UK referred to above has illustrated the age-related discrimination experienced. For example, the Australian study of day options for older people with disabilities discussed in Chapter 6 found prevailing attitudes towards older day program participants reflected pathological and traditional views of the association between ageing and disengagement. Older participants were viewed as more likely to be 'observers rather participants'. Despite survey data completed by service providers revealing that compared to younger participants a lower proportion of those that were older had high support needs and two-thirds of the older group not having health-related support needs, providers considered that increased resources were required to take account of these same older people's higher support needs (Bigby et al. 2001). Contrary to current policies reflecting an active concept of ageing, 92 per cent of respondents considered that older participants required a more relaxed and less demanding environment.

Walker and Walker (1998) also suggest that the application of dominant negative and stereotypical views of ageing to those with intellectual disability means that the paradigm of care and dependency prevalent in the residential aged care system relevant to the 'old old' informs approaches to younger older people with intellectual disability rather than one of support and interdependence that is applicable to younger people with intellectual disabilities.

Analysis of Australian policy and service system responses to older people with intellectual disability suggests another source of disadvantage. Neither system has a clear responsibility to respond to this group, and neither has developed systematic policy or program structures to guide the responses and delivery of support. Too often older people with intellectual disability fall between the two systems, victims of each system's poor knowledge base about ageing with a disability. They are regarded as 'too old' by the disability service system that has little experience or knowledge of ageing and as 'too young' for the aged care system that is geared towards the frail aged and has little experience or knowledge of people with lifelong rather than age-associated disability (Bigby 1999b; Bigby 2002b). Possibilities of falling between service systems are heightened in the climate where in both systems demand for services outstrips supply and available resources.

The voices of people with intellectual disability

The collective voices of people with intellectual disability, their views on ageing, how they would like to be supported to lead a better quality of life, and what they regard as successful ageing are major omissions from this book and the body of research in this field. This silence makes it difficult to counter negative assumptions and means that the views of others, most predominantly service providers, policymakers and academics, dominate the agenda of successful ageing and the nature of support to achieve it.

Current principles of equity, choice and self-determination, participation and inclusion, and human rights found in both Australian and UK policy reinforce the importance of providing mechanisms for garnering the views of people with intellectual disability of all ages and ensuring greater levels of participation and control by them in development and evaluation of policy and programs. However, referring to the experiences and views of all ages of people with intellectual disability, Ramcharan and Grant suggest 'there remain large gaps between policy, action [practice] and knowledge' (2001, p.357). The legitimacy and use of qualitative and participatory research methods that involve in-depth interviewing, narrative and ethnographic approaches are slowly gaining ground and may in the future redress the silence of older people with intellectual disability about their own lives and aspirations.

The very few studies that have sought to tap the experiences of older people with intellectual disability provide insights that strongly counter prevailing views held by service providers. Edgerton's seminal ethnographic study traced life in the community from young adulthood to old age for a cohort discharged from a US institution (Edgerton 1994; Edgerton and Gaston 1991). This suggests that as people aged they become less dependent on benefactors and more competent than at any other stage of their lives but experienced major problems of access to adequate healthcare, intensified by their poor communication skills and any understanding of this by the community. The older people in this study wanted the freedom to chose what suited them, to exercise control even if this meant opting out of participation in formal programs and leading a more restricted life-style. They also wanted the right to associate with their friends however defined, whether disabled or not. This latter view is echoed in a small ethnographic study by Mahon and Mactavish (2000) which indicates that the distinction between friends with and without disability was unimportant for older people with intellectual disability. Edgerton's study also pointed to the importance of acquaintances to the identity of older people, their security, sense of belonging and being recognized in their environment.

Several studies have sought the views of older people about retirement and later life activities (Ashman, Suttie and Bramley 1995; Bigby *et al.* 2001; Hand and Reid 1989; Sutton, Sterns and Schwartz 1991) or more specifically views on ageing (Erickson, Krauss and Seltzer 1989). These point to an active conception of ageing by people with intellectual disability, where few can imagine doing nothing and many are in fact fearful of retirement and its expected implication in terms of loss of meaningful activity, social contact and friendships. Bigby's (2000) study highlighted the opportunities relished by some older people with intellectual disability who perceived later life as a period when they were free to pursue their own interests and relationships unrestricted by parental protectiveness.

A study by Todis (1992) of an older married couple with intellectual disability provides a compelling comparison between the views expressed by formal services providers and family members that the couple is well supported and that of one member of the couple who sees himself as not being supported at all. This man has led a life relatively free of formal services and resents the withdrawal of family support and contact that has coincided with formal services as well as his loss of autonomy and the degree of control by others that resulted from the use of formal services.

Although still sparse, rather more studies have sought the view of older parents and their co-resident, middle-aged adult children about their lives and service provision. These are discussed in Chapters 8 and 9, but again reinforce the disparity between service users and service providers and magnify the importance of taking the perspectives of the user into account in designing and providing support.

Countering discrimination through an individualized approach

Ageism is:

> a matrix of beliefs and attitudes which legitimates the use of age as a means of identifying a particular social group, which portrays the members of that group in negative, stereotypical terms and which consequently generates and reinforces a fear of the ageing process and a denigration of older people. (Hughes 1995, p.42)

The consequences of ageism are found in social and economic policies, and the attitudes and values of community members that shape treatment of and behaviour towards older people (Hughes 1995). As suggested earlier in this chapter, older people with intellectual disability are particularly at risk of and affected by ageism:

> If older people with intellectual disability are to have positive futures, then as an essential starting point, the implicit age discrimination that regards older people with intellectual disability as having lesser needs than younger ones should be tackled, root and branch within all service provision agencies. (Walker, Walker and Ryan 1995, p.241)

Neither age stereotypes nor chronological age should dominate the life chances of people with an intellectual disability or create arbitrary points to exclude them from active participation in life and support from specialist services. Countering ageism does not mean disregarding age but requires a more concerted focus on the individual and their needs rather than just their membership of stereotyped groups such as the 'aged' or 'disabled'.

Approaches to individualized support

A focus on tailoring services to individual needs as a prime objective in service delivery for both older people and those with a disability has evolved in the last 30 years (Baldock and Evers 1991). This has been largely driven by the shift in the balance of care from institutions to the community and has become so central that Mansell and Beadle-Brown suggest in relation to people with intellectual disability: 'there is now no serious alternative to the principle that services should be tailored to individual needs, circumstances and wants' (in press, p.6). Whilst many varieties and nomenclatures are found, the fundamental notions of case management and individual program plans have been the primary vehicles used to achieve more individualized packages of care and support. Assessment, planning, implementation, monitoring and review comprise the core components of these approaches for which an impressive array of techniques and tools have developed. Legislative requirements to formulate individualized plans either across all life areas or particular domains are found in some jurisdictions. For example, the Intellectually Disabled Persons' Services Act 1986 in Victoria requires the preparation of a General Service Plan and Individual Program Plan for clients of disability services funded by this Act. However, the emphasis has been on rights to a plan rather than implementation and access to the resources to achieve this (DHCS 1995; Mansell and Beadle-Brown in press).

Individual plans and case management potentially provide powerful mechanisms to counter negative stereotypes and ensure older people with intellectual disabilities have a sense of significance – of being recognized as an individual and a person of worth. The essence of this approach is a focus both on core needs such as health and safety, as well as an understanding of what is important to a person, and the design and delivery of services and support that reflect these.

The depth, breadth and intensity of planning and case management required to identify needs and aspirations and organize the support to achieve these varies. The strategies used must also be tailored to each individual. Challis (1999) suggests that, although variation is found in the manner in which case management is implemented in the UK, it is characterized by an undifferentiated approach that takes little cogniscene of differences in the complexity of individuals' circumstances and the depth and intensity of planning and coordination required. This is despite research among community care recipients that suggests intensive professional case management which combines planning and coordination with a supportive therapeutic role is most effective for the relatively small group with complex and changing support needs (Challis 1999). It also indicates that less intensive strategies such as key workers or service coordination can be effective for those with less complex needs.

Individualized planning can occur at many and various layers in a person's life: from a broader whole of life perspective, such as where to live, with whom, or how to spend one's time to specific life domains such as health issues; and at the micro level of daily life such as if and how support is given to participate in domestic chores and what station, if at all, the radio is on during breakfast. Linkages and interconnection between plans at various levels are fundamental however, to ensure coherence and that support provided reflects interests and capacities across all aspects of a person's life, rather than their existence being segmented into unconnected parts. For example, passion for a particular type of music should be reflected not only at home through the choice of radio station but also in leisure pursuits such as concerts or festivals. A classic example of the restrictions on lifestyle that can flow from such disconnections is given by Goodley (2000) who recounts a woman living in supported accommodation who every week is placed in a taxi to travel a short distance to a self-advocacy meeting because it has been determined that she has no sense of road safety. However when she alights from the taxi, she crosses the road, buys a litre of milk and recrosses to attend the meeting and fulfil her role as caterer for the group.

Staffing/organizational plans too, such as those used to plan 'active support' by staff, are a means of individualizing support but should also be clearly linked to the broader lifestyle plans of the individuals with whom staff are working. Thus an overarching lifestyle plan may be connected to a series of more detailed, specific plans relevant to different spheres of their lives.

Person-centred planning

One individualized approach to planning and case management, 'person-centred planning' is given a central place in the UK White Paper on services for people with intellectual disability (DH 2001). This approach is suggested as being 'essential to deliver real change to the lives of people with learning disabilities' (p.5), and to the improvement of service coordination, outcomes and better partnerships between professionals and families. Person-centred planning has been described as:

> a process of continual listening, and learning; focused on what is important to someone now, and for the future; the acting upon this in alliance with their family and friends...the person will be at the center, working in partnership with family and friends, the plan will clearly identify what the person's capacities are, what is important to her, and what support she requires; there will be actions that have a bias towards inclusion, and the learning and reflecting are ongoing. (Sanderson 2000, p.11)

> Put simply, person centered planning is a way of assisting people to work out what they want the support they require and helping them get it. (Routledge and Sanderson 2002, p.12)

The plan itself is not the outcome, but rather a vehicle for recording learning and acting on it. Once a plan is formulated the challenge is to identify how the learning can be kept alive and meaningful and used to achieve the type of life the person desires. Person-centred planning seeks to explore two fundamental questions: Who is the person? How can they and others involved in their life achieve a better life now and in the future? Answering who the person is requires their firm location within and an understanding of their history, social relationships and immediate and broader social context, as well as their capacities, interests and aspirations. The central and most important perspective is that of the person themselves which is complemented by the views of those close to them, family, friends and professionals. As suggested in the quote above, listening and learning are central to the process of working out who the person is. Answers to this question provide the basis for negotiation, problem solving and mobilizing support to achieve those things identified as important.

Various creative and specific methods of planning and tools have been developed to facilitate person-centred planning. These include, Person Futures Planning (Mount 1992), MAPS (Forest and Lusthaus 1989), and Essential Lifestyle Planning (Smull and Burke Harrison 1992). They all have a similar set of premises which Sanderson (2000) suggests are:

- the person at the centre

- family members and friends are partners in planning

- the plan reflects what is important to the person, their capacities, and what support they require

- the plan results in actions that are about life, not just services, and reflect what is possible, not just what is available

- the plan results in ongoing listening, learning and further action.

Person-centred planning is suggested as quite distinctive from previous forms of individualized planning (Holburn and Vietze 2002). By placing the person with the intellectual disability at the centre of the planning process it signifies a shift in power, with the person gaining more power and control over both the process and its outcome. Stressing partnerships with family and friends places the person firmly in the context of their social network but also emphasizes the actual and potential contributions of informal networks, and recognizes both commitments and detailed knowledge about the person held by network members. Person-centred planning reverses the traditional orientation of planning by focusing on a person's capacities, rather than their deficits. It is concerned with what they can and want to do and any support required to achieve this rather than what they can't do and how they must change in order to fit into a narrow range of potential services. The dominant perspective is one of 'wants' led by the views of the person themselves and others close to them. This contrasts to traditional models that are led by assessments by professionals of 'needs'. In a person-centred approach professionals should focus more on process and problem solving. Their role is more one of technical expert, providing advice and strategies on how to make things happen rather than as experts on the person.

For all ages, but older people in particular, an important role for professionals is to put on the agenda and ensure attention is paid to the more invisible issues such as health that underpin and mediate other aspects of life. Plans should not be just based on the type of services that are available, nor constrained by resources. They should create tensions between what is happening now and what is important that will drive change and design of support around the individual. Because of the principles on which such planning is based, actions will have a bias towards inclusion, development of relationships and the use of informal as well as formal sources of support. Finally, person-centred planning is a dynamic, ongoing process that should be characterized by continuous listening, learning and action.

Reflecting on the history of planning in the disability sector, Shaddock (2002) suggests it has shifted from planning for people with intellectual disabilities to planning with them and is now moving towards planning by people themselves. He suggests a useful metaphor for thinking about person-centred planning is that of 'owner builder', where a person is empowered by their dream of what they want to build, but without the expertise to do it on their own and requires an array of different types of supports welded together in different configurations to achieve the desired construction.

Scepticism and outcomes

The traditional association of planning with skill development combined with negative age-related stereotypes can mean little value is accorded to planning with older people (Bigby *et al.* 2001). In addition direct care workers and professionals are sometimes sceptical of possibilities of ascertaining aspirations or improving the quality of life of people with more severe disabilities. Sanderson provides a detailed example of the implementation of person-centred planning in the context of a supported accommodation service, which illustrates the value of planning and addresses possible scepticism. She recounts the reflections of a worker on the planning process:

> I thought it was crazy. I thought Kath and Dave could not even communicate...
> I thought 'what more can they do?' I have been amazed at what they can do.
> Now, it feels like we were just doing the bare necessities for existing. I was very
> wrong – they have so many interests and preferences. (Sanderson 2002, p.117)

The example documents the impact of person-centred planning on two people's lives. Prior to planning they were seen as a group. Decisions about activities were based variously on what staff thought was good, weather conditions and staff preferences. They were not involved in household activities and support was inconsistent. After a planning process, they were seen as individuals each with their own views and interests. More consistent individual support was provided. Decisions were based on what staff knew was important to each person that was recorded in their plan. They were more involved in household activities. The number of people seen regularly other than staff doubled and opportunities increased to try new activities in the community.

There are however no magic bullets and, as Emerson (2003) suggests, the field should be aware of far-reaching claims regarding the capacity of new paradigms or mechanisms to deliver so much more on quality of life outcomes than those that have gone before. The development of individualized planning and case management has occurred in tandem with significantly increased resources in the field of intellectual disability and shifts to much smaller more localized services (Mansell and Beadle-Brown in press). The relative contribution of these factors to improvements in the quality of life of people with intellectual disability over the last three decades is not clear. No large evaluative studies of person-centred planning or case management for people with intellectual disabilities have been conducted to date and, as suggested earlier, more generic studies of case management suggest it is most effective for those with high complex needs (Challis 1999; Emerson personal communication; Mansell and Beadle-Brown in press).

Both research, the views of advocacy groups and policy commentators indicate the limited success of mandated, individualized planning schemes, pinpointing problems with coverage, implementation and quality of plans (Auditor General 2000; Cummins et al. 1996; DHCS 1995; Felce et al. 1998). These issues may be related not to the tools or technologies of planning, but resource or skill constraints:

> Thus where goals have resource implications – moving from a residential home to supported living, for example – expenditure constraints may prevent their achievement. Where they are concerned with changing individual experience without major new resources – such as helping a person with severely challenging behaviour to shop more independently – skill shortages among staff may do so. Both situations are likely to lead to individualised planning becoming a paper exercise with little impact on real life. (Mansell and Beadle-Brown in press, p.11)

The efficacy of the various modes of individual planning and case management, in particular the current new paradigm of person-centred planning, is largely untested and evidence from more generic community care populations suggests problems of implementation, translating plans into actions. Effectiveness may be improved by strengthening the rights and entitlements of people with disabilities to funding or supports and shifting the focus to implementation and outcomes, evidenced by person-centred action (Mansell and Beadle-Brown in press). Perhaps closer attention should also be given to differentiating the nature of planning offered, matching complexity of needs to the breadth, depth and intensity of planning offered.

These issues should not mean that individualized planning is discounted but rather that it be regarded as one tool among many for combating ageism and tailoring supports to individual needs. Other strategies must include education and training of staff to counter stereotypical attitudes and to develop the skills necessary to engage older people in the everyday activities of life, as well as systemic changes that aim to ensure the overriding culture of both specialist disability and mainstream health and support services are person centred and regard each older person as a unique individual.

Summary

This chapter has discussed the diverse groups that are ageing with a lifelong or pre-existing disability, sketching in a more detailed profile of people with intellectual disability. A striking feature is their vulnerability to discrimination on the basis of their age, which can substantially reduce the opportunities they are afforded and restrict their lifestyle. Another feature is the absence of the perspective of people with intellectual disability themselves on issues associated with ageing from research and the literature. The chapter concludes by discussing individualized planning and case management as mechanisms to counter negative, age-related stereotypes and ensure supports are tailored to individual needs. Person-centred planning is highlighted as a central core of UK policy which has the potential to help to ensure each older person achieves a sense of significance and has their voice heard in regard to the type of lifestyle they want to lead.

Further reading

Australian Institute of Health and Welfare (2002a) *Older Australians at a Glance*, 3rd edn. Canberra: Australian Institute of Health and Welfare.

Edgerton, R. and Gaston, M. (1991) *'I've Seen It All': Lives of Older Persons with Mental Retardation in the Community.* Baltimore: Brookes.

Fact sheets on ageing with intellectual disabilities: www.thearc.org/ageing.html

Up-to-date sources of demographic data

Australian Bureau of Statistics: www.abs.gov.au

UK Office of National Statistics: www.statistics.gov.uk

Part 1

Vignettes

Elements of successful ageing

The vignettes below describe five older people with intellectual disability who have had very different lives and experiences of ageing. They provide an opportunity to highlight the diverse lives of older people and to reflect on the various ways each person could be considered to be ageing successfully. The vignettes also challenge the reader to think about how, for each older person, the principles of equity, choice and self-determination, participation and inclusion and human rights might have been better realized in the past or applied to their current situation to optimize their quality of life and increase their sense of security, continuity, belonging, purpose achievement and significance.

Catherine Deaver

Catherine is 69 years old and has lived in the hostel section of a large retirement village in a semi-rural setting for the last four years. She has her own room that is decorated with rugs she has knitted and photos of her extended family. Catherine is a slight woman, who has become quite frail following a fall several years ago when she fractured her hip. She gets around the hostel slowly with the aid of a walker. Aside from a long-term skin disorder she has no major health problems. Catherine's meals are provided and she takes care of most of her own personal needs, but needs some help with showering. A hairdresser visits regularly to do her hair and she sees a chiropodist every two months. Her meals are provided in a central dining room.

Catherine doesn't go out independently but participates in the regular trips organized by the village. In recent times she has been to the circus, a musical in the city and a restaurant. She always has some knitting on the go and splits her time between her chair in the common room, her own room where she has a television and regular craft sessions with an occupational therapist. She eats in the dining room with the same group of ladies every day, whom her niece says all 'make a fuss of her'. Her niece suggests that Catherine enjoys living at the hostel, doing her own thing and making her own decisions. She said, 'She's enjoying her independence now and she copes really well. She does things that she would never have dreamt of doing once upon a time. She's been to shows. She's very content with her situation as it is now.' Catherine's life revolves around outings, knitting, watching television and contact with members of her extended family.

Before she moved to the hostel Catherine had always lived at home with her mother in an inner city suburb. Encouraged by her sister, Catherine had spent several short respite periods in group homes during which she found she could do things on her own that she wasn't allowed to do at home, such as choosing her own clothes and vacuuming. Catherine had attended the same day centre for adults with disabilities from her early twenties until she moved to the hostel. She talked about her friend Gwen with whom she had grown up at the centre but had not seen since she left four years ago. Apart from the day centre Catherine has not had any contact with the disability service system. When she was in rehabilitation with a fractured hip, the hospital social worker was in contact with her and her family and provided advice about aged care facilities.

Her sister negotiated her move to the retirement village when she was released from rehabilitation. Catherine had visited the village prior to the decision and understood that as her mother was in hospital with a terminal illness she was not able to return home. Her sister continues to oversee her affairs and visits at least once a week. Catherine has a niece and three nephews, and at least eight grand nieces and nephews. She has most contact with her niece and her family who live close by. She has dinner with them at least once a week and they support her to attend all the frequent family functions such as birthdays, christenings and Christmas. Catherine named all the members of her extensive family who feature in the photos in her room, and talked a little about each of them.

Catherine's sister paid a refundable entry fee to the village of $70,000, out of her mother's estate. After paying a fortnightly accommodation and service fee Catherine has $50 of her pension left to buy personal items and cover other expenses. The hostel accommodates over 100 older people, most of whom are in their eighties.

Questions

1. In what ways do you consider Catherine is ageing successfully?

2. What other housing and support options might have been considered when Catherine's mother was in hospital?

3. What are the strengths and weaknesses of Catherine's informal support network?

4. To what extent does Catherine have a sense of continuity? How could this be increased?

5. What might have been possible roles for disability support services during Catherine's transition to the hostel and whilst she is resident there?

Gino Castellini

Gino is 73 years old and part of a large Italian family. He lives in the men's hostel section of a large aged care facility run by the church in the inner city. He has lived there for the past ten years. Gino has his own room, which is next door to his friend Jeff. Gino is a well-built, friendly man with good communication skills. He is generally in good health but suffers from high blood pressure, which means he gets out of breath after walking for any distance. He had a cataract operation two years ago which has significantly improved his sight. Gino has passable social skills but requires reminding about aspects of personal care and hygiene such as changing his clothes. He gets around on the public transport system and daily travels to a centre for people with disabilities. He has been at the day centre for 34 years, which has been his only contact with disability services. He participates in a range of recreational activities both the centre and at several community-based clubs for older people. His main enjoyment, however, is spending social time with his friends at the centre. He emphatically said that he did not want to retire from the centre although they have a policy of retirement at the age of 70 years.

Gino worked in the family restaurant until his parent retired, when he was 36 years old, at which time he started going to the day centre. Gino's father died 20 years ago and he continued to live with his mother. When she was in her eighties his mother was diagnosed with Alzheimer's disease. For several years Gino helped her cope at home, with the assistance of family members who dropped in regularly. During this period, thinking about his own future, Gino told his sister-in-law that he wanted to move to the hostel where his friend Jeff has moved with his mother. Gino continued to express this wish despite the offer from his brother and sister-in-law that he could live with them.

As his mother's health deteriorated Gino provided more care for her, and neglected his own until the stage where he had large ulcers on his legs that required hospitalization. Eventually, he was offered a place at the hostel and his mother went to stay with Gino's brother. She is now in a nursing home, where Gino visits her every week, although she no longer remembers who he is.

Gino's sister-in-law said the best things that had happened to Gino were finding the day centre and then his move to the hostel. She said, 'The day centre enabled him to find friends of his own outside the family and since the move to the hostel he has become much more his own person.'

Gino has two brothers and a sister, nieces, nephews and grand nieces and nephews. He is closest to his sister-in-law who since his mother's incapacity has supported him to make decisions and overseen his affairs. She has now moved to the country but he talks to her on the phone at least once a week and sees at least one of his relatives every week.

Questions

1. In what respects do you think Gino is ageing successfully?

2. How could Gino's sense of purpose be increased?

3. What could replace Gino's attendance at the day centre if he were forced to retire?

John Wheatley

John is a 60-year-old man who uses a wheel chair for mobility. At the age of five John moved to a large residential institution. Two years ago he moved out of the institution to a new group home in the community that he shares with four other residents. John likes living there, particularly being able to have a room to himself. He understands much of what goes on around him but has only a very few words to communicate his views on the world. One of his chief interests is football and he has been following the Hawthorn team for many years. He also loves to eat and is a bit overweight. John does a minimal amount of exercise following a program prepared before he left the institution.

For the last ten years John has attended an arts and drama program for people with intellectual disabilities which is based in a community college. Here he participates in drawing, cooking, watching videos and in at least two drama performances a year. Recently, the new house supervisor organized for him to 'retire' so now he only attends three days a week and is at home for other two days. On these two days a staff member is available to support him in whatever he chooses to do. So far they have gone for a walk in the local park, visited a friend, gone shopping and are investigating opportunities to go fishing.

John has limited movement in his arms and his reliance on a wheelchair makes participation in domestic chores difficult. Anyway the kitchen benches are too high to be accessible to anyone in a wheelchair. He gets around independently in an electric wheelchair and can transfer himself to and from his chair. He requires assistance with all personal care tasks but with modified plates and cutlery he can feed himself.

John knew the four other residents from the institution and is particularly friendly with one of them. He also has a friend at the day program who just recently he has begun to visit at home. The pace of the household has slowed since they first moved into the community and the search for activities in the local area has scaled down.

John's mother lives in a country town, two hours drive from the house. She visited him regularly whilst he was in the institution and has continued to be very involved in his life. However, her vision problems mean she can no longer drive and she is reliant on staying in touch by phone now. John is an only child and his father is dead.

In the two years since John moved all the staff in the house have changed. The first house supervisor created a spotless, well cared for home and mothered all the residents. She left after a year, to be followed by a series of short-term appointments. The new house supervisor has a very different approach, much more focused on building each individual's life than the state of the house. He has some very definite views about the rights of people with disabilities to retire, just like everyone else.

Questions

1. In what respects is John ageing successfully?

2. How could an optimal level of health and fitness be maintained for John?

3. How is John's sense of continuity and belonging under threat and in what ways might this be tackled?

4. Do you think John should retire? What factors might you consider in reaching this decision?

5. If he does retire, what type of lifestyle might he adopt?

6. What obstacles might be encountered to John ageing in place?

Ben Cavendish

Ben is 59 years old and for the past three years has lived in a 60-bed private supported accommodation facility, which mainly caters for older people. It is located in the outer southern suburbs, quite distant from the city and has a poor public transport service. Ben's range of skills has developed in the last few years, assisted by an outreach worker from disability services. He manages his own weekly spending allowance, shops for his own clothes and gets himself around on public transport, although he cannot read or add up money. He manages all his own personal care. He has never had the opportunity to learn domestic or household management skills. Ben spends quite a bit of time helping out in the kitchen, where he washes up and has learnt to chop many different kinds of vegetables. He gets the newspaper from the local shop for two older residents every day and sometimes goes shopping or visits his friend across the other side of the city. There is an art and craft session every day but he chooses not to go to this. Ben is in good health.

Ben has substantial private means that were left to him by an aunt and his parents, but despite this he has had a difficult time in the last few years and is very unhappy with his present lifestyle. After his parents died his brother found him a place in a private boarding house where he lived for ten years. Eventually it was closed down for failing to meet accreditation standards. Ben talked about eating the same food every day, not being allowed seconds, not being allowed to go out and having to share his clothes with other residents. During the process of closing the boarding house, Ben was allocated a caseworker from disability services. This worker found Ben his current accommodation, organized an outreach worker to help him learn how to use public transport and found him a citizen advocate. She stayed involved with Ben for three months until he was settled in the new accommodation.

Ben was befriended by the proprietor of his new accommodation, who though she has now left stays in touch with him. She feels that disability services wrote Ben off as he was over 50 and were reluctant to help him find a job. They had located various groups for him to attend but he hadn't like mixing with groups of people with disabilities. Reflecting on his current situation Ben said 'I'd like to move somewhere else close to the city or to Grantly. Here is too far away from everything. I have to get a couple of buses and a train to go anywhere. Not into another place like this if I can help it, somewhere where there are young people. They are all too old here I think for me. I'd like to be somewhere where they are my own age. Not so many old people around. When they die they get me down a bit. It's too quiet for me. I'd like to go out more often if I can. I've got a camera. I take photos every now and again. I listen to cassettes when I'm lonely.'

Ben's only relative is a brother whom he dislikes as he is always asking for money. He sees his new citizen advocate once a fortnight and they share outings. The advocate recently took Ben to look at his old family home, and they bumped into one of neighbours who remembered him. Ben has no other friends aside from the two men he sits with at mealtimes and the ex-proprietor, Jenny. He visits Jenny regularly and they sometimes go to the opera or the zoo. She says that she tried to support him and is trying to get disability services to find him a case manager so alternative living options can be explored.

Questions

1. In what respects do you think Ben is ageing successfully?

2. How could Ben's sense of belong and continuity be increased?

3. What other housing and support options might Ben have aside from shared supported accommodation with older people?

4. How might a sense of purpose and achievement be achieved for Ben?

5. Have any aspects of ageing had a substantial impact on Ben's life?

Eileen Neave

Eileen is a 63-year-old woman who loves to chat. She lives on her own in a small house in the inner city, where she has lived for the past 50 years. Her brother and his family live half an hour drive away. They were keen for her to sell up and buy a flat near them when her mother died. However, Eileen was adamant that she wanted to stay put. 'I wanted to stay in the house and look after the cats. I like this house and the area.' Since that time her interests have broadened and she has built new relationships in the community. She said, 'I used to look after Mum. I couldn't get out then like I do now to different places. I like what I'm doing now. I'm never home, only on Mondays.' Two days a week Eileen goes to a day centre for senior citizens that provides a base for outings and social activities. One morning a week she goes to an exercise class with her nextdoor neighbour who is a single woman about her age. One afternoon a week she is learning to read and write at a specialist class run by the local college. Other days she stays at home, does the housework, cooks and watches TV or listens to the radio. She said, 'I've got lots of friends, the next door neighbours, the one over the road, Jenny, she's a good friend. Hilary down the street and Mrs M. I'm lucky I've got such good neighbours. I see a lot of nice women down at the centre. It's been real good I've met nice people, nice women. I've met a couple of chaps that come with us.'

The caseworker from disability services who initially helped to plan support with Eileen only sees her rarely now. However, a support worker visits once a week to help with budgeting, paying bills and buying provisions for the week. Also a handyman from the local council comes once a month to tidy up the garden and do any household jobs that needs doing. Eileen visits her GP every six months for a check-up.

Eileen stays in touch with her brother and sisters-in-law by phone and they drop in when they are in the area. She is close to her brother, who used to come down every week and help her pay bills. Her brother says that he felt he was edged out by the worker and is concerned about Eileen's ability to manage alone, if the support services she has are withdrawn, as she really doesn't understand money. He is worried about the future. His health hasn't been good and as Eileen's other brother died last year he is the only one left.

Questions

1. In what respects is Eileen ageing successfully?

2. How could her brother's anxieties about her security be dealt with?

3. What potential obstacles to ageing in place may occur for Eileen as she gets older and how might these be resolved?

Physical and Psychological Needs

Chapter 3

Healthy Ageing

The higher age specific mortality rate and reduced life expectancy of people with more severe disabilities means that many do not survive to old age. As a group therefore older people with intellectual disabilities have less severe disabilities than their younger counterparts and have superior adaptive behaviour and functional skills (Walker *et al.* 1995, 1996). Edgerton (1994) suggests that in later life people with intellectual disabilities are more competent than at any other stage of their life. Moss (1991) speculated the 'healthy survivor' effect would operate in regard to health and that older people with intellectual disabilities would be healthier than their younger counterparts. However Cooper (1997a, 1998) demonstrated that biological changes and increased health risks associated with ageing mean that older people with intellectual disabilities have poorer health than their younger peers. Incontinence, reduced mobility, hearing impairment, arthritis, hypertension and cerebrovascular disease are all more common in older than younger people with intellectual disabilities.

People with intellectual disability experience many of the same age-related biological changes and associated health risks as older people in general. However, due to diverse factors directly or indirectly associated with their disability they generally have poorer health and experience some significant differences in health status and needs compared to older people without disabilities. The Appendix at the end of this book provides a brief overview of the biological changes associated with ageing and the major health conditions that affect all older people. For readers with limited knowledge in regard to ageing, this provides useful background for this chapter, which looks specifically at some of the particular health challenges that confront older people with an intellectual disability.

Compared to older people in the general community, older people with intellectual disabilities experience greater health-related functional decline and risk of poor health: 'The cumulative evidence suggests that older adults with intellectual disability have rates of common adult and older age related conditions that are comparable to or even higher than that of the general population' (Evenhuis *et al.* 2001, p.181). As a group older people with intellectual disability have an increased frequency of thyroid disorders, heart disorders and sensory impairments (Kapell *et al.* 1998). Older women with intellectual disability are twice as likely to report fair to poor health compared to those in the general population (Anderson 2002).

Particular subgroups of people with intellectual disability, most notably those with Down's syndrome and cerebral palsy, may experience a unique ageing trajectory and 'syndrome specific' risks. Recognition of variability and avoidance of health-related assumptions are critical however. As Adlin notes:

> In the general ageing population, there is more variability both within the individual and between individuals than among younger persons. Older individuals with developmental disabilities probably encompass an even greater heterogeneity than is found in the general ageing population. It is difficult, therefore to discuss physical ageing in persons with developmental disabilities in general terms. Every older person needs to be evaluated individually in the context of his or her unique history and special concerns. (Adlin 1993, p.51)

Nevertheless, the overriding challenge and goals of health promotion, the prevention, detection, treatment, management of health conditions and minimization of their impact on well-being are similar for all older people. These goals have been summed up as being health promotion, health surveillance and healthcare (Moss *et al.* 1998).

People with intellectual disability embark on the ageing process from very different and often quite disadvantageous starting points. Factors such as genetic make-up, lifestyle, health conditions and treatments, disadvantaged socio-economic status and the poor healthcare experienced in earlier parts of their lives singly or in combination impact detrimentally on the ageing process. In addition to these pre-existing factors the continuing impact of their disability may affect the ageing process or impede access to effective healthcare. However, as Flynn and Hollins point out: 'We must not concede the inevitability of these disadvantages. We have the means and an obligation to do better' (2002, p.216). Understanding the factors behind disadvantage can nevertheless equip professionals with the means to begin to overcome them.

Whilst recognizing that health is not just the absence of disease but rather a complex interaction of physical, mental, social and psychological elements, this chapter focuses on physical health. The first part focuses on health risks specific to older people with intellectual disabilities. It examines the reasons why they have a high risk of ill health in later life and outlines some of those high risk conditions. The latter part of the chapter considers issues of death, dying and palliative care, the impediments to optimal health and effective healthcare experienced by older people with intellectual disabilities and possible strategies for health promotion.

Disadvantageous starting points for ageing

Interrelationship of existing conditions with age-related changes

The pre-existing health conditions of some people with intellectual disability may increase their risk of or the impact of age-related diseases. For example, many people with Down's syndrome experience sensory loss in childhood. Thus for them the impact of age-related sensory change will be much higher than if no previous loss has been experienced. Long-term inactivity as a result of cerebral palsy may increase the risk of osteoporosis in women. For people with epilepsy the long-term use of medication to control seizures may also increase the risk of osteoporosis. Already chronic medical conditions may be compounded by age-related changes. For example, younger people with cerebral palsy experience high rates of bladder and swallowing problems that may be exacerbated by age-related change to muscles, the digestive and urinary systems (Noonan Walsh and Heller 2002).

Syndrome specific differences in health risks or ageing trajectories

People with specific syndromes may show a different pattern of ageing or higher risk of particular age-related diseases. The most commonly recognized are the signs of premature age-related changes and the high risk of early onset Alzheimer's disease found in people with Down's syndrome. Others are the increased risk of mitral valve prolapse and musculoskeletal disorders for people with Fragile X, and increased risks of diabetes, cardiovascular disease and obesity for those with Prader-Willi syndrome (Evenhuis *et al.* 2001). Syndrome specific differences in the ageing process are discussed further below in relation to people with Down's syndrome and cerebral palsy.

Lifestyle risk factors

The lifestyles of many people with intellectual disability are not health conscious. A high proportion lead sedentary lives, have little exercise, poor diets and are overweight or obese. For example, in the USA half of all people with intellectual disability are overweight compared to a third of the general population (Janicki *et al.* 2002; Rimmer 1997). They have higher rates of nutritional problems and higher cholesterol levels than the general population (Heller and Marks 2002). A sense of the low level of physical activity and exercise amongst adults with intellectual disability is provided by Emerson and his colleagues (1999) who found that the inactivity rates of adults with intellectual disability living in a variety of supported residential settings in the UK were equivalent to those of non-disabled people over the age of 75 years.

As a result of unhealthy lifestyles people with intellectual disability embark on the ageing process with poor levels of fitness and, like others who are overweight and sedentary, are at high risk of age-related disease such as diabetes, hypertension, heart disease, stroke, arthritis and respiratory disease.

In addition, as many as a third of all people with intellectual disability take antipsychotic medication over extended periods of time. As well as a high risk of polypharmacy, this medication has numerous side effects such as blurred vision and a dry mouth that impact on everyday quality of life. It also has longer term health risks such as constipation and urinary retention, increased risk of infection, weight gain and heart problems. For example, in a sample of 1254 people with intellectual disability in the UK residing in supported accommodation, 31 per cent were prescribed antipsychotic medication and 22 per cent were at substantial risk of polypharmacy (Emerson 2002).

On the positive side however, some aspects of their lifestyle such as low use of alcohol, low rates of smoking and not driving may reduce health risks for people with intellectual disability.

Social, economic and environmental factors associated with poor health

As well as lifestyle factors, the social circumstances of people with intellectual disabilities are not conducive to good health. They generally have poor informal support networks, low socio-economic status, low labour force participation and encounter a range of obstacles in accessing healthcare (AIHW 2002b). People with intellectual disabilities are not generally included in health promotion programs and have poor access to screening programs and accessible information about health (Heller and Marks 2002; Howells 1986; Lennnox *et al.* 2001).

The primary healthcare needs of adults with intellectual disability are not well met and their experiences of health services are 'confusing at best, hurtful at worst' (Fernando, Cresswell and Barakat 2001; Gill and Brown 2002, p.147). For example, findings from an Australian survey of General Practitioners suggest that three-quarters felt they had been inadequately trained to provide treatment for people with intellectual disability (Lennox, Diggens and Ugoni 1997). Yet GPs are the primary providers of healthcare to people with disabilities. Indicative of the difficulty of accessing effective healthcare are high rates of undiagnosed and untreated medical conditions (Beange *et al.* 1995; Wilson and Haire 1990). Even where adults live in supported accommodation that is part of the disability sector and where the potential exists for health needs to be monitored and health advocacy undertaken by staff, they are still at considerable risk of poor health and fitness levels (Emerson 2002).

Clearly adults with intellectual disability embark on the ageing process from a position of vulnerability rather than strength. Inevitably this amplifies the impact of age-related changes and increases the risk of age-related disease.

Syndrome specific ageing trajectories

Down's syndrome

People with Down's syndrome are likely to experience premature ageing with marked biological age-related changes occurring from about 40 years. Some people begin to experience degenerative changes of the spine as early as their twenties (Seltzer and Luchterhand 1994). They have a high risk of early onset Alzheimer's disease, and by age 60 just over half will have signs of the disease. For example, one US study found that 22 per cent of adults with Down's syndrome over the age of 40 years had Alzheimer's disease, rising to 56 per cent after the age of 60 years. This compares with 3 per cent and 6 per cent respectively in the general population (Janicki and Dalton 2000). Chapter 4 has a more detailed discussion of Alzheimer's disease.

The particular health conditions that affect younger people with Down's syndrome continue to have an impact in their later years. Their high level of pre-existing sensory impairment compounds the impact of later changes and in later life they have very high rates of vision and hearing loss and eye disorders. They also have a higher risk of cardiovascular problems, dermatological problems, heart disease and thyroid disorders (Evenhuis *et al.* 2001). For example, the risk of cardiovascular problems in older people with Down's syndrome is six times higher than that of the general population (Lantman de-Valk, Schupf and

Patja 2002). These include heart valve disorders that show few symptoms (Moss *et al.* 1998). They also have exceptionally high rates of periodontal disease – 96 per cent (Seltzer and Luchterhand 1994).

Women with Down's syndrome experience menopause three to five years earlier than other women (Carr and Hollins 1995). Like other women who experience early menopause, they have a higher risk of osteoporosis as a result of the cessation of oestrogen production.

Cerebral palsy

Whether due to early ageing processes or the progressive effects of disability, the physical condition of people with cerebral palsy begins to deteriorate as early as middle age. People with cerebral palsy report reduced mobility, increased pain, bowel and bladder problems from their forties (Balandin and Morgan 1997; Overeynder *et al.* 1992). The long-term effects of muscle tone abnormalities, overuse of some joints and immobility of others means they have increased risks of bone, muscle and joint related diseases such as scoliosis, spinal stenosis, arthritis. As mentioned previously, reduced muscle tone may exacerbate swallowing problems and recurrent reflex oesophagitis may increase the risks of cancer of the oesophagus. Poor long-term posture may increase the risks of respiratory disease as well as arthritis. Existing bladder and bowel dysfunction and associated incontinence or urinary tract infections are likely to be further exacerbated by age-related changes. Immobility, small body size, poor diet and prolonged use of anticonvulsant drugs all contribute to increased risk of osteoporosis and high risk of falls and fractures. All these changes impact on the functional ability of people with cerebral palsy, in particular their mobility, and many report increased reliance on wheelchairs for mobility as they age.

Whilst all older people with intellectual disability have high levels of dental and gum disease, those with cerebral palsy are particularly at risk. This is due to their poor access dental attention, difficulties experienced with brushing and often long-term use of medication associated with gum disease.

Issues of dying and access to palliative care

Decision making

Dilemmas exist across the life course in respect to decisions regarding the provision of healthcare for people with intellectual disabilities – its initiation, continuation, withholding and withdrawal. Issues arise in regard to the clarity, transparency, legality and review of decisions and decision-making processes. These include, questions of capacity and informed consent, who makes decisions for the person, when are alternative legal decision-making processes necessary, and on what basis are decisions made by others – notions of best interest or substituted judgement. Many of these issues are particularly relevant to older people in regard to whom decisions such as the withdrawal of active treatment, transition from curative to palliative care and where to die will be confronted more often as they are supported to die.

The unique circumstances of each individual should determine the nature of decisions about medical treatment and appropriate decision-making processes. However, these should be informed by general principles indicative of practices surrounding a 'good' death. Throughout their life, many decisions for people with intellectual disability are informally made by others, usually parents, without recourse to formal legal processes, informed by the principle of the least restrictive alternative (Creyke 1995). Reliance on the informal may however be more difficult for an older person whose parents have died and for whom an obvious and undisputed informal substitute decision maker may not be apparent. To ensure speedy decisions that do not disadvantage the older person by delaying appropriate treatments or actions, decision-making processes and preferences articulated by the person themselves or others close to them should be clearly documented and acknowledged by all those involved with their care. Brown, Burns and Flynn (2002) suggest that decisions about day-to-day care should be made by those carers most involved with the person and this approach documented in a care plan. Decisions that depart from normal clinical pathways or other significant end-of-life decisions, such as cessation of active treatment, should be made in a formal case conference involving those providing care and others who are close to the person. Where controversy arises, the appropriate formal legal alternative decision-making processes should be used. Such processes differ with jurisdiction; for example, in Victoria such provisions are governed by the Guardianship and Administration Act and administered through the Guardianship list of the Victorian Civil and Administrative Tribunal, which will hear urgent applications at any time. All those involved in end-of-life care should make themselves aware of alternative decision-making mechanisms, which are also avenues to challenge informal decisions that are considered not to be in the person's best interests. Situations such as the example given by Brown *et al.* (2002) where a parent who was minimally involved with her son made a decision to withhold curative treatment and excluded staff who knew the person well would not happen if both formal and informal carers were more aware of decision-making processes.

Ensuring a good death and access to palliative care

Todd suggests that for people with intellectual disability 'death and dying remain largely neglected issues, screened off from wider appreciation in a private and impenetrable zone of expression' (2002, p.226). These issues, which as well as grief have always impacted on families, are slowly being addressed by professionals in the field of intellectual disability (see Chapter 4 for further discussion around grief and loss). One such example is the formation in the UK of a National Network for the Palliative Care of People with Learning Disabilities that seeks to promote access to and share best practice in respect of palliative care.

One of the few pieces of research about death was conducted by Brown *et al.* (2002) who found that while specialist intellectual disability services were willing to accommodate death and support people to die at home, they were generally unprepared for the issues that arose. Their research suggests a number of signposts that indicate good practice:

- prompt diagnosis and provision of curative treatment when practicable and feasible

- treatment based on evidence and decisions based on informed choices or the person's 'best interest'

- appropriate transition from curative to palliative care

- access to palliative care as required

- clear decision-making procedures

- carers and family members having knowledge of and being prepared for the likely course of the illness

- death occurring at home or in a hospice where a person's social bonds can be maintained and acknowledged

- good management of physical symptoms and pain, adequate pain relief, in accordance with standard expectations where a person is unable to express their needs

- good management of psychological symptoms, disclosure of illness and impending death handled sensitively, and if necessary clarity as to by whom and when disclosure can be made to the person, assistance to prepare for death

- ability to negotiate and quickly access variation in resources to enable the person to remain in place.

McEnhill and Blackman (2002) suggest that people with intellectual disability are particularly susceptible to late diagnosis of terminal conditions such as cancer and undertreatment compared to the general population, which makes access to palliative care particularly important. Palliative care is defined as:

> the active, total care of patients at a time when the disease is no longer responsive to curative treatment and when control of pain of other symptoms and of social, psychological and spiritual problems is paramount. Palliative care affirms life and regards dying as a natural process; it neither hastens nor postpones death. It offers a support system to help the person to live as actively as possible until death and help the family to cope during the illness and in bereavement. Palliative care is multidisciplinary in its delivery and its encompasses the patient, the family, and the community in its scope. (European Association of Palliative Care, cited by McEnhill and Blackman 2002)

People with intellectual disabilities should have the same access to palliative care as other members of the community, although its provision must take particular account of their social context and communication difficulties. For example, the focus of palliative care is usually the patient and their family, but for people with intellectual disability living in supported accommodation this may have to be broadened to include paid support staff and other residents. Support staff may have little knowledge or experience of death and dying and require the opportunity for their anxieties to be shared and addressed through both education and emotional support. Major challenges for support staff are identified as supporting other residents, managing pain, supporting the person who is dying and breaking the news of illness or death to others (Read 1998). Staff are often fearful of knowing what to say, saying the wrong thing or actually finding a dead person.

Many of the challenges that arise in provision of palliative care to people with intellectual disability stem from limited communication abilities and should be informed by good practice applicable across many issues and parts of the life course. Alternative non-verbal means of communication should be used to assist a person to understand and be involved in their illness and its treatment or to express their emotions and feelings about death. Creative ways to explore feelings may include the use of drama, creation of a person's life story, drawings or photos. This may include not only support to express feelings but also to identify and fulfil final wishes. A particularly difficult issue for people with intellectual disability is identification of pain and expression of the need for pain relief. Read (1998) suggests that carers must be keen observers of non-verbal indictors of distress.

At a programmatic and service system level, partnerships such as those fostered by the UK National Network need to be formed to educate and resource both the palliative care and disability sectors about the particular issues affecting people with intellectual disability. One strategy suggested is the development of link workers from either sector with additional training who can straddle the two sectors (McEnhill and Blackman 2002).

Impediments to optimal health

Many of the impediments to optimal health for older people with intellectual disability are no different from those encountered in earlier parts of the life course, although may be compounded by age-related factors. They stem from both individual characteristics and the social context. The nature of formal supports, in particular the skills and knowledge of support or medical staff involved in individual planning and delivery of personal care, are critical. These in turn are closely allied to the nature of organizations, service systems and the socio-political context that guide their actions and development.

Identification and diagnosis

Communication problems often make the identification of ill health or pain, and in turn diagnosis, more difficult in people with intellectual disability. The difficulties of trying to communicate what is happening in one's body, the way it feels and the discomfort experienced are magnified for people with communication problems. Identification of a problem is therefore often reliant first on observation of physical or functional changes by those who know the person well, and second on further investigation being instigated and followed through.

Diagnosis may be more complex and time consuming. Even when medical practitioners are skilled in communicating with people with intellectual disability, additional time is required and heavy reliance may have to placed on second-hand descriptions of symptoms and changes. Placing these in the context a person's medical history may also be difficult. For those who live in supported accommodation, too often staff turnover or the process of deinstitutionalization means that a person's history has been lost or forgotten (Bigby et al. 2002). The interactions of age-related change with long-term conditions may mean atypical presentation of conditions which add to the difficulty of diagnosis.

People with intellectual disabilities often have little understanding of the ageing process and may have had poor experiences of medical treatment in the past. Lack of health knowledge or understanding of procedures diminish the person's confidence and can result in confusion and a lack of cooperation. These factors combined with cognitive and communication difficulties can make it dif-

ficult to administer standard tests such as those used in visual or hearing evaluations. The physical inaccessibility of equipment or examination rooms for people
with physical disabilities add to the difficulties of diagnosis.

Many people with intellectual disability are not included in screening
programs for age-related conditions such as prostate cancer or breast cancer. It is
not clear whether the reasons for this relate to their omission from databases and
therefore a failure to invite participation or whether such invitations are not seen
as relevant by them or staff supporting them. One small UK study suggested the
former may be the case (Davies and Duff 2001). The result of this may be that
conditions are not identified until they are well advanced, meaning that treatment
may be more invasive or less effective.

Treatment and adaptation

As suggested earlier the impact of health-related changes will be greater when
compounded or interrelated with pre-existing health conditions or physical and
sensory impairment. The impact may also be greater because of the reduced
adaptive capacity of people with intellectual disability. For example, difficulties
of adapting to or learning to use aids such as hearing aids, glasses or walkers may
be exacerbated in people with intellectual disability. Staff attitudes and support to
learn or persevere with such aids are critical in this respect. If staff underestimate a
person's potential for social engagement, they are unlikely to encourage the
wearing of spectacles or a hearing aid.

Socio-economic factors

People with disabilities are particularly vulnerable to poverty and the restricted
access to medical, dental and allied health services that stem from this. Limited
financial resources create obstacles to accessing healthcare from simple problems
with transport to the more complex of accessing second opinions or specialist
care. Availability of medications, alternative therapies, aids and environmental
modifications may also be beyond their financial resources.

Strategies for ensuring good health

Good health is the outcome of the complex interaction of a multiple of factors
stemming from both the individual and their environment. Clearly access to
quality healthcare is a necessary but not sufficient condition for maintaining
health into later life. Rather multiple strategies that address prevention, surveillance, treatment and adaptation are necessary. The recent emphasis on health pro-

motion has made more explicit the importance of environmental and lifestyle factors to good health. It is estimated, for example, that as much as 80 per cent of chronic illness that affects older people in the general community is related to social, environmental or behavioural factors and that 90 per cent of near fatal or fatal strokes and heart attacks are preventable (Hooyman and Kiyak 1999, p.117).

Health promotion has expanded the focus of strategies for good health to behaviour/lifstyle change, creation of healthier environments and alteration to cultural attitudes and expectations. Ensuring good health then requires an array of strategies that impact on the individual and the multiple layers of their social environment. The following sections give some examples drawn from each of these different levels.

Individual behaviour and adaptation

Supporting older people with intellectual disability to change aspects of their lifestyle and health behaviours is an important strategy. Participation in structured exercise programs, restructuring everyday life to extend the amount of physical activity and health education all have the potential to build a healthier lifestyle. Research by Tamar Heller and her colleagues has demonstrated the ability of older people with intellectual disability to participate and enjoy structured exercise programs as well as exercise choice and gain new knowledge and skills (Heller *et al.* 2000; Heller, Hsieh and Rimmer 2002). Aspects of daily life can be structured to involve more physical activity, for example, dispensing with the automatic channel changer, using stairs instead of lifts, walking to the next rather than the nearest bus stop, using a watering can instead of a hose. Simple resources such as the 'lets get active' program in Victoria have been developed to provide ideas to staff about building activity into everyday life (DHS 2001).

Education about the ageing process and expected changes are a fundamental right of people with intellectual disability and will enable them to identify symptoms earlier, understand changes and be less reliant on the observations of others.

However, older people with intellectual disability have very little general health or sex education and thus limited knowledge on which to build understanding of age specific issues. For example, work by Michelle McCarthy demonstrates clearly the absence of knowledge about menopause and its symptoms amongst women with intellectual disability (McCarthy 2002). In her research staff and family members suggested that specialist materials adapted for use with older women with intellectual disability were important in explaining and supporting older women through this change of their lives. Though staff were aware of the need to support and explain menopause to women, they cited lack of time and their own limited knowledge as creating obstacles. This work serves as an exemplar of obstacles in supporting learning about age-related issues for individuals, and the importance of supportive staff or family members who in turn have access to education, support or specialist materials.

Adequate surveillance of individual health conditions by regular participation in health screening and comprehensive health checks are essential to early detection and treatment of health conditions. For example, it is recommended that people with intellectual disability have an annual health examination (RCGP 1990). It is also recommended that, like the general population of older people, they have regular screening for age onset conditions such as breast, skin, prostate, cervical and colon cancer, diabetes, and regular hearing, dental and vision evaluations (Evenhuis *et al.* 2001). In addition, blood pressure, cholesterol and iron levels should be regularly checked. A proactive approach to such health screens by building them into a yearly calendar will help ensure regularity and reduce reliance on sometimes inefficient invitations from health providers. Policy directions in both the UK and Australia suggest the importance of formulating a health plan for every adult with intellectual disability. This should be done as part of a person-centred planning process and will help to formalize and monitor regular health screening. Older people should be a priority group for plan formulation, but like other types of plans they are worthless until resources are directed to implementation, monitoring and review.

Use of assistive devices and aids were mentioned previously as an important in helping older people adapt to age-related changes. Here too often poor use or rejection of aids such as spectacles or hearing aids is ascribed to choice rather than poor fitting or lack of support to get used to the unfamiliar. Adapting to hearing aids, for example, takes a lot of practice as they not only amplify the main sounds but background noise as well.

Adapting and modifying the immediate social and physical environment

Elements of good practice in working with people with intellectual disability are similar across all stages of the lifecycle. For example, attention to communication strategies and simple adaptations to the environment can optimize involvement and social interactions of people with intellectual disability and their ability of to engage in everyday activities. Similarly, these elements can compensate for age-related changes, particularly those of a sensory nature. The 'communication environment' can be improved to compensate for hearing and vision loss (Bagley 1997; Flax *et al.* 1997). An effective method is elimination of background noise such as that of TVs or radios which are a feature of so many supported residential environments, or setting aside quiet space away from noise. Individual communication partners can alter their behaviour by ensuring they have the person's attention before speaking, being closer to the person when speaking, facing them directly, speaking slowly and repeating or rephrasing important points. Additional lighting will assist hearing as well as vision. Lighting should be task focused, that is specific to particular activities or parts of a room rather than of a general overhead nature. Increased use of contrasting colours will highlight stairs and structural obstacles, although blue and green combinations should be avoided. Items should be organized more carefully, clutter avoided and minimal changes made to regular room layouts or furnishing to enable regular patterns of movement to be sustained. Reduction of glare by minimizing shiny or highly polished surfaces will assist with vision. Use of non-slip strips, contrasting colours on stairs, installation of handrails and avoidance of rugs will assist in mobility and avoidance of falls.

Programmatic and service initiatives

Many of the individual, social and physical changes and modifications suggested above rely on support from the family or staff with whom an older person lives or interacts during the day, and responsive service systems. There is little point, for instance, in regular health checks with a general practitioner who has few skills and little interest in working with people with intellectual disability. The roles of staff and family are also fundamental in observing and investigating physical and behavioural changes that may indicate the onset of health-related conditions. They are vital interpreters, informants and advocates for the person with an intellectual within the primary health system to ensure appropriate care is received.

Staff require support and training and families require resourcing to carry out these roles successfully. It is the role of service organizations to provide resources to enable staff and families to implement reactive individual strategies. It is also important that service systems develop initiatives to enable issues to be tackled in a more proactive programmatic manner. Disability policy is forging inclusion of people with disabilities into mainstream or generic health services. To achieve this, however, resources, training, consultation and support are necessary, which are often best achieved initially through joint initiatives with the specialist disability sector.

Specific additional resources may need to be allocated to the health system to develop expertise and provide an avenue to trial best practice in relation to older people with intellectual disabilities. This can be achieved by, for example, the appointment of a community health nurse based in a local health centre or Aged Care Assessment team to develop expertise around healthcare for older people with intellectual disability, build links and consult with other healthcare professionals and assist older people with disabilities to navigate the healthcare system and receive optimal services. Initiatives such as this could facilitate outreach or proactive strategies that seek to actively engage older people with disabilities with aspects of preventative healthcare. Another approach is the employment of clinical nurse specialists by the disability system to work directly with people with disabilities in planning their care, liaising with health services, and systematically resourcing and educating health professionals in mainstream services.

Comprehensive geriatric assessment services are variously configured in different service systems, but share a common role in providing multidisciplinary assessment and comprehensive treatment or rehabilitation plans for older people. One strategy to develop expertise in this type of mainstream service has been the establishment of specialist geriatric assessment services for older adult with developmental disabilities. For example, the Ageing and Developmental Disabilities Clinic at the Waisman Centre at the University of Wisconsin-Madison (Seltzer and Luchterhand 1994) and the ID/DD Comprehensive Adult and Geriatric Assessment Clinic affiliated with the University of Rochester School (Henderson and Davidson 2000). These services provide secondary consultation to primary healthcare providers, provide interdisciplinary training for students and health professionals, undertake research and provide direct assessment services in complex cases. Seltzer and Luchterhand (1994) suggests that mainstream professionals working in geriatric services do not feel competent in assessing older adults with developmental disabilities and specialist programs are necessary to train professionals.

Another strand of innovation has been the development of health-related educational materials designed specifically for people with intellectual disability. Many of these materials are developed in partnership with people with intellectual disability. For example the 'Books Beyond Words' series developed by Shelia Hollins and her colleagues at St George's Hospital in the UK deal with issues such as death and dying, visiting a doctor and dealing with cancer. Pavilion, also in the UK, are beginning to publish a range of accessible material on health-related issues such as a package on menopause aimed at older women with intellectual disabilities developed by Michelle McCarthy (McCarthy and Millard 2002). Such resources are a valuable resource for both individual support and more formal educational programs. Allied to this could be further development of peer education programs such as 'Paps I Should' to cover age-related issues.

In addition it is important that older people with disabilities are included in mainstream initiatives that support healthy ageing and their images included in health promotion material. Their inclusion will not only help educate people with disabilities but also send strong messages to families and staff both about health needs.

Summary

Overarching social and economic policies that respond to societal poverty and inequality, in particular in relation to healthcare and the disadvantaged position of people with disabilities, will inevitably underpin the types of health promotion strategies discussed above. Addressing the mediating factors of physical health such as inclusion, participation, robust social networks and mental health which are discussed in other chapters are also vital strategies to ensure good health. Although many people with a lifelong disability age in a similar manner to the general community as a group, they begin to age from a disadvantageous position, have high risk of poor health and experience multi-faceted obstacles to attaining effective healthcare. Greater understanding of the issues they face and multi-level support strategies will help to overcome some of these.

Further reading

Books Beyond Words Series. Jointly published by St George's Hospital Medical School and the Royal College of Psychiatrists, 17 Belgrave Square, London SW1X 8P. www.rcpsych.ac.uk/publications

Evenhuis, H., Henderson, C., Beange, H., Lennox, N. and Chicoine, B. (2001) 'Healthy ageing – adults with intellectual disabilities: Physical health issues.' *Journal of Applied Research in Intellectual Disabilities 14*, 3, 175–194.

McCarthy, M. and Millard, L. (2002) *Supporting Women with Learning Disabilities through the Menopause.* Brighton: Pavilion. www.pavpub.com

Prasher, V. and Janicki, M. (2003) *Physical Health of Adults with Intellectual Disabilities.* Oxford: Blackwell.

Chapter 4

Psychological Ageing and Emotional Well-being

Psychological aspects of ageing include age-related changes to cognitive functioning – intelligence, memory and learning ability, as well as coping with the developmental tasks and adjustment to the changes that confront an ageing person. Many of these changes are associated with loss; death of loved ones, physical or cognitive capacity, home, locality, status or social roles. Each person confronts his or her own set of psychological challenges from a unique position, determined by the life experiences, the coping resources and the external opportunities and supports available to him or her. An indication of the magnitude of psychological tasks associated with ageing is the high risk of mental health problems such as depression and anxiety experienced by all older people.

Theories of personality development suggest the various tasks that confront individuals in later life and the manner in which their personality adjusts and responds to these. The most well-known theorist is Erikson (1973) who suggests a stage theory of personality development. From this perspective the final task confronting older people is one of achieving 'ego integrity versus despair'. This involves the acceptance that one's life has had a meaning whether or not it has been 'successful' and the acceptance of one's own mortality. Strategies for achieving this include the processes of reminiscence and life review.

Jung's (1959) theory of personality suggests that changes occur in later life such as greater introspection and decreased sex-typed behaviour. Empirical research suggests that age-related changes in personality result in greater nurturance, more introversion and reduced aggressiveness. It also suggests that ageing is associated with greater difference between individuals, as people develop unique styles of interaction and become less concerned about societal expectations (Valliant and Valliant 1990).

Despite strong myths to the contrary, older people in general are not less intelligent than younger people and have a continuing ability to learn. Most do not experience significant cognitive decline unless affected by the onset of particular disease states. Most people experience a classic ageing pattern of cognitive functioning whereby overall IQ performance begins to deteriorate after the age of 60 years but major changes rarely occur until at least the mid-70s (Hooyman and Kiyak 1999). However, like physical and social changes, those relating to cognitive functioning do impact on aspects of people's lives. For example, cognitive decline may affect performance in work and leisure activities, relationships with informal network members and a person's ability to deal with stresses and the demands of their social and physical environment.

Very little is known about the psychological functioning and developmental processes of people with intellectual disability across their lifespan (Thorpe, Davison and Janicki 2001), nor about how they make sense of their world and cope with its challenges. This chapter brings together and explores various aspects of psychological ageing for people with intellectual disability, drawing on the limited research specific to this group and material extrapolated from the general population. It begins with a discussion of cognitive changes associated with ageing and then considers general psychological tasks of ageing and evidence that people with intellectual disability are particularly vulnerable to adverse outcomes. Grief and loss is used as an exemplar to illustrate the obstacles to coping experienced by people with intellectual disability and strategies to overcome these and support coping. The last part of the chapter discusses characteristics and strategies for supporting people with Alzheimer's disease, the type of dementia to which people with Down's syndrome have a particularly high risk.

Cognitive and adaptive changes in later life

The potential exists for continued improvement to the intellectual and adaptive functioning of many people with intellectual disabilities across their lifespan right up to their mid-sixties (Eyman and Widaman 1987). However, such development is clearly dependent on the social and physical environment and availability of opportunities. It is also affected by genetics. For example, people with Down's syndrome display a pattern of cognitive decline different from that of classic ageing that characterizes the general population and other people with intellectual disability. Whilst for most people abilities do not begin to decline until 65 years, those with Down's syndrome can experience decline as early as 45 to 50 years (Zigman 1994). This pattern is no doubt related to the greater risk of premature ageing and early onset Alzheimer's disease experienced by people with Down's syndrome.

Changes to memory, intellectual and learning capacity do not occur in a uniform fashion, rather decline is differential, affecting some aspects of capacity more than others. For example, in relation to IQ, people over 65 years score worse on performance scales that measure fluid intelligence, which includes things such as speed of response and may reflect non-cognitive changes such as sensory decline. In contrast scores on verbal scales that measure chrystallized intelligence, which reflects the ability to recall stored verbal information and use of abstract reasoning, remain fairly stable for people over 65 years, showing no significant decline until advanced old age or affected by diseases such as dementia.

Like some physical changes in later life, cognitive decline is most marked amongst people who do not use their abilities. It is also particularly associated with poor physical health, such as cardiovascular problem, hypertension and nutritional deficits, poor mental health, such as depression and anxiety and sensory loss.

Short-term memory is likely to be most affected by age-related changes, characterized by a reduced ability to remember unfamiliar or new material. Long-term memory may also become less efficient in terms of the ability to retrieve information.

Strategies to reduce cognitive decline or minimize its impact

Research by Lifshitz (1998; Lifshitz and Rand 1999) demonstrates not only that people with intellectual disabilities can continue to learn as they age but that the use of planned interventions can enhance their cognitive capacity. She suggests that the notion of self-actualization in later life, which sees old age as a period of renewed personal and psychological growth, is equally applicable to people with intellectual disability and their potential for change should not be written off.

Although the nature of Lifshitz's suggested 'cognitive intervention programs' are not well articulated, her research reinforces the importance of both positive attitudes by staff and families towards the potential of older people with intellectual disability and provision of continued opportunities for an active and challenging lifestyle. Clearly also the ongoing use of one's capacities is a strategy to combat decline. The relationship between physical and mental health and cognitive capacity is fundamental and strategies that optimize health will also impact positively on functional abilities.

Adaptation of teaching strategies and environmental modifications can compensate for both cognitive and sensory changes and optimize learning and functional capacity. For example, learning modes that permit a person to go at their own pace and allow longer reaction times are most suited to older people. Physical environments that, for example, exclude background noise and have optimal lighting can compensate for sensory losses and support learning. Environmental cues such as use of pictorial representations, colour and texture can compensate for memory deficits.

Psychological tasks associated with ageing

As suggested earlier little empirical data or theoretical work exists in relation to the psychological functioning of adults with intellectual disability. The focus has been on understanding and working with behavioural rather than emotional aspects of their lives; a trend that is clearly reflected in the predominance of behavioural rather than psychodynamic approaches and support to mediate signs of personal distress. Seltzer (1993) suggests that ideological forces and an emphasis on people's humanity drove the shifts towards provision of more normative life opportunities, acquisition of human rights and the minimization of stigma for people with intellectual disabilities based on assumptions that such changes would increase development and life satisfaction. Such changes were not underpinned by theoretical understanding, and there has been little focus on how people with intellectual disabilities might cope differently from others, understand or make sense of their world. As a result of this dearth Seltzer suggests much work in this area is extrapolated from research on the general population.

Seltzer (1985) conceptualizes the developmental tasks of ageing for older people with intellectual disabilities as:

- adjustment to losses
- reduced physical capacity
- restructuring of roles
- reassessment of self-concept
- interaction with societal prejudices
- acceptance of mortality.

The resolution of these tasks Seltzer suggests is mediated by individual character-istics, life experiences, social and environmental conditions. Outcomes are con-ceptualized as dichotomies of adaptive versus maladaptive behaviour, functional versus dysfunctional thought and life satisfaction versus discontentment.

Seltzer (1993) speculates that although the tasks of ageing for people with intellectual disabilities may be similar to those of the general population, the challenges may be different in terms of the timing, problem-solving capacity and the meaning of experiences. People with intellectual disability may be severely disadvantaged in terms of the availability of internal and external resources to buffer stress, adapt to change and support coping with loss. For example, their poor cognitive abilities, lack of informal social supports, low status in society and often disadvantaged and restrictive life experiences leave them poorly prepared or resourced to adapt to loss and change. The high rates of mental health problems among older people with intellectual disability are an indication of the greater impact on them of the psychological challenges of ageing and the adverse outcomes on their emotional well-being they are likely to experience.

High rates of psychiatric problems

Older people with intellectual disabilities have a higher risk of psychiatric problems than their younger peers, and older people in the general population. Their rate of problems is two to four times higher than that of other older people (Tor and Chiu 2002), and is partly due to a high incidence of dementia, particu-larly Alzheimer's disease, that accounts for approximately one-fifth of all condi-tions amongst older people with intellectual disability (Cooper 1997c).

In the UK Cooper found that 69 per cent of people with intellectual disabil-ity aged over 65 years had some form of psychiatric problem, compared to 47.9 per cent in younger age groups (Cooper 1997d). She also found that behavioural disorders persist into later life with older people having similar rates to those in younger age groups (Cooper 1998). Similarly in the USA Janicki et al. found that psychiatric conditions increase with age up to at least 70 years (Janicki, McCallion and Dalton 2000).

Although rates of psychiatric illness are higher amongst older people with intellectual disability, the overall trends replicate those found in the general aged population; that is psychiatric disorders increase with age and the most common conditions are depression and anxiety (Cooper 1997c). Also in common with the general older population only a very small proportion of psychiatric conditions are identified and actively treated.

The problems of identifying and diagnosing psychiatric conditions are similar for both older and younger people with intellectual disability. Communication problems may lead to atypical often behavioural symptoms, difficulties in conveying how the person is experiencing their world and diagnostic overshadowing may mean any symptoms are simply ascribed to the intellectual disability itself. In addition, for older people behavioural changes or other symptoms may be erroneously identified and associated with ageing; therefore not judged as warranting any further investigation (Tor and Chiu 2002).

Increased vulnerability to psychiatric problems

As suggested earlier and demonstrated in the figures above, older people with intellectual disability are particularly vulnerable to mental health problems in later life. Moss suggests this is due to two factors: negative past experiences such as separation in childhood, social stigma, neglect, abuse, limited opportunities; and their current adverse circumstances such as loneliness, lack of choice and autonomy, poor social networks (Moss 1999). The list of negatives and therefore increased biological, psychological, social and developmental risk factors likely to have impacted on the lives of people with intellectual disability is extensive and will not be laboured further here. A more extensive consideration is found in Cooper (2000) who conceptualizes the increased risks as stemming from a three-fold combination of factors: those that affect all people; those that affect people with intellectual disability; those that affect older people. Perhaps the fundamentally important point to be made, one that is repeated throughout this book, is that earlier life experiences and opportunities substantially impact on the processes and chances of successful ageing.

Dealing with grief and loss

Deaths of family and friends are perhaps the losses most commonly associated with ageing. The challenge of dealing with ensuing grief is one area of emotional coping that has begun to be explored in relation to people with intellectual disability. This area exemplifies the obstacles encountered by this group in coping with difficult emotional issues and possible supportive strategies to assist in dealing with these in later life.

Grief and the tasks of mourning

Grief is the experience of significant loss and mourning the process of adaptation to loss. The manner of a person's death, for example, whether it was sudden, the result of suicide, accident or expected after a prolonged illness and the nature of relationship with the dead person are key factors that affect grief reactions. A wide range of feelings may be experienced, including shock, disbelief, helplessness, guilt, frustration, anger, low self-esteem, anxiety, sadness, panic and confusion.

The course of uncomplicated grief is relatively predictable, with symptoms occurring within the first month and generally lasting for less than 12 months. The distress associated with grief will not normally disrupt normal day-to-day functioning. Grief however, takes time, varies in length and depends on situational factors, personal characteristics and support available. In some instances the period of grief may be prolonged and become pathological. In such cases, emotions may be overwhelming, leading to maladaptive strategies and leaving the person with long-term depression, delusional, unsettled or alienated (Botsford 2000; Deutsch 1985). Of the various models of the grief process the most well known is probably that of Kübler-Ross (1969) who suggests a number of stages: denial, anger, bargaining, depression and acceptance. Progress through stages may not be linear and shift may occur backwards and forwards between stages. Four key tasks are identified as being fundamental to mourning (Deutsch 1985):

- acknowledging the loss
- experiencing the pain of loss
- adjustment to an environment (external, internal and spiritual) without the deceased
- relocation and memorialization of the deceased.

These tasks require finding another place for the deceased, which whilst providing opportunities to remember them allows the person to reinvest some of their emotional energy in existing or new aspects of their life.

People with intellectual disability coping with grief and loss

There is little doubt that people with mild or moderate intellectual disability understand death and its essential features: universality, inevitability and irreversibility (Hollins 2000; Wadsworth and Harper 1991). An understanding of this concept increases with chronological age and is not related to developmental stage, as emotional intelligence can be more advanced than cognitive development (Lipe-Goodson and Goebel 1983). Similarly, the capacity for grief is not dependent on intellectual ability and thus people with intellectual disability experience similar emotions associated with loss to the rest of the population.

Research indicates however that while the reactions to grief for people with intellectual disability may be typical, their experiences and expression of grief are not. The onset of grief may be delayed, it may last for a prolonged period and is more likely to become 'pathological'. The strong emotions associated with grief are more likely to be expressed through behaviour rather than verbal communication (Bonnell-Pascual *et al.* 1999; Hollins 2000). For example, Bonell-Pascual *et al.* state: 'the response to bereavement by adults with learning disabilities is similar in type, though not in expression, to that of the general population. Learning disability is a significant predictor of mental health problems following bereavement' (1999, p.348).

Studies by Hollins and her colleagues have found that following the death of a parent adults with intellectual disability showed significantly increased aberrant behaviour and increased psychopathology. For many their symptoms lasted well over 12 months and could be classified as prolonged depressive reactions, mixed anxiety and depressive reactions, predominant disturbance of conduct or mixed disturbance of conduct and emotions (Bonnell-Pascual *et al.* 1999; Hollins and Esterhuyzen 1997). A very early study by Emerson (1977) found a clear association between perceived difficult behaviour and death of loved ones, in that half the adults referred for behavioural problems had experienced a significant loss in their recent past. Clearly each individual will differ in their expression of grief, but common behaviour may include prolonged searching, withdrawal, sleep disturbance, loss of appetite, inability to concentrate and aggression.

The communication problems experienced by many people with intellectual disability that make the expression of emotions difficult means the process of mourning and expression of grief are more challenging. They may be unable to verbalize and therefore share or understand their feelings. Both limited experiences and cognitive ability mean that some people may find it more difficult to adapt to changes in relationships. In addition, death of a close family member may result on catastrophic life changes and many losses that compound and magnify the tasks involved. For example, for some adults who have lived at home with parents all their lives, the death of a their last surviving parent can also mean a sudden residential move and involve the loss of their home, familiar routines, locality and social network.

Attitudes of support staff and family members

One of the most challenging problems that may be encountered by adults with intellectual disability in dealing with grief is however the attitudes of support staff and family members – their lack of acknowledgement, support and understanding of the grief process. Their inadequate knowledge can lead to the exclusion of people with intellectual disability from the rituals of death and mourning and misinterpretation of grief-related psychological distress or behaviour (Botsford 2000; Hollins 1995; Hollins and Esterhuyzen 1997; Read 2001). Ignorance, fear and misplaced hope of shielding from stress may also account for the failure to clearly inform people with intellectual disability about serious illness or death of a loved one and the use of euphemisms for death that are incomprehensible and confusing. Oswin captures the issue well, suggesting that the emotions and grief of people with intellectual disability may be caught up in the double taboo of death and intellectual disability and lost in a 'muddle of misconceptions' (1990, p.6).

Misconceptions by others include belief that people with intellectual disability do not understand the concept of death; that they are incapable of forming attachments and so do not experience grief; that their poor memory and sense of time means they will forget about people if they don't see them; a sense that by not including or informing them they will somehow be protected from distress and grief; and the assumption that changes in behaviour are due to intellectual disability itself or personality (Deutsch 1985; Hollins 2000; Kennedy 1989; McDaniel 1989).

In their study of adults who had lost a parent, Hollins and her colleagues found a significant lack of understanding by staff of the bereavement process or its impact, and a failure by both staff and other carers to attribute increased behaviour problems to grief (Hollins and Esterhuyzen 1997). They also found support for adults living in supported accommodation following the death of their parents to be both haphazard and unplanned.

Misconceptions by staff and family mean that too often people with intellectual disability are unprepared and unsupported in dealing with grief and denied the opportunity to explore, express and resolve their grief. It should be no surprise then that intellectual disability is a strong predictor of pathological grief reaction (Bonnell-Pascual et al. 1999). One UK study suggests however that as exposure to death and associated grief increases, staff knowledge and attitudes may be changing. A small survey by Murray, McKenzie and Quigley (2000) found that a majority of health and social care staff had supported a person with intellectual disability through the grief process, had an accurate knowledge of the grief process and could recognize the emotional and behavioural impact of the loss on their clients.

Strategies for supporting the expression of grief and adaptation to loss

People with intellectual disabilities cannot be protected from the emotions surrounding death, nor should they be excluded from the relevant cultural rituals. They have the right to be supported to express their grief and adapt to life without the deceased person, irrespective of whether the relationship was that of family, friend or paid carer. It is crucial that support is planned around the circumstances and skills of each individual taking particular account of their communications skills. Broad strategies discussed further below are drawn from the work of Botsford (2000), Deutsch (1985), Harper and Wadsworth (1993), Hollins (1995) and Read (2001) and include:

- education and preparation for death
- honesty and involvement in process and rituals of death
- listening, observation and support to express emotions
- avoidance of change or skills assessment for 12 months
- education of families and professionals
- resolution and negotiation of different approaches with families
- identification of the need for and acquisition of specialist help if necessary.

Preparation and education about death should be available to all adults with intellectual disability. This should include information about how death occurs, its vocabulary, different cultural rituals associated with death, culturally acceptable expressions of grief and visits to places associated with death such as churches, crematoriums and graves.

Use of appropriate communication techniques to convey information so it is meaningful is a fundamental skill required to work with people with intellectual disability of all ages. Finding ways to communicate information and the feelings that surround death and grief is perhaps the greatest challenge that confronts all professionals.

People with intellectual disability require honest and concrete information about serious illness and death of their loved ones. Where possible they should be given the opportunity to make visits to hospitals, to say goodbye and be informed of the death when it occurs. Information should be conveyed as simply as possibly, using means accessible to the person and avoiding euphemisms that may be misleading and could lead to guilt or anger. For example, if a person is told their parent has gone to live with God they may assume this means the parent has chosen this course of action because of something they have done or in preference to living with them. People with intellectual disability should be included in funerals, wakes and other rituals associated with death and burial. Other family members may not feel able to support the person or be wary of their reactions at funerals. In such cases, an alternative support person such as a staff member or friend may have to be found. A support person to attend such rituals can be important to assist in understanding what is happening, answering questions and dealing with misgivings of relatives.

Support with catharsis, the expression of feelings, is critical, as is recognition and acknowledgement of behaviour that may be used to express emotions. Here too, informed and creative use of communication techniques are critical. Aids and alternative means of communication such as photos, pictures, books, drawings and life books may be useful in assisting the expression of feelings and helping the person to remember and relocate the deceased in their own life. An understanding of the person's life history and their relationship with the deceased may be very important in interpreting emotions and assisting the person to make connections between current feelings and past events. Non-verbal rituals such as tree planting, selection and establishment of a memorial, choice of photos and mementos are all a means of assisting the expression and recognition of feelings. Acknowledgement of anniversaries and support with searching by visits to places such as graves are also important.

Small groups of adults with intellectual disability have been used as a medium for sharing experiences and emotions, providing information about grief processes, making people aware their reactions are not unique and assisting adaptation and resolution of grief. Cognitive behaviour therapy is suggested as means to explore the interpretation of events from the person's point of view and a way of supporting alternative meanings or ways of responding to what has happened.

Education for professionals and families is an important strategy to ensure they can acknowledge and understand the impact of grief and provide support. In the longer term such education may avert the misconceptions held about grief and remove some of the obstacles these present to the resolution of grief. It may also avoid the need for professionals to confront and resolve differences between themselves, a person with intellectual disability and family members regarding appropriate strategies to adopt in supporting a person through bereavement. The extent to which the wishes of others should be respected to exclude a family member with intellectual disability from the rituals of death can be a difficult issue to resolve. In doing so staff must consider the unique aspects of each individual's situation, their relationships with family members, creative options or alternative strategies available, and the potential impact of disregard of wishes and possible alienation from family members.

Very practical and concrete strategies are the avoidance of significant changes in a person's life for at least 12 months following bereavement. For example, decisions regarding long-term future accommodation should be delayed, change in staff and routines should be minimized and no attempt should be made to assess a person's level of skills. Most importantly specialist help should be sought where there is any indication that the person is not coping with their emotions, that the impact of grief is overwhelming, or that those supporting the person consider they lack appropriate skills and additional support is required.

Research is beginning to suggest that mainstream bereavement counsellors have the capacity to support adults with intellectual disability through the process of grief, but they may require additional support with issues of informed consent and non-verbal communication strategies (Read 2001). In Australia some residential services are beginning to tackle these issues by putting in place planned approaches aimed to identify early when a resident is likely to confront death of a close family member, strategies to ensure involvement and support throughout the process (Missingham 1999). Such plans should be an integral part of all support services.

Summary: Minimizing the risks and supporting adaptation to loss and change

The obstacles experienced by people with intellectual disability in dealing with grief following the death of loved ones, stem both from the misconceptions of others and from their own individual characteristics such as communication difficulties and negative life experiences. They exemplify many of the factors that lead to the heightened risk of psychiatric problems for this group. If older people with intellectual disability are to negotiate and cope with the multiple changes and losses that occur in later life, a crucial first step is the acknowledgement of them of as emotional beings, with similar feelings and needs to express and resolve them as others. This means the adoption of strategies across the lifecycle to increase protective factors and bolster their coping skills, prevent the incidence of life experiences that result in high risks of poor mental health, and the provision of resources and skilled support to facilitate adaptation and adjustment to change and loss:

> With increasing age, gerontological research has validated the expected belief that engagement and minimisation of life stressor have preventative value and can lead to prolonged life and stable health status. Life factors that provide for sound nutrition, access to valued activities, safe and pleasant domicile, and intellectual challenge can minimize stress organic or environmentally derived psychopathology and reactive behaviours. A quality old age among persons with intellectual disabilities will be based on the same factors that provide for quality old age among other persons. (Thorpe *et al.* 2001, p.225)

By normative standards people with intellectual disability will have fulfilled few of the standard life goals in terms of occupation, family formation or social status. This reinforces the importance of a person-centred planning process to identify goals that in turn will serve as life markers and achievements.

Preventative strategies must commence early in life and be complemented by prompt identification and recognition of problems, assessment and appropriate treatment throughout life. As with physical health, a key to ensuring good mental health is good communication, an orientation by professionals and family that is sensitive to and fully explores any changes in behaviour and a dogged approach to ensuring appropriate investigation occurs, and treatment and support provided. In relation to ageing this may necessitate combining knowledge and understanding from multiple sectors, intellectual disability, mental health, dual diagnosis and pyschogeriactrics.

Understanding Alzheimer's disease

Alzheimer's disease is one of the most common psychiatric conditions among older people with intellectual disability and particularly those with Down's syndrome. Its course is predictable and unlike many other conditions it is incurable. The final part of this chapter concisely summarizes the incidence, characteristics and progression of Alzheimer's disease and highlight some of the key issues it raises for professionals. A significant amount of work in this area has been undertaken by the Special Interest Group on Ageing and Developmental Disabilities of the International Association for the Scientific Study of Intellectual Disability (IASSID), led by Janicki. This section draws substantially on this work (Janicki *et al.* 1996; Wilkinson and Janicki 2002).

What is Alzheimer's disease

Alzheimer's disease is the most common form of dementia. It causes progressive deterioration of mental functioning, leading to the impairment and eventual loss of cognitive and adaptive skills necessary for everyday functioning. People forget how to carry out everyday tasks and have no capacity to relearn. Deterioration in skills is accompanied by changes to mental status and behaviour, such as depression, psychosis, aggression and irritability. Alzheimer's disease eventually leads to a total loss of function, the requirement for 24-hour nursing care and death from acute causes such as heart failure or pneumonia (Janicki and Dalton 1999). A useful way to characterize the types of changes that occur is suggested by Sloane:

- amnesia – memory loss

- apraxia – loss of ability to coordinate learned movements

- aphasia – inability to speak or understand

- agnosia – inability to recognize what is seen (Sloane 1997, cited in Janicki *et al.* 2000).

The disease follows a predictable irreversible progression that lasts from between three and twenty years. High rates of psychiatric symptoms, particularly delusions and hallucinations (Cooper 1997d), chronic health problems and late onset seizures are found amongst those with Alzheimer's.

People with Down's syndrome have a higher risk of Alzheimer's disease at an earlier age. Janicki and Dalton (2000) report a rate 22 per cent among people with Down's syndrome aged over 40 years and 56 per cent for those aged over 60 years, with onset generally occurring in the early fifties. In the UK context the rates of Alzheimer's disease among people with Down's syndrome reported by Prasher (1995) are 2 per cent between 30 and 39 years, 9.4 per cent between 40 and 49 years, 36 per cent between 50 and 59 and 54.5 per cent between 60 and 69 years. This is significantly higher than in the general population where the rate is 0.1 per cent between 30 and 59 years increasing to 1.4 per cent between 65 and 69 years and only reaching 13 per cent in those over 80 years.

Nevertheless, it must be remembered that not all people with Down's syndrome will have symptoms of Alzheimer's and almost half of those who survive to age 60 show no symptoms at all. The course of Alzheimer's disease for people with Down's syndrome is atypical, onset is earlier and its course is more rapid, lasting between one and nine years.

Reported figures for the rate of Alzheimer's disease among people with intellectual disability over 65 years without Down's syndrome differ. Cooper's

(1997d) research suggests a higher rate of 22 per cent compared to between 5 and 10 per cent found in the general population. Janicki and Dalton (2000) report a rate of 6 per cent which is comparable to that found in the general population.

Diagnosing Alzheimer's disease

The early symptoms of Alzheimer's disease are very similar to those of various other conditions, many of which can be treated. These include depression, thyroid dysfunction, urinary tract infections, diabetes, poor diet and sensory loss. It is critically important therefore to pursue a thorough diagnostic procedure to identify such conditions rather than assume a person has the untreatable Alzheimer's disease. Initially diagnosis should focus on the exclusion of all other possible causes of the observed changes and symptoms. These imperatives are complicated by the inherent difficulties of diagnosing Alzheimer's disease in people with intellectual disability. Essentially diagnosis involves identifying a pattern of change in a person's functional capacity over time, and must therefore use previous levels of functioning as the benchmark. Standard measures of functioning and diagnostic tests based on population norms are not appropropriate for use with people with intellectual disability. Given their diverse functional capacity there are no standard tools for diagnosis that can be used. Heavy reliance is placed on accurate, reliable accounts of functional changes from those who know the person well. For people who live in supported accommodation this type of information may be limited, particularly where there is high turnover or use of casual staff. Regular monitoring of adaptive skills conducted by health professionals to complement other medical screening is proposed as a method of ensuring benchmark information exists upon which to make judgements about changes. It is suggested that such monitoring should occur at regular intervals from the age of 40 years for people with Down's syndrome and 50 for others with intellectual disability (Janicki et al. 1996).

Initial symptoms of Alzheimer's disease are gradual and include mild memory loss and minor changes to emotional and cognitive functioning. Sudden changes to functioning are likely to have causes other than Alzheimer's. As well as tracing patterns of functional change, diagnosis should include full physical and neurological assessments including tests such as thyroid and liver function. Full assessments should be conducted by geriatric specialists available in a range of settings such as memory clinics or aged care assessment teams.

Progression of the disease and strategies for adaptation

The course of Alzheimer's disease is often broken into three stages: early, mid and late. Table 4.1 summarizes the characteristic symptoms experienced in each of these stages and the broad range of responses that may be required from professionals and formal support services. The overarching approaches to supporting people with Alzheimer's disease are however similar to those applicable to other aspects of ageing, including compensation for loss, adaptation of an individual's social and physical environment to changes, preservation of skills and optimal function, and a planned proactive approach to program design and individual support.

Throughout the progression of the disease, the nature of support provided and the social and physical environment will need to be continually adjusted to take account of the changing needs of the individual. An understanding of the nature of Alzheimer's disease provides an indication of likely changes but specific changes to individual needs must determine adjustments to care and support. Flexibility and responsiveness of support and resources are fundamental. A focus should be on preserving an individual's functional capacity as long as possible by maintaining their existing skills and engagement in hobbies and activities of daily living. Compensation for loss, protection and safety issues must be balanced with the need to preserve continued function. For example, whilst regular routines should be maintained and change avoided, where possible tasks should be simplified to make them less demanding, choices reduced, or more prompting provided. Every effort should be made to maintain communication, support continued independence, and understand and resolve behaviour problems. The Edinburgh Principles for support of people with intellectual disability and dementia suggest that the right should exist for people to remain in the community with sufficient and appropriate supports and not be subjected to inappropriate or premature institutionalization (Wilkinson and Janicki 2002). A variety of well-designed resources have been developed that provide comprehensive and sensitive ideas for tackling these difficult tasks (see Further Reading at end of chapter).

Care must be taken throughout the course of the disease to treat all coexisting medical and psychiatric conditions to ensure optimal physical and mental health. Services and individual professionals must adopt a long-term, planned, proactive approach to supporting individuals with Alzheimer's disease. Person-centred planning and subsequent care or support plans will require collaboration from a range of health, disability and community care professionals drawing on the particular expertise each has to offer. Members of informal social networks should also be involved in planning and responses over time so their energies can be tapped in the provision of emotional and practical support.

Table 4.1 Summary of characteristics and responses at the three stages of Alzheimer's disease

Early stage: mild memory loss and deterioration of skills – 1–5 years, less for people with Down's syndrome	Mid stage: pronounced and severe decline of skills – 5–15 years, less for people with Down's syndrome	Late stage: complete loss of functioning and basic skills – 3–5 years, less for people with Down's syndrome
	Characteristic symptoms	

• short term memory loss
  ◦ difficulty remembering facts, faces and words
  ◦ forget where going
  ◦ forget what doing
  ◦ repetition of the same conversation
• language disturbances
• difficulty organizing behaviour
• mild deterioration of everyday living skills
• odd, inappropriate or unusual behaviour
• loss of interest in hobbies
• confusion
• puzzlement re behaviour
• mild disorientation
	• disturbed perceptions, especially spatial and depth
	• problems with language and speech
	  ◦ loss of conversational logic
	  ◦ inability to understand instructions or name familiar objects
	• significant memory loss
	  ◦ unable to recognize familiar people
	  ◦ unable to remember what to do with objects
	• loss of functional and self-care skills
	• inability to complete day-to-day tasks without support
	• increased apathy, inactivity and withdrawal
	• disorientation, time, place, person
	• depression, delusions
	• aggression, irritability
	• wandering, rummaging, shadowing
	• personality change
	• late afternoon agitation, (sundowning)
		• loss of skills
		  ◦ eating, drinking, swallowing
		  ◦ ability to control motor movements
		• loss of mobility, ability to walk and balance
		• incontinence
		• lack of awareness of surroundings
		• loss of affect
		• loss body weight
		• long periods inactivity
		• greater risk seizures
		• greater risk infections
		• death from acute causes, heart failure, pneumonia

Response strategies

• minimize change to environment and daily routines
• maintain activity and engagement
• compensate for memory loss and disorientation
  ○ simplify activities
  ○ provide additional cues
  ○ provide more guidance and supervision
  ○ structure support to maintain daily activities
  ○ more explicit direction and prompts
• ensure safe environment
• optimize everyday successes
• monitor changes
• understand diagnosis
• plan for predictable progression of the disease
  ○ staff education
  ○ staff and other resources
  ○ environmental adaptations to allow safe wandering, physical cues, maximize surveillance
  ○ ageing in place or move in later stages
• inform and educate family and significant others, particularly co-residents
	• continuous adaptation to changes in ability, skills and self-care
	• maintain physical and mental activity
	• minimize agitation and maintain communication
	  ○ validation techniques
	  ○ understand behaviour in context of past
	  ○ calming, reassuring, talking
	  ○ remove mirrors
	• redirect and understand repetitious behaviours
	• watch for triggers to agitation
	• don't take behaviour personally
	• understand impact of hallucinations and failure to recognize familiar people
	• closer supervision
	• maintain physical health
	• ensure adequate nutrition and fluid intake
	  ○ maintain independent eating
	  ○ use of finger foods
	  ○ adjust eating times when more alert
	  ○ allow longer time for eating
	• maximize surveillance and restrict access to private spaces
	• continuous attention to environmental adaptation, simplification, cues
	• consider care plans for end stage
	• consider advance directives re active treatment and resuscitation
	• consider decision-making processes
		• total 24-hour care
		• primary nursing care and medical management
		• preventative care and comfort
		  ○ prevent dehydration
		  ○ prevent choking
		  ○ prevent aspiration
		  ○ prevent, ulcers, bedsores
		  ○ prevent infections
		• constant direction and supervision with
		  ○ eating
		  ○ washing
		  ○ grooming
		  ○ personal care

Individual and service system issues

As the progress of Alzheimer's disease is relatively predictable, services should be well prepared for the changing nature of support needs and aware of the issues with which they have to grapple. Two major issues to be resolved at an organizational level are the extent to which supported accommodation or in-home services can become dementia capable, and whether they are prepared to offer support to individuals to 'age in place' through the course of the disease. Resolution of this later issue is linked to the model of dementia support adopted by the broader service system.

A dementia capable service is one that is competent and equipped to provide support to people with Alzheimer's disease, whether in the initial stages or for its entire progression. Dementia capability requires staff to have an understanding of the nature and course of Alzheimer's disease, its likely effect on day-to-day functioning and a grasp of the repertoire of strategic and everyday responses for minimizing the impact on the person affected and other residents. Dementia capable services will have the ability to modify the physical environment, not only to ensure safety but also to provide relevant cues to maximize independent movement and minimize agitated behaviour. For example, eliminating shadows, installing switches on cookers that shut off automatically, using colour, texture and photos as cues to delineate specific areas or pathways in a house. Such environments should not be reliant on access to upper storeys by stairs which due to spatial and mobility problems will become increasing difficult for a person with Alzheimer's disease to navigate. Dementia capability also requires the capacity to redeploy staff as necessary, and have flexible and responsive staff resources that can be attuned to changing support needs.

If a planned proactive approach to supporting an individual with Alzheimer's disease is adopted, then organizations that provide residential support must decide their position in regard to 'ageing in place'. The fundamental questions to be addressed include whether they are willing and do they have skills and sufficient access to flexible resources to support a person in their home until death. Ageing in place for a person with Alzheimer's will inevitably require the provision of full-time nursing care for a period of time. Factors to be taken into account in reaching such decisions are the organization's mission, philosophy and policies, the impact on other residents, physical design of the house, staff and other resources, and the possibly changed nature of the house over time, particularly if more than one resident has the disease.

Alternative models to ageing in place involve at least one residential move for the individual, to either a generic nursing home type facility or to specialist supported accommodation for people with intellectual disability and Alzheimer's disease. Critical issues here are the stage at which such moves take place, in order to minimize the impact of change, and the transparency of the decision-making process to instigate such a move and mechanisms for involvement of significant others and seeking review. A more detailed discussion of the various options for accommodation support is presented in Chapter 7. Evidence to date suggests that older people with intellectual disability are at risk of institutionalization in later life, which is often premature, and that generic nursing care facilities do not have the staff skills or resources to provide quality care for this group. In light of this the report of the Growing Older with Learning Disabilities Programme in the UK recommended the best option for older adults with intellectual disabilities to remain within a service system that has expertise about their disability (Foundation for People with Learning Disability 2002).

Further reading

Davidson, P., Prasher, V. and Janicki, M. (2003) *Mental Health, Intellectual Disabilities and the Ageing Process.* Oxford: Blackwell.

Janicki, M. and Dalton, A. (1999) *Dementia, Ageing and Intellectual Disabilities.* Philadelphia: Brunner/Mazel.

Janicki, M., Heller, T., Seltzer, G. and Hogg, J. (1996) 'Practice guidelines for the clinical assessment and care management of Alzheimer's disease and other dementias among adults with intellectual disability.' *Journal of Intellectual Disability Research 40,* 374–382.

Resources

Cathcart, F. (1994) *Understanding Death and Dying.* Kidderminster: British Institute of Learning Disabilities.

Dodd, K., Turk, V. and Christmas, M. (2002) *Resource Pack for Carers of Adults with Down Syndrome and Dementia.* Kidderminister: British Insititute of Learning Disabilities. www.bild.org.uk

Hollins, S. and Sireling, L. (2001) *Understanding Grief: Working with Grief and People who have Learning Disabilities.* Brighton: Pavilion. www.pavpub.com

Working Resources List on Dementia Care Management and Intellectual Disability. Preparing Community Agencies for Adults Affected by Dementia – 'PCAD' Project. Available from Rehabilitation and Research Training Centre on Ageing and Developmental Disabilities at the University of Illinois in Chicago. www.uic.edu.orgs/rrtcamr/

Useful organizations

Australian Alzheimer's Society. www.alzheimers.org.au

UK Alzheimer's Society. www.alzheimers.org.uk

Vignettes

Doug Oliver

Doug is 57 years old but looks much older. His hair is very grey, his skin wrinkled and he has little control over his movements. Eight weeks ago he moved into a nursing home and since then has gradually lost his ability to walk. He is in the final stages of Alzheimer's disease and is no longer really aware of his surroundings. Most of his day is spent strapped into the chair by his bed. Every day at least one member of his family drops in, but he no longer recognizes anyone.

All his life Doug has lived at home as a valued member of a large Greek family. His mother had 13 sisters and he is the youngest of 5 children. There were always family around the home – cousins, nephews and nieces and more recently great nephews and nieces. Doug's sister said, 'Doug was just one of the family, his social life was ours.' His sister stayed at home after she married and eventually cared for both her elderly mother and father until their deaths within several years of each other. Doug hadn't needed any care. He looked after his own personal needs and helped around the house, sweeping, making beds and sometimes doing some gardening. He enjoyed playing golf with his brother-in-law and had never used any disability services.

His sister said she would have liked to have known about some of the services. She said, 'We didn't know they were around. We never had any need until he started to deteriorate. He could have gone to a day centre, because he likes people. He could have seen some new faces, different faces, mingled a bit and had a bit of a social life.'

About three years ago things began to change for Doug. He began to forget what he was doing sometimes and had trouble going up stairs. When his bedroom was flooded and had to be redecorated he became quite confused, wandering the house looking for his room saying things like 'I'm going home now'. He began to wander outside, so his sister kept all the doors locked. He needed prompting to have a shower and get dressed in the right clothes. In a fall down the stairs Doug broke his leg, which required hospitalization, during which time he was referred to a geriatrician who after completing a range of tests and several long interviews with his sister about his previous skills diagnosed Alzheimer's disease.

Doug came home but his skills continued to deteriorate until the stage where he needed assistance with all personal care tasks. His sister found it progressively more difficult to provide the level of physical care that Doug required. He became incontinent, needed assistance to walk and get in and out of the shower and had to be fed all his meals. With much regret the family decided to find a nursing home place for him. Since his move eight weeks ago his condition has deteriorated and now he cannot walk at all and requires total nursing care. His sister has been trying to ensure he comes home one day a week and after the last visit said, 'It took all my feelings of guilt away. He's there now. I can't look after him. I can't lift him, he's too heavy. He can't walk. He sleeps most of the day. He has to be fed every meal. He can't do much for himself at all.'

Questions

1. In what respects has Doug aged successfully?

2. How could Doug's sister have adapted the house to compensate for the loss of adaptive skills, poor memory and perception of depth?

3. In what way if any could the need for the move to a nursing home have been avoided?

Marg King

Marg is 67 years old and for the last ten years has lived in a nursing home run by a large church organization in a very pleasant inner city suburb. Marg is tall and well built but not overweight. She has a short concentration span and tends to flit from one conversation or activity to another. She loves going out to places where there are lots of people, shops or activity. Marg has diabetes that is controlled by daily injections of insulin and adherence to a very strict diet. She requires assistance with the injections and to regulate her diet. Marg's mother also had diabetes, which meant she had very poor blood circulation to her feet and toes. As a result of this and a cut that became infected which was not picked up in time she had to have one of her legs amputated when she was in her eighties. Her brother,

Joe, is very concerned about Marg's health and wants to avoid what happened to their mother by ensuring Marg receives the best possible care.

Marg spends most days around the nursing home chatting to staff and other patients. She sometimes goes to the occupational therapy sessions but never really lasts very long there. She goes on outings organized by the home and once a month goes on an outing with a social group for people with disabilities. Joe collects her every week and they have a look around the shops and a coffee. Her other brother and various nieces drop in occasionally. Once a year at Christmas her brother takes her to visit old haunts like the country town where they spent their childhood.

When Marg's parents died she continued to live in the family home with an elderly aunt who had always lived with the family. After several years Joe was concerned that his aunt could not provide enough support for Marg with personal care tasks. He organized to sell the home and in accordance with his parents' will established a trust fund to support Marg. Marg and her aunt moved to a private shared supported accommodation facility, and her aunt died several years later from stomach cancer. Marg stayed in the facility, but after it was sold to new proprietors her brother was concerned that the quality of care was deteriorating. He felt the facility did not provide either the standard of care or the longer term security Marg needed. Joe was very pleased to get Marg into the nursing home, where his mother had been. In his mind this is the best place for Marg. The home has an excellent standard of both medical and personal care, good food, and the staff are able to monitor Marg's diet.

A question was raised by a new director of nursing a couple of years ago as to whether the nursing home was the most suitable place for Marg. Joe was worried that a move might be contemplated. However, disability services told the home that Marg was really too old for their services and the issue was never followed up. Joe said, 'If we could find some sort of small community home and get her medical care and injections every day we'd be thrilled to bits, but where do you find a place like that? I think she's better off medically with her care, she's better off being well fed, because at the nursing home they have got folk that are watching everything you eat, a balanced diet is put in front of you. There's less worry regarding her ongoing position and what's going to happen tomorrow.'

Questions

1. In what respects is Marg ageing successfully?

2. What do you think is the most appropriate support and housing option for her?

3.   What are the risks associated with diabetes for an older person?

4.   How would you describe Marg's informal social network?

5.   What role might disability services play in Marg's life?

6.   How might Marg's sense of purpose and achievement be improved?

Isabella Morgan

Isabella is 74 years old and lives in a group home in the community with four other residents. She is a quiet woman who enjoys knitting and is often seen to be fairly unsociable. She likes to sit in the lounge but doesn't go out of her way to converse with other residents or staff. Although Isabella's mobility is very restricted, she is able to get around slowly with the aid of a walking frame. Isabella finds it hard to take the initiative, but will happily join in activities if she is encouraged. Isabella has been on medication for epilepsy for many years and, following a series of falls that have resulted in broken or fractured limbs, she has been diagnosed as having osteoporosis. There is little doubt that her falls were exacerbated by her poor vision as a result of cataracts that went unnoticed for several years.

Isabella attends a day centre for older people two days a week where she participates in craft activities, various games and a gentle exercise program. She loves going to the program and is always up and ready well before it is time to leave. On the other days she spends most of her time in the lounge, watching the television or knitting. The other residents in the house are of a similar age and at home for most of the day.

Isabella moved to the group home three years ago, having spent 40 years living in a large institution. Since the move she does more for herself and now takes care of most of her personal care and grooming. When she first moved into the house staff noticed she bumped into things. After one incident when she fractured her arm, staff sought a thorough medical assessment during which it was discovered that she had cataracts which were subsequently removed.

Isabella has known the other residents for many years but has not seen anyone else from the institution since she has moved. She has a sister who rings every fortnight and talks on the phone but has not yet visited the house.

Questions

1. In what respects is Isabella ageing successfully?

2. How could Isabella's sense of continuity and belonging be increased?

3. What steps could be taken to avoid further falls at home or in the community?

4. What factors could account for Isabella's perceived lack of sociability?

5. How could Isabella be assisted to have a greater sense of purpose?

6. How could Isabella's opportunities for choice and self-determination be increased?

Edwin Jones

Edwin died in a nursing home several months ago. He was 53 years old and although the cause of death was pneumonia he had been suffering from Alzheimer's disease for about four years. A tree in the garden of the group home where he lived for the last three years of his life has a plaque commemorating him.

Edwin had spent most of his life in a large institution, where he worked in a catering business that was part of supported employment services. At his own request, which was supported by his mother, Edwin was included amongst a small group of residents who moved out of the institution three years ago. The decision to move was first made six years ago, at which time Edwin's health was not a major problem. He had always had gastric reflux and asthma but these were well controlled. When he was about 45 he had developed rheumatoid arthritis that particularly affected his hands, making it difficult to grip the knife when he cut vegetables.

Both Edwin and his mother were very excited about the move and were kept informed of progress during the long process of purchasing land and building houses. Whilst the building was in progress staff began to notice that Edwin was becoming very forgetful and losing some of his independent living skills; for example, forgetting to shower or what particular kitchen implements were for. He also began to lose interest in his work, which he had always enjoyed in the past. Initially staff thought he was depressed as the move was taking so long.

It took over 12 months and several visits to a neurologist for a diagnosis of Alzheimer's disease to be reached, by which time Edwin had moved into the community house with the others and continued to attend his place of work. However, it took him much longer to adjust to the new house than the other residents and he had difficulty remembering where to put things away in the kitchen and where his room was. He sometimes became quite confused about where he was, which made him upset.

He continued to lose his skills and all interest in going to work. Eventually it was decided that he should give up work and remain at home. By this time Edwin had been in the house for two years and was an important member of the household. The staff as a group made a decision to try and support him at home as long as possible, despite suggestions from the regional disability services team that he should be moved to a nursing home. Edwin's mother supported the decision to keep him at home. In her view he was extremely well looked after, although as he needed more and more help with personal care she felt the staff could have used additional equipment such as hoists to help with the heavy lifting. Staff spent time explaining to other residents what was happening with Edwin and they seemed to accept that some routines had to change to accommodate his needs. Staff rosters were reorganized to ensure a staff member was always available to support Edwin. He remained at home until four weeks before his death, when he contracted a severe chest infection and the GP advised that he required hospital care. Staff organized an unofficial roster with his mother to ensure one of them was with him at all times, and all the residents had a chance to visit him in hospital. Edwin died during the night whilst his mother and the house supervisor were there. All the house staff and residents attended his funeral and a counselling service was contracted to work with both residents and staff about issues of grief and loss.

Three months after his death Edwin is still regarded as a valued member of the household. Pictures of him are still on the noticeboard with other residents and he is often talked about. No one has taken his place, although a new resident is currently being selected by the regional disability team.

Questions

1. What arguments can be made for and against Edwin making the move into the community at the time he did?

2. How could the house have been adapted to compensate for the predicted changes in Edwin's needs as his disease progressed?

3. What more does it take than a committed staff group to ensure a resident can age in place?

4. What strategies might have been used by the counselling service to help the other residents deal with their grief?

PART 3

Social Dimensions of Ageing

Chapter 5

A Sense of Belonging

Informal Support from Family, Friends and Acquaintances

The nature and availability of informal support plays a significant role in the social, psychological and physical well-being of all older people. The bulk of support required by older people is provided by informal sources. For example, Australian statistics show that among older people who require assistance with activities of daily living, 89 per cent receive help from informal sources, 59 per cent formal sources and 43 per cent from both sources (AIHW 1999). Deinstitutionalization and community care policies of the last two decades have emphasized the complementarity of formal and informal sources of support, moving from implicit to explicit recognition and interaction between the two. The primary focus however has been on 'carers', those perceived as pivotal in informal networks of support and who provide hands on, day-to-day care for older people. Formal supports such as respite care and carers' groups have been established to assist carers to continue in their roles. Carers are most likely to be spouses, daughters or daughters-in-law.

The focus on carers has draw attention away from a broader understanding of informal support and the diverse ways in which relationships with a network of family members, friends, neighbours and acquaintances contribute to the quality of life of older people. As well as direct and indirect helping through, for example, the provision of care, advocacy and negotiation with formal services, informal relationships provide older people with valued social roles such as that of great aunt or club member, companionship and avenues to social activities and contribute to their sense of self-esteem, belonging and community integration.

In the last decade, with the shift to paradigms based on citizenship, community membership and inclusion, the disability sector too has given greater recognition to the informal sphere. Primarily this has focused on carers and supporting families to continue caring and building community connections for adults, particularly those relocated to the community from institutions. Despite this emphasis however, formal and paid relationships predominate. Although many more adults with intellectual disability are present in the community, most do not have close relationships with others in the community (Chappell 1994).

As a result of their life experiences, the informal support networks of older people with intellectual disabilities are quite different from those of other older people. Most significantly, the majority will lack a spouse and children. Their closest relatives are siblings and more distant relations such as cousins, nieces, nephews, aunts and uncles. With the loss of parents and increasing age, most do not have an informal 'carer' who provides day-to-day support to enable them to continue living in the community. Nevertheless, some older adults do have robust informal networks, with committed family and friends who play key roles in their lives. However, as people age their networks are dynamic, and particularly vulnerable to shrinkage and disruption due to moving house, retirement and the failure by others either to acknowledge the existence of or provide support to maintain relationships.

This chapter begins by examining conceptualizations of informal support, its significance to well-being and factors that influence its provision. The characteristics of informal support networks of older adults with intellectual disability are considered, and finally strategies examined that may reduce the vulnerability of networks as people age, build new or maintain existing relationships.

The significance of informal support

Informal support is a multidimensional concept often imprecisely defined. Terms such as social support, support networks, informal care, or social relationships are used interchangeably. Its defining characteristic however is support provided in the context of an unpaid relationship based on the personal tie between individuals. The depth and quality of informal relationships varies considerably, as does the basis of the tie. Personal ties stem from common membership of a kinship system – family, personal affinity and common interests – friendships, geographic propinquity or use of common spaces – neighbours and acquaintances (Bulmer 1987).

Types of informal exchanges

Informal support covers a multitude of different types of exchanges that have been conceptualized in different ways. One of the most common is the dichotomy between instrumental and affective support. Instrumental support is direct and indirect: hands-on assistance with tasks such as personal care, domestic tasks, or household maintenance tasks; and intangible tasks such as advocacy, negotiation, facilitation, coordination of formal services and information collection. Affective support is less practical generally involving spending time together, shared activities or celebrations, companionship, listening or reassuring. An alternative conceptualization suggested by Dalley (1988) is that of 'caring for' and 'caring about'. Caring for tasks are associated with direct hands-on support, whilst caring about is expression of affection, or concern and concrete actions such as monitoring service quality to ensure a person's overall well-being.

Value of informal support

Having a social network and receipt of informal support from family and friends is related to 'higher morale, less loneliness and worry, feelings of usefulness, a sense of individual respect within the community and a zest for life' (Hooyman 1983, p.139). Availability of informal support appears to be have protective aspects and is associated with lower mortality, better survival and recovery rates from acute conditions and reduced institutionalization (Mendes de Leon et al. 1999). The mechanisms at play are not clear, although it is suggested that it is the quality and not quantity that is important and that the perceived availability of support may be a crucial factor (Krause 2001). Informal support does not simply equate with presence of relationships, rather it is the salience and nature of the relationships that are important. For example, an older person may have an extensive family network but only be in contact regularly with one member.

Bayley (1997) discusses the cognitive and emotional needs met by informal relationships that he suggests include:

- attachment and intimacy where relationships allow the expression of feelings freely and without which loneliness as distinct from social isolation may be experienced
- social integration where common concerns and interests are shared often by means of joint activities
- opportunities for nurturance, whereby relationships provide an opportunity to give back and achieve a sense of being needed

- reassurance of worth where relationships affirm competence in a social role either at work or in the family

- reliable assistance where network members provide direct assistance

- obtaining guidance from respected others to assist in life decisions

- the exercise of choice, which is fundamental to a sense of autonomy, human worth and dignity.

Bayley suggests that a single relationship is unlikely to meet this range of needs and further that inappropriate behaviour and strain on relationships may occur if too much is expected of anyone. He suggests therefore that various relationships of different styles and intensities are required to fulfil an individual's range of needs.

As suggested earlier, the paradigm of community membership has created emphasis on informal relationships between people with intellectual disability and members of the community. Inclusion in the informal sphere is seen as fundamental to citizenship, of equal important to formal rights, for example, the opportunity to be both a worker and a colleague (Reinders 2002). Perkse (1993) suggests: 'It is not enough merely to place persons with disabilities in the neighbourhood – they must be connected to it socially. Their lives must interweave emotionally with the lives of others.'

The emphasis on valued social roles, community inclusion and social relationships with members of the community who are not disabled has detracted from the value of friendships between people with intellectual disabilities (Chappell 1994). As Knox and Hickson (2001) suggest it is more often the view of outsiders that decide whether and in what way relationships are meaningful and scant attention has been paid to the meanings that people with intellectual disabilities themselves give to relationships. Research suggests that friendships between people with intellectual disability can have depth, richness and longevity. The types of friendships classed as 'good mates' play a pervasive and pivotal role in people's lives (Knox and Hickson 2001). Relationships between people with intellectual disabilities also provide the basis for furthering collective interests through means such as self-advocacy organizations (Chappell 1994). What is important however is to distinguish friendships between people with intellectual disability based on common interests and choice from mere groupings of people whereby individuals although proximate to each other have no common bonds.

Some of the functions played by informal support, particularly direct hands-on assistance, are replicated by formal support services. In some instances paid relationships between workers and people with intellectual disability can replace the informal without loss of quality. However, formal organizations and relationships cannot replicate all the tasks and find it particularly difficult to fulfil those that require long-term commitment, are non-routine and idiosyncratic. These are the 'caring about' tasks that provide affective support, manage and mediate relations with formal services and undertake advocacy. These latter functions are crucial to the quality of life of older people who live in shared, supported accommodation and rely on formal support to meet their day-to-day needs. In situations such as this sources external to formal organizations fully committed to the individual and without divided loyalties are required to monitor and negotiate quality of care, advocate and oversee the well-being of the older adult and their affairs. Formal structures such as standards monitoring, case management, statutory guardianship and advocacy services are in place but undertake only fragments of these tasks for short periods and often work reactively rather than proactively. Formal services cannot provide the same continuing comprehensive commitment to an individual and oversight of their well-being that informal sources can (Bigby 2000). The inability of formal services to substitute for some of the key roles fulfilled by informal network members emphasizes the vulnerability of those people whom as they age lack strong informal networks of support.

Factors affecting networks of support

Litwak's (1985) theory of task specificity argues that family, friends and neighbours each have particular characteristics that differentiate the type of support they are best able to provide. For example, neighbours are characterized by close proximity but loose or non-affective ties, and thus are well suited to support that requires low commitment but either speedy response or proximity such as emergency assistance, monitoring an empty house or feeding the cat. In contrast relationships with spouses or other close family members are characterized by proximity, face-to-face contact on a daily basis and high degree of commitment. They are often the only ones in a network in a position to provide support with primary care tasks, which require these characteristics. Other family members may not be geographically close but still have a strong commitment and be suited to tasks that don't require frequent day-to-day contact such as administration of financial affairs, advocacy or negotiation with formal organizations. Friendships are characterized by affective ties but often not proximity or long-term commitment and may be better suited to tasks such as emotional support, companionship or shared activities that require intermittent contact with a low level of commitment.

Clearly, this delineation of characteristics and functions is based on ideal types. Both relationships and the tasks fulfilled by informal network members are mediated by factors such as gender, social context, individual resources, personal histories, life course stage and negotiated commitments. Nevertheless, Litwak's ideas can provide indications of which functions may not be well performed by a person's network. However, the idea of task specificity together with the absence of close family, traditionally regarded as spouse and children, from the network of older adults with intellectual disability potentially leaves a substantial vacuum. With fewer expectations as to the roles of remaining family members in the support networks of older people, substantial room is left for creative negotiation of roles based on affinity rather than obligations or kinship. This opens up the possibility of non-normative roles being played by more distant family or friends.

The notion of a 'convoy of social support' suggests that the history of supportive relationships is central to understanding present relationships, and that people move through life surrounded by a convoy of others with whom they exchange social support (Antonucci and Akiyama 1987). Convoys are lifelong but dynamic, varying across time and situations. The model is a useful framework to organize factors that determine the structure and functions of an individual's support network over the life course. The properties of the individual, their demographic characteristics, personality and abilities are one set of factors. The properties of the situation, external aspects of the environment, roles occupied, place of residence, organizational membership and life events are another set. Both sets affect the structure of the convoy, its size, connectedness, stability, complexity and homogeneity. The convoy structure in turn affects its functions; the actual support given, received or exchanges by members of the convoy. By stressing the dynamic nature of convoys this model emphasizes changes that occur to social networks over the life course. This highlights the vulnerability of networks as individuals and their convoy members age, and as a result of environmental or situational age-related changes.

Understanding networks

The concept of networks is a framework for analysing informal relationships. A network approach examines relationships between the individual and others in their network, in terms of the origin, duration and strength of ties and the frequency, nature and location of exchanges. It provides a means of understanding the whole as well as the individual components. For example, the structural properties of a network can be described in terms of size, the age, gender and relational balance of members and density, the extent to which members are known to each other. Research has shown that the structural characteristics of informal networks are often predictive of the nature of support provided informally

(Wenger 1994). Thus, an understanding of a network per se is useful for considering how it may be vulnerable on the one hand to disruptions by formal supports, or on the other strengthened or complemented by formal services.

Informal networks in later life

In regard to informal networks of support, as for health, adults with intellectual disability embark on the ageing process from a position of weakness rather than strength. A proportion of the current and several future cohorts of older people will have spent much of their lives in institutions dislocated from family and community before relocation to small-scale, supported living in mid or later life. Strategies to build informal relationships for this group with community members are still evolving, but to date have had little success. Research suggests that among adults with intellectual disability moving to the community from institutions 'friendships are frequently non existent' (Rapley and Beyer 1996) and 'most are still not really part of their communities. The majority of these people have few if any friends' (Amado 1993, p.279).

However, adults who live in supported accommodation or in more independent options in the community tend to have larger networks that include more friends and are less dominated by family members than adults who have remained at home with parents. This latter group has smaller informal networks, characterized as family dominated and community insulated (Grant 1993). Friends are likely to be shared with parents and, as a result, their networks are likely to be dense and comprise people from their own or an older generation. Ramcharan, McGrath and Grant (1997) suggest that despite a high proportion of adults that live with family identifying a wish to have more friendships and community activities, opportunities for this are constrained by the attitudes of parents and ensuing difficulties of negotiation encountered by care managers or support workers. Clearly, for some adults with intellectual disability who remain at home with family a form of trade-off exists between opportunities for friendships and the exploration of independence and things such as security, continuity of care and unconditional commitment by family.

The influence of earlier life experiences is demonstrated by research findings that people who have stayed at home with parents have stronger relationships with family members in later life than those who have left home at an earlier age (Bigby 1997a; Skeie 1989). For example, Bigby (2000) found that 92 per cent of older people who had lived with parents till middle age had at least twice yearly contact with a family member. In comparison an earlier Australian study found that only just under half of older people from all backgrounds had contact with family members (Ashman *et al.* 1993).

The nature of informal networks of older adults with intellectual disabilities are largely uncharted. Some writers have characterized them as the familyless elderly (Gibson, Rabkin and Munson 1992; Hogg, Moss and Cooke 1988), suggesting that unlike their peers they will have no significant others and no friends. Others suggest that family members such as siblings largely replace the roles of parents (Janicki and Seltzer 1991). A study undertaken by Bigby (2000) in Australia provided some in-depth understanding of the informal networks of a group of 62 older people who had all stayed at home with parents until middle age. The findings from this study provide the basis for the following sections.

Dynamics of networks when parents die

The informal support network of adults who have remained at home changes dramatically with the death of their parents. At minimum they will lose their source of primary care but often also a dominant force in their lives that was the major source of advocacy and negotiation with formal service systems. As discussed in Chapter 8, after the loss of their parents some adults remain at home, with various sources of in-home support and some move to live with other family members, but over time as people age the majority move to supported accommodation. Thus in later life a characteristic of their informal support networks is the separation of caring for and caring about tasks, both of which were previously performed by parents. Formal services are much more likely to be involved in caring for tasks, whilst other family members and long-term family friends often alter or intensify their roles to absorb some of the caring about tasks. In particular siblings may assume greater responsibility for more concrete caring about tasks, as well as continuing to be an important source of social contact and companionship for older adults with intellectual disability. A defining characteristic of older people's informal networks is the existence of a 'key person' who takes responsibility for oversight of their well-being. Key people have a close long-term relationship with the older person, demonstrate considerable commitment to their well-being and play a plethora of caring about roles, combining them in some instances with primary care. Their role is discussed further in the section below.

The networks of older adults have many similarities to those of middle-aged adults at home. Networks are small, with between 0 and 20 members and an average of 6 members who have contact at least twice a year. They continue to be dominated by family members comprising the entire network for a third of older people. Very few people have no family, whilst a third have no friends. The most common form of support is affective in the form of visits and outings. However, three-quarters also get some form of instrumental support from network members, although this is usually from one member only. Types of support included:

1. *Caring for:*

    o   provision of hands-on, day-to-day care

    o   development of skills.

2. *Caring about:*

    o   decision making

    o   financial management

    o   adoption of formal or legal roles

    o   mediating, negotiating and advocating with service systems

    o   monitoring service quality

    o   supervision of medical needs

    o   coordinating support from other network members

    o   provision of back-up or short-term replacement of other members

    o   emotional support

    o   listening

    o   advising

    o   visiting and companionship.

Although roles such as grandparent or mother-in-law were missing from their networks, in later life these older people had new roles of aunt and great aunt. Incidental contact with family often decreased when they left the parental home but involvement with family at times of celebration like birthdays and Christmas was an important aspect of informal support.

Indeed for many older people the loss of their parents signified a shift to an adult rather than child role and the opportunity for new – in some instances for the first time – intimate friendships. Key people from a different generation to parents with different attitudes often actively sought out and encouraged new horizons and opportunities for the older adult, having previously felt powerless to counter protective attitudes of parents; yet at the same time understanding and respecting parental stances, acknowledging the different historic and value context in which they gave birth and raised a child with a disability. In addition restrictions and responsibilities placed on an adult with intellectual disability from living with a frail parent who required care or monitoring were also lifted. New opportunities for activities and meeting people were sometimes also offered by the supported accommodation service to which some people moved.

The role of key people

Three-quarters of the older people in Bigby's study had a key person in their informal network. Roles played by key people were fluid and responsive to events and changes that were happening in the older person's life. The defining characteristics were oversight of all aspects of the person's well-being and strength of commitment. This role was acquired when parents died or become incapacitated. Although in some ways it resembled parental roles, it was less protective and intense. Key people were in touch with the older person regularly and as well as companionship undertook at least three instrumental tasks.

Although key people are most commonly siblings, it was a negotiated role based on strength of feeling and commitment rather than family ties or obligation. Where a person had more than one sibling, the role was assumed by the sibling with the closest relationship rather then the oldest and where a poor relationship with siblings existed the role was taken on by a family friend or more distant relative. Parental 'key person succession plans' had often negotiated the adoption of the key person role with an informal network member. The importance, nature and success of such plans are discussed in Chapter 9. Key people were the most stable element in older people's networks, but as they were from the same or an older generation did on occasion predecease the older person. In such cases some key people had planned their own succession and were replaced by another person, most often a niece or nephew. However as people aged, the chances of losing a key person and not having them replaced increased. This loss leaves some older people very vulnerable, as it means they have no one outside formal services who can oversee their well-being, to proactively ensure the quality of services and that any decisions are made in their best interest.

Family relationships

Few older people had a parent alive, and the parents of those who did were often frail and resident in a nursing home. For this group staying in touch on a regular basis was important. Eighty per cent of the older people in this study had at least one sibling, and the majority had at least twice yearly contact with a sibling. As suggested above, a common relationship with the closest sibling is that of key person. Other types of relationships with siblings ranged from friendly regular monthly contact, undertaking some instrumental tasks such as financial management to indifference or no contact at all. As with other older people, later life relationships tended to replicate those forged earlier in the life course. In some cases even where siblings were not geographically close they maintained regular contact and involvement in the older person's life. Siblings-in-law, particularly sisters-in-law were important and their stance in relation to the older person was also a determining factor to the type of relationship. Some siblings-in-law remained in contact with the older person after the death of their spouse.

Relationships with more distant relatives varied and tended to reflect family traditions, and whether an active role of kin keeper operated in the family to ensure members remained in touch and celebrated key occasions together. Nieces and nephews of key network members often have a close relationship to the older person, having known and been involved with them all their lives.

Friends and acquaintances

On average the older people in Bigby's study had two people whom they or another person named as their friends. This is probably an underestimate as it is clear that friendships with others who have an intellectual disability are discounted by informants. Relationships with friends, other than those who occupied a key person role, were generally affective and involved companionship and shared activities rather than instrumental support. For those who lived in shared accommodation, other residents with whom they sat at mealtimes or for whom they did errands were often named as friends. Many friendships were specific to a particular context such as accommodation, or a day centre attended by the older person. It was the exception that friends met outside of this context. Some older people, particularly those who involved in church communities, continued in be in touch with shared parental friends after the death of parents.

Older people were likely to refer to unnamed groups of people whom they saw regularly as friends. This might be neighbours in the local area, members of a football club or other patrons at a café. Such relationships give people a sense of identity and being known. The importance of acquaintances that are friendly but distant without reciprocity was also noted by Grant *et al.* (1995) in their study of community inclusion of older people with intellectual disability.

Vulnerability of networks

The characteristics of older people's networks and the nature of their relationships mean they are particularly vulnerable to disruption and loss. The context-specific nature of friendships means they are disrupted by moving house, leaving a day program or retirement from employment. People with intellectual disability often require support to stay in touch and share activities with friends. Unless this is forthcoming cessation of regular proximity means friendships are lost. For example, none of the people who had retired from day programs or who had moved to aged care accommodation had retained contact with friends from other settings. Very few people retained contact with neighbours when they moved from the locality. The lack of intergenerational members mean that networks are particularly vulnerable to loss through the death or incapacity of members from the same or an older generation.

Maintaining and building networks in later life

Whilst formal services and paid relationships with support workers cannot replicate aspects of informal support, such as long-term commitment and affective support, they can support and foster development of informal relationships. However, formal supports can also, through neglect and ignorance, unwittingly obstruct and disrupt informal relationships. Evidence suggests that formation of friendships is reliant on opportunities and the nature of the social environment which for older people with intellectual disability are often fashioned by and reliant on the attitudes and skills of support workers (Landesman-Dwyer and Berkson 1984). In this regard there is a disparity between the importance that workers attach to development of friendships and their perceived responsibility for actions in this regard. For example, an Australian study suggested that although workers in day and residential programs rated the development of friendships as very important, they were not confident of their skills and success in this area and most did not see it as central to their roles (DHS 2002b).

Strategies that can be adopted to support informal relationships and build new ones range from consciousness raising, the reorientation of everyday structures and support to implementation of more formal 'network building programs'. At the very basic level it is crucial that support staff and professionals at all levels recognize and value the range of informal relationships of older people. This means actively mapping and understanding the network of family, friends and acquaintances surrounding each person, knowing the history and significance of relationships. This approach will foster a proactive stance to supporting relationships and mean that account is taken of the potential impact on informal relationships when lifestyle changes are considered. For example, if a change of residence or day activity is being contemplated or is unavoidable, active strategies must be planned and implemented to maintain contact with friends. It is not necessary to see a person every day at a day centre or live with them to be a friend. Provision of support for activities with one or a small group of friends in a community venue or visits to homes will help maintain friendships. Private space in shared houses for friends to share time together is an important factor. Involvement of a whole household in a visit may not only be overwhelming but also obstructive to maintaining individual relationships. Regular mapping of relationships with the person with intellectual disability will also ensure relationships aren't lost when staff or other changes occur. Similarly, family relationships may need active support as relatives age and encounter problems with driving or use of public transport. Again a proactive approach to maintaining contact and supporting visits that adapts to changed circumstances will help to keep relationships alive.

The way in which day-to-day activities are structured can create opportunities or obstacles to building friendships. Whilst the development of friendships cannot be scripted, chances of friendships are increased when people are known as individuals, when others are encountered on a regular basis, when interests are held in common and activities shared. Outings in large groups on an irregular basis to impersonal venues that provide little opportunity for individual interaction are unlikely to lead to the development of new relationships. Yet it is these very sorts of outings to anonymous public spaces in groups that occupy much of the time that people with intellectual disability spend in the community (Bigby, Frederico and Cooper 2002; Walker 1995). An overriding consideration of any planned venture by staff, be it mundane or not, should be the opportunities it presents to meet others and develop friendships or acquaintances. The location, continuity, regularity, size of group and meaning of the activity to the individual are all key considerations in whether obstacles or opportunities are created in everyday lives for friendship development.

Various examples are found in the literature of innovative models specifically designed to support the formation of informal relationships for people with intellectual disability. This approach can complement everyday structures and focus intensive and specific resources on relationship building. Models include the planned lifetime advocacy network (PLAN), circles of support, volunteer companions, citizen advocacy and initiatives such as community builders (Etmanski 2000; Gold 1994; Jameson 1998; Kultgen, Harlan-Simmons and Todd 2000).

Although these models work at the individual level, they are also important avenues for community development and changing attitudes towards people with intellectual disability that in the long run will have implications beyond a particular individual.

Comprehensive network building around an individual is the common approach taken by circles of support and PLAN. For example, PLAN is a Canadian parent-run organization that supports the development of a 'personal network' around an individual with a disability (Etmanski 2000). The aim is to build a web of relationships, achieving not only individual relationships but the collective identity and strength of a network. A paid facilitator oversees a three-stage establishment process that recruits and supports network members. The facilitator is a person with knowledge of and connections to the local community and compatibility with the person with a disability and their family rather than a human service professional. After an exploratory phase with the person and their family, potential network members are recruited by the facilitator; goals, strategies and commitment are made and the network fashioned. Over the long term the facilitator supports regular meetings of network members, ensuring follow-through on commitments and that adaptations to change are made. It is estimated that initial network formation takes up to 40 hours of facilitator time over an eight-month period, with ongoing support taking about two to three hours a month. Keys to this type of network development are a vision of what is possible, the willingness to look beyond traditional social service systems and the ability to ask for support and involvement of others. Development of such networks is used as a means of planning for the future of the adult with a disability. A major challenge for parents may be stepping aside and making room for the involvement of others in the lives of their adult child.

Other examples of formal programs that support the formation of relationships stem more from the community membership/inclusion perspective. They are based on the premise that participation in community-based activities or acquisition of valued social roles are the means to individual relationships. An example of this type of approach is the Community Membership Project in Indiana (Harlan-Simmons *et al.* 2001; Kultgen *et al.* 2000). This program uses person-centred planning techniques to build up a picture of the person with a disability, their capacities, interests, aspirations, strengths and preferences. A paid 'community builder' gets to know the person and explores the local community for sites and activities where the person may play a valued role or contribute to community life. The community builder facilitates the person's introduction to activities, seeks out and fosters the development of natural supports within them.

The degree to which friendships develop depends on attentive listening, strategy, persistent support and sometimes luck. Community builders are risk takers, creative and flexible with an ability to take an unbounded approach. Approaches such as this require significant investment of time, intensive in the exploratory stage and less so but often continuing in the long term. This project estimated an investment of up to ten hours a week for each person.

Programs that seek to build and support informal relationships demonstrate the intensive and lengthy processes involved that require planning, commitment, resources and a positive outlook. Common tasks are assessment of strengths and interests, exploration of opportunities, negotiation of entry, ongoing support to the individual or those in the social environment and review.

Summary

The foundations of the relationships that older people with intellectual disability have with family and friends, like so many other aspects of ageing, are built during the life course and reflect their earlier lifestyle and opportunities. Although many older people continue to have at least one strong and committed relationship with a family member, the chances of such a relationship decrease with age. The absence of the younger generation from the networks of older people with intellectual disability make them particularly vulnerable to social isolation and undue control and decision making by formal service providers. Supporting, nurturing and building a breadth of informal relationships, each of which will contribute in different ways to their quality of care, social well-being and quality of life, is a vital role for formal services.

Further reading

Bigby, C. (2000) *Moving On Without Parents: Planning, Transitions and Sources of Support for Older Adults with Intellectual Disabilities.* New South Wales: Maclennan and Petty.

Etmanski, A. (2000) *A Good Life for You and Your Relative with a Disability.* British Columbia: Orwell Cove and Planned Lifetime Advocacy Network.

Kultgen, P., Harlan-Simmons, J. and Todd, J. (2000) 'Community membership.' In M. Janicki and E. Ansello (eds) *Community Supports for Ageing Adults with Lifelong Disabilities.* Baltimore: Brookes.

Reinders, J. (2002) 'The good life for citizens with intellectual disability.' *Journal of Intellectual Disability Research 46,* 1, 1.

Chapter 6

Achieving a Sense of Purpose

Retirement or Supporting Lifestyle Choices

Retirement at a specified age was a cultural marker of old age in Australia, the UK and USA for much of the twentieth century, denoting older people's disconnection from the paid workforce and their greater amount of free time (Atchley 1976). Although the postmodern era has brought greater flexibility to notions of retirement that mean its nature and timing are more open to negotiation and less tied to a specific chronological age, labour force participation still decreases significantly with age (Blaikie 1999). For example, in 1998 in Australia, the proportion of people employed or actively seeking work dropped from 78 per cent of those 45 to 54 years, to 59 per cent for those 55 to 59 years and to 6 per cent for those 65 years and over (ABS 1999).

The event of retiring from a central daytime activity, whether it be open or supported employment or attendance at an activity centre for people with disabilities, has wide-ranging implications for an older person's quality of life, the nature of support required at home, friendship networks, financial well-being, sense of purpose and social participation (Budge 1998). Janicki suggests that 'inimically it [retirement] presents an immediate change in lifestyle; maximally, it may threaten one's living situation, health, social and financial supports and friendship networks' (1990, p.123).

The focus of this chapter is the concept of retirement for older people with intellectual disability and the debates that surround it. The chapter moves beyond a focus on the type of 'day program' best suited to older people to thinking about the processes and structures necessary to support an older person to pursue the lifestyle of their choice.

Time use by older people in the community

Little data exists regarding the time use of older people with intellectual disabilities, but time use studies of older people in the general community can provide a context for considering social roles and time use by those with intellectual disabilities. Compared to those of working age, older people have a much greater proportion of time that is free, unstructured or uncommitted to paid work. Surveys indicate that 30 per cent of older people's time is 'committed time', devoted to unpaid child care, voluntary work, personal care, shopping and domestic activities (ABS 1999). Older people are the single largest volunteer group within the community. Their contributed time often reaps rewards in terms of social connections and relationships, as well providing a sense of purpose. Approximately 40 per cent of older people's time (74 hours a week) is 'free' when they have greater opportunity to exercise choice and pursue leisure activities (ABS 1999). More than half of their leisure time (65%) is passive, involving activities such as talking, reading, watching TV or videos and relaxing. A smaller proportion is taken up by activities such as socializing, attending cultural and religious venues or community meetings. In a 12-month period, 67 per cent of older people attended at least one cultural event, with the three top venues being cinemas, libraries and botanic gardens. In a similar period 42 per cent of older men and 33 per cent of older women participated in some type of sports or physical activity. The most common of these activities are walking and lawn bowls. Older people have low participation rates in formal education but high rates of participation in non-award education courses (ABS 1999).

Only a small proportion of older people, primarily the frail aged, participate in formal or structured day programs. For example in the USA only 10 per cent attend a social day centre or nutrition site (LePore and Janicki 1997). Structured day programs, such as Adult Day Activity and Support Services (ADASS) aim to support the frail aged and those with dementia to remain in the community and provide respite for carers. Formal assessment is commonly required and tight eligibility criteria are applied.

Aside from very structured programs for the frail aged, a spectrum of programs, services, organizations, clubs and societies offer activities targeted at older people. In addition, they participate in social, leisure and cultural activities available to people of all ages. The activities undertaken differ in their degree of structure and formality but are in the main chosen and accessed independently by older people themselves.

Leisure time

Leisure is a key feature of retirement, central to later life satisfaction and success-ful ageing (Hawkins 1993; Hogg 1993; Parsons *et al.* 1997; Rogers, Hawkins and Eklund 1998). It is broadly conceptualized to encompass the development and strengthening of social networks, improvement of skills, exercise of choice, participation in decision making and maintenance of good physical and mental health. Leisure is a more active concept than free time and is defined as 'freely engaged in, intrinsically satisfying meaningful activity of one's own choosing' (Rogers *et al.* 1998, p.122).

Ideas about leisure provide useful ways of thinking about the use of time and the value of different kinds of activity and participation. For example, Kelly (1983, cited in Moss 1993) suggests a core and balance use of leisure time, whereby the core of a person's leisure time is home based involving activities such as reading or watching TV. Such activities tend to be fairly stable across a person's life course and are balanced by more specialized participatory activities that shift and change over the life course. He suggests that the quality rather than the quantity of activities is important to life satisfaction. Drawing on the work of Nash, Hogg (1993) suggests a balance needs to be achieved between four types of leisure engagement:

- creative participation
- active participation
- positive emotional participation
- killing time, amusement, entertainment or escape from monotony.

People may engage in similar activities but their level of engagement and thus the significance of the activity for them may differ. For example, watching a soap opera may be just killing time for a person who has not followed the drama from week to week, but involve active emotional participation for another who knows all the characters and is involved in their life stories. Thus, the value of leisure and the nature of engagement are related to the person, their sensory strengths and personality, the history of the activity rather than just the kind of activity under-taken.

'Retirement' aspirations and reality for people with intellectual disabilities

As suggested in Chapter 2, evidence suggests that a high proportion of older people with disabilities value continued active engagement with their world. They express the desire to continue working, continue learning, participate in more leisure activities and place a high value on structured activities (Ashman *et al.* 1995; Bigby 1992, 1997b; Heller 1999). This is in stark contrast to the many anecdotal stories that older people just want to 'stay at home and put their feet up'. Older people with disabilities who are working seldom express the desire to retire and are concerned about loss of income and social isolation if they cease working (Ashman *et al.* 1995; Sutton *et al.* 1991). One US study found that the majority of people who had retired wanted to return to work (Rogers *et al.* 1998).

Despite their aspirations however, older people with intellectual disabilities experience few opportunities to participate in meaningful day and leisure activities of their choice (Bigby 1992, 1997; Grant *et al.* 1995; Hawkins 1999; Rogers *et al.* 1998). 'Retirees' days were often filled with diversionary activity rather than leisure that was valued and meaningful to participants. Furthermore, they were not provided with opportunities to retain contact with previous friends or develop new social contacts' (Rogers *et al.* 1998, p.127). Choice of activity is likely to be determined by carers and is often more dependent on management of group needs rather than individual preferences (Glausier, Whorton and Knight 1995; Rogers *et al.* 1998). The lack of individual choice is accentuated by the congregate nature of activities undertaken. Even when people are at home, involvement in day-to-day domestic household activities tends to drop off for the older age groups (Wilson 1998).

Because of their characteristics and the nature of their physical or cognitive impairments, people with disabilities often require support to choose, initiate or engage in everyday domestic, personal care and leisure activities or access community facilities. Very simply, many are reliant on others to present opportunities, provide support to exercise choice and take up opportunities to participate in meaningful activities. However, for all three dimensions formidable barriers – contextual, financial, physical and attitudinal – exist (Fitzgerald 1998; Glausier *et al.* 1995; Hogg 1996; Messant, Cooke and Long 1999). Family and friends are the chief medium through which older people participate in leisure activities. Poor social networks and a lack of friends without disabilities are characteristics of older people with intellectual disabilities and identified as one of the major obstacles to their participation in leisure activities. Residential staff have limited time available after undertaking mundane housekeeping and caring tasks. Difficulties in accessing transport and the cost of activities are also common hurdles. Attitudes of the public, staff and other program participants restrict opportunities offered, obstruct access to community leisure facilities and create barriers to accessing generic programs for older people such as day centres (Glausier *et al.* 1995; Grant *et al.* 1995; Heller 1999; LePore and Janicki 1997). Individual characteristics such as poor motivation, choice, lack of skills, knowledge or preparedness may also hinder participation in activities. However, Hawkins argues that interpersonal factors are the least important in the pursuit of leisure and that structural and contextual elements such as the absence of staff support are more important (1999).

It is clear that in engaging in leisure and social activities older people with intellectual disabilities are heavily dependent on access to support and other external elements in their social environment (Bigby 1992; Hogg 1993; Jones *et al.* 1999). The question must therefore be asked as to why the concept of retirement is applied to an older person who is attending a day or employment program or even open employment that provides such external supports. The utility and advisability of seeking to replicate retirement as both an event and life phase for people with disabilities, particularly those with tenuous connection to the workforce, have been subject to much debate.

Is retirement a useful concept for older people with intellectual disability?

Labour force participation amongst people with intellectual disabilities of all ages is low (Gleeson 1998; Heller 1999). Very few of the older people with intellectual disabilities, located as part of an Australian national survey, had any experience of the workforce. Instead most had participated in day programs orientated to health, craft, hobbies, basic community and self-care skills (Ashman *et al.* 1995). The applicability of retirement, particularly for those who have attended day centres for most of their lives, is questioned: first, from a normalization perspective and the possible replication of disadvantageous 'norms'; second, from the perspective of whether retirement is meaningful and necessary or driven by system rather than individual needs.

An application of normalization theory to older people raises questions as to the desirability of replicating retirement and the resulting devalued status and vulnerable position of older people in the general community for people with disabilities (Wolfensberger 1985). Reflecting on the situation in the UK, Hogg summarizes the debate:

> Clearly the marginalised state of many older people could hardly be taken as a model... Decline in income maintenance, or still worse poverty, social isolation, and inadequate provision for physical or mental health, all typify the lives of a substantial number in our aged and elderly population. (1993, p.206)

Common themes in regard to the necessity of retirement for people with intellectual disabilities are 'why?' and 'retirement to what?'. The point being strongly made is that notions of retirement must involve the replacement of support and compensation for roles, social relationships, life meaning or activities that have been lost as a result of cessation of attendance at a day activity centre or program (Janicki 1990; Seltzer and Krauss 1987; Star 1987).

The necessity for older people to retire from day centres or substantially to change the nature of programs or pattern of service provision by, for example, reduced and more flexible hours of attendance is sometimes justified on the basis of the changes that occur to people's needs as they age. Factors such as the declining skill level of older people, their reduced abilities or the increased time required to perform tasks, their need for a quieter less boisterous environment and the incompatibility of interests and needs of younger compared to older program participants are all suggested as reasons for retirement or the development of specific programs that cater for older people (Bigby *et al.* 2001; Lambe and Hogg, 1995). Arguments are also put forward that neither day programs for younger people nor their staff have the skills, knowledge or resources to respond to the needs of older people. It is suggested that more flexible funding and specialist knowledge of both the ageing process and service systems than staff actually have in age-integrated disability services are required to provide appropriate programs for older people (DH 1997; DHS 1999a).

It could be argued, however, that if existing day services are addressing each individual's needs through individual program plans, they should be sufficiently flexible to accommodate people of all ages (DH 1997). In many instances the rationale for retirement is not strong and based on stereotypical negative images of ageing rather than individualized assessment of needs. The assumption is too often made that simply getting older is sufficient reason for instituting changes to a person's lifestyle and daytime activities (Gatter 1996).

Some imperatives for change derive from the types of service system available to younger and middle-aged people with disabilities. For example, a cross-national review suggested that one of the main imperatives to develop retirement programs in the US system was the strong training/developmental focus of day programs. In contrast, in the UK a broader approach to day programs that encompasses support for leisure and recreation meant that more flexibility and adaptation could occur within existing programs (Bigby 2001). Thus the nature of day programs or employment available to people as they begin to age is very influential in determining whether the direction should be retirement or adaptation. The notion of 'retirement from what?' may be as important in framing and answering the 'to what?' question. Retirement may also be a mechanism for managing demand on other parts of the service system by, for example, the creation of vacancies for younger people.

Aims and outcomes of day programs

Though sometimes framed in different ways, considerable agreement exists regarding the aims of day programs for older people with intellectual disabilities and the outcomes sought. Table 6.1 summarizes the views of researchers on this matter. A central theme is the high expectations that opportunity for active engagement and expression of creativity rather than passive leisure should be offered. It is clear that programs are expected to be more than just about filling in time.

The most commonly sought suggested outcomes of day programs for older people with intellectual disabilities are:

- exercise of choice
- strengthening of social networks
- participation in the community
- skill maintenance
- development of self-expression or creativity.

These reflect the dimensions captured by Nolan, Davies and Grant (2001) when they suggest that achieving a sense of purpose and achievement are important for older people, and replicate almost exactly the five accomplishments – community presence, choice, competence, respect and community participation – seen by O'Brien as central to the quality of life for people with intellectual disability (Russell 1995).

Table 6.2 summarizes the 'means' – the suggested characteristics of services or programs required to achieve outcomes.

Table 6.1 Aims and outcomes of day support services for older people with intellectual disabilities

Researcher	Service aims or outcomes sought for participants Services should provide opportunities for/to:
Catapano, Levy and Levy (1985)	• peer interaction • stimulation • participation in leisure activities • improve meaningfulness of life • challenges • prevent regression • minimize mental and physical deterioration due to ageing processes • enhance quality of life • develop and sustain skills to remain in the community
Seltzer and Krauss (1987)	• continuity and stability in interpersonal relationships • new opportunities for age-appropriate retirement activities • develop new skills • maintain existing skills
Hawkins and Kultgen (1990)	• tackle the vulnerabilities of older people with disabilities • companionship/friendships • compensation for lack of networks • community integration • improve physical function/physical fitness • adjustment to retirement
Bigby (1992)	• access and participation in activities in the local community • age-appropriate activities • social interaction • stimulation • maintenance and development of skills • sense of achievement • individual choice
Community Services Victoria (1992a)	• social interaction • skill maintenance and development • enjoyable and stimulating activities • participation in valued social roles

Foote and Rose (1993)	• development and maintenance of relationships • enjoyable leisure activity
Factor (1993)	• prevention of skill loss or regression • skill development • enhancement of community living, socialization and leisure skills • participation in natural community activities
Hawkins (1993)	• participation in leisure activities that provide an opportunity for self-development and creative expression • expression of choice • involvement in community
Moss (1993)	• maintain and enhance self-care and community living skills • lively activities to maintain physical and mental alertness • stimulating environment • social contact with friends and exploration of religious questions • exercise of mastery and choice over activity • social interaction and social support
Moss (1994)	• maintenance of autonomy • potential to make choices • develop close personal relationships
Grant *et al.* (1995)	• improve quality of life • foster choice • emotional engagement in leisure activities
Wilson, Angelo-Forrest and James (1997)	• balance choice and keeping motivated • maintain skill and confidence • involvement in day-to-day chores and everyday living tasks
DH (1997)	• access to education • access to leisure • socialization and development of skills

Rogers *et al.* (1998)	• adjustment to ageing changes • intrinsically meaningful daytime activity • develop, support and strengthen social networks • improve existing skills • participate in decision making • maintain good physical and mental health • self-determination
Walker *et al.* (1998)	• reflect individuality rather than age stereotypes • foster expression of own need • participate in community • increase competence • individual choice • gain self-esteem • sustainment and widening of friendships
Lambe and Hogg (1995)	• maintenance of maximal functioning in order to live full independent life • continuing opportunity for development and to be stretched • the opportunity for growth
Heller (1999)	• development of relationships and friendships • exercise of choice and control • ensure quality of life
Bigby (1999b)	• exercise of individual choice • opportunities for community inclusion • optimally challenging range of social, skill development and leisure activities

Table 6.2 Suggested service or program characteristics	
Researcher	**Service or program characteristics** **Programs should/offer/have:**
Catapano *et al.* (1985)	• variety of activities to reflect needs and interests • highlight strengths and abilities • prevent segregation though promotion of integration into both community and intergenerational programs
Hawkins and Kultgen (1990)	• components of therapeutic intervention • normalized and engagement in daytime routines
Riddick and Keller (1990)	• a continuum of recreational options • a range of settings, both integrated and not • focus on mainstream where possible • age-appropriate activities that can be pursued in general community • utilize interagency cooperation • be underpinned by a strong planning model
Segal (1990)	• extensive use of expressive therapies
Bigby (1992)	• facilitate access and participation in activities in the local community • age-appropriate activities • opportunities for social interaction • opportunities for stimulation • maintenance and development of skills • a sense of achievement • individualized
Community Services Victoria (1992a)	• flexible • activities selected according to choice, interest and abilities • reduced emphasis on formal training, vocational training or skill acquisition than programs for younger people • age-appropriate activities but not preclude age-integrated activities • choice attendance, full or part time

Heller (1999)	• commensurate with the paradigm of community membership • emphasize the community and family as resources • individualized lifeplans and person-centred programming
Rogers *et al.* (1998)	• effective support to engage in leisure
Walker and Walker (1998)	• regular review • flexible • offer recreational and occupational activities • respect creativity
Zarb and Oliver, cited in Walker and Walker (1998)	• user led • proactive rather than reactive • provided in a context of rights and entitlements • creative options
DH (1997)	• provide a diversity of options • develop partnership with health services • not be part of a move to ration day services between older and young people
Lambe and Hogg (1995)	• non-threatening environment • provision of stimulating activities • tailored and responsive to individual needs • flexible, optimize opportunities for involvement in generic services for the elderly and wider community and to extend social networks
Bigby (1999b)	• flexible choice of activity • flexible in regard to eligibility criteria, particularly age of entry • accessible to all people regardless of service history • community development orientation to facilitate systemic access • linkages with third age programs • sensitivity to ageing and intellectual disability issues by staff

The most commonly suggested required program characteristics are:

- availability of a wide choice of activities
- availability and choice of integrated or segregated activities both in respect of disability and age

- an individualized and planned approach to service delivery
- flexible eligibility requirements
- part-time and flexible hours and days of attendance
- use of therapeutic interventions.

The importance of a community development approach, linkages between aged and disability programs are also emphasized by several writers (Bigby 1999a; Heller 1999; Lambe and Hogg 1995). Engagement in daytime routines and domestic tasks are suggested as being a fundamental component of day programs (Hawkins and Kultgen, 1990; Wilson *et al.* 1997) indicating that activities can be located both in and external to a person's place of residence.

Frameworks for considering day programs

Debates about applicability of normalization and desirability of integration into generic aged care programs have provided the framework for considering the nature of day support options for older people with disabilities. A national survey in the USA of programs serving older people with intellectual disabilities conducted by Krauss and Seltzer (1987) suggested three basic program options:

1. *'Age integration'* including older people in programs for younger people with disabilities; for example, continued attendance at a day activity centre for people with intellectual disability, lifestyle support packages and brokerage programs such as Western Australia's Local Area Coordination.

2. *'Generic integration'* including older people with disabilities in programs for the general aged population; for example, attendance at senior citizens' centre, day centres for the frail aged, community leisure and recreation programs.

3. *'Specialist programs'* developing specialized programs for older people with disabilities; for example, day centres dedicated to older people with intellectual disabilities, combined accommodation and day support for a group of older residents, outreach programs that target older people with disabilities in supported accommodation in the community.

Table 6.3 summarizes the views of different researchers on these options and comments on the prevalence of the different options.

Table 6.3 Strengths and weakness of different approaches to day programs

Program option	Strengths	Weaknesses	Comments
Age integration Inclusion of older people in programs for younger people with intellectual disabilities e.g. sheltered workshops, day activity centres, supported employment	• Minimizes change and disruption for those attending non-vocational day occupations • Continuity of social networks (CSV 1992) • More likely to offer individualized programs, more educational input, more involvement in community leisure pursuits (Moss, Hogg and Horne 1992) • Focus on support and not care (Walker *et al.* 1996) • Active treatment programs to challenge continued development • More varied social experience, cross-age peers • Avoids labelling people as 'old' (Seltzer 1988)	• Activities not age appropriate, too difficult, not attuned to health needs, too pressured, not sensitive to age-related changes, inflexible, lack of age peer group with similar interests and levels of energy (Seltzer 1988)	• Most commonly found in 1993 national survey of Australia (Ashman *et al.* 1993) and in a Queensland survey (Buys and Rushworth 1997) • Dominant model in UK (DH 1997; Moss 1993) • Argue if service is individualized should be flexible enough to continue to address (DH 1997)

Program option	Strengths	Weaknesses	Comments
Specialist programs Development of specialist programs for older people with intellectual disabilities e.g. dedicated day centres for older people with disability, non-centre-based community access programs	• Staff specialist in ageing and disability • Greater potential to be individualized and flexible • Less pressured to skill acquisition, foster peer relationships based on age and skill (Seltzer 1988)	• Potential to isolate and segregate from both younger people with intellectual disability and old people in the community • Limited community integration • May separate from previous friendships • Concern that services less stimulating, with fewer choices, and low level of expectation (Seltzer 1988) • Stereotype and label as older and unproductive (Catapano *et al.* 1985; Seltzer 1988) • Choices are based on age and breadth of choice available to older people is reduced (Bigby *et al.* 2001)	• Few examples in Victoria • Specialist enclaves within age-integrated service are a variant of this model

Program option	Strengths	Weaknesses	Comments
Generic integration Inclusion in programs for older people in the general community e.g. use of senior citizens centres, adult day centres, generic community leisure and recreation programs	• Age appropriate activities and environment • Normalized social environment • Wider integration (Seltzer 1988) • Possibilities of new friendships, wider range of activities and choice • Fosters links into the community • Break from routines • Positive effect on behaviour and emotions • Forestall deterioration (Janicki and LePore 1997) • Spin off for older people in general community (Robertson, Moss and Turner 1996)	• Issues re access, range of barriers (attitudinal, etc.) • Lack of case and individual orientation of generic aged services (Janicki and LePore 1997) • Can be en masse attendance (Bigby 1998) • Lack of staff training • Lack of receptiveness by other service users • Inappropriate programs, geared to too high cognitive level, or too large (Hogg 1993; Seltzer 1988) • Not always available or accessible • Cost may be prohibitive (Janicki 1990) • Use of poor quality services with already devalued groups (Wolfensberger 1985) • Few options re structured programs, most focused on old 50–70 (Walker and Walker 1998)	• Most commonly found in Victorian study, included people unknown to disability services (Bigby 1998) • Dominant model pursued in USA, mandated joint planning (Moss 1993) • Demonstrated can be successful but rarely just happen, require considerable input, development (Janicki and Lepore 1997) • Not pure, may involve specialist program to facilitate access (Bigby 1992)

Conceptualizing service options in this manner suggests that the central questions are whether new or specialized programs should be designed for older people with disabilities or whether they should utilize programs already available to people with disabilities of all ages or those available to other older people in the community. These questions and the three options may however be somewhat misleading as the aged care system may not have generic programs but rather only specialist programs for the frail aged. Furthermore, for many people to successfully achieve the generic aged integration option, as has been clearly demonstrated by programs in the USA, it is necessary to establish specialist programs such as peer companions or community access or provide additional funds, staff or consultancy to the generic from the disability sector. This suggests another option – generic programs 'topped up' with specialist disability services (CSV 1992a; Gatter 1996).

Although the generic integration option fits most closely with dominant service philosophies, both Janicki (1990) and Seltzer and Krauss (1987) suggest service systems should encompass the complete spectrum of options, to ensure the individual exercise of choice and to take into account the diversity of the population in question. Janicki suggests that suitable generic aged programs may not always be available within a person's community. This point is highlighted by the relative absence of day programs for the younger old and the focus of generic aged programs on the frail aged (Bigby 1999b; Walker and Walker 1998). In addition, generic aged programs may not always be appropriate for people with intellectual disabilities and in some instances the cost may be prohibitive (LePore and Janicki 1997). Janicki and colleagues from New York have written extensively on the processes involved in supporting access and integration into generic programs for older people with disabilities, which follow simple principles to that applicable to younger adults. They suggest that the functional limitations of the person and the extent to which the intensity of day support as well as the nature of the generic programs available affect and inform the viability of integrating a person into a generic program (LePore and Janicki 1997).

Reframing day programs as lifestyle support
Segmentation of lives

Traditionally, in the disability sector day programs have been equated with a 'day placement' at a specialist segregated centre, for five days a week, from 9am to 3.30pm during school term times. Centre attendance may be interspersed with activities in the community that are negotiated and supported by centre staff.

Such day placements have fulfilled the complementary purposes of providing respite for family carers, ensuring the safety of those potentially at risk alone, skill development and/or a meaningful daytime occupation for adults with disabilities once they have left school. The experience for many individuals has been one of spending five days a week away from their home from their early school years to older adulthood.

Support required by adults with intellectual disabilities to pursue active or passive leisure interests, outside standard hours, at weekends and in the evenings has been outside the parameters of day programs and provided by parents, residential staff or specialist leisure services. As a result similar support may be provided under the guise of different programs, day, leisure and residential. This paradigm of day programs neatly divides people's lives into service types. Until recently, little questioning has occurred as to the potentially restrictive nature of such divisions and the possible overlap of purpose between these three types of programs.

Neither have purposes of day programs been explicit and thus their quality has been confounded by multiple purposes: respite for informal carers, safety monitoring and quality of life aspects. This has been particularly the case for people who require constant monitoring and safety support who do not have 24-hour accommodation support. For this group the safety monitoring functions are shared between accommodation and day programs, with the potential to undermine quality of day programs by having to stretch support over a long period of time.

New paradigm for day programs

The shift during the 1990s to individualized funding and the paradigm of community support and membership has challenged the traditional day placement model, providing a different frame for thinking about day programs. The new framework is based on person-centred planning principles whereby support is planned around an individual rather programs into which individuals are slotted. In this framework the scope of day programs is broadened, becoming more flexible in regard to times of the day or week support may occur, the places it may be delivered, the mode of delivery and activities involved. Across Australian states and territories new terms such as 'lifestyle options' and 'lifestyle support packages' have emerged to replace traditional day programs and, in some cases, combine day and residential programs. For example, in its brochure for people with disabilities and their families, the Victorian Department of Human Services (1999b) suggests that day programs are a service or 'package of services' that offer people with a disability opportunities to develop skills and increase independence, either as individuals or in small groups. The variety of activities offered and the locations in which they take place are diverse.

Distinctions between day, residential and leisure services have blurred with the suggestion that day support can occur outside the traditional hours of 9am to 3.30pm and be located in a person's home or the community as well as at a day centre. The new framework suggests that support can be provided in groups or individually, involve any activity of choice, be it passive or active, can differ from week to week and day to day and be on a regular, episodic or intermittent basis for as few as one or two hours or for substantial parts of the week.

Lifestyle support for older adults with intellectual disability

While the reconceptualization of day programs is applicable to all age groups, it has particular significance for older adults as it holds possibilities for accommodating their suggested age-related requirements for greater flexibility, less than full-time programs, greater choice, and home rather than centre base. A fundamental aspect of a lifestyle approach is the notion of planning support around an individual to take account of and adapt to their changing needs. For older people this means avoiding stereotypical attitudes that curtail opportunities and assumptions about reduced capacity and interest. However, it does mean that particular attention can be paid to physical or health restrictions and selection of activities to ensure an older person is making optimal use of the capacities they do have. It also involves compensating for interests they may have difficulty pursuing by finding alternatives.

A lifestyle approach is centred on the individual and clearly distinguishes the different purposes of support, respite, safety monitoring and optimizing qualify of life. By making the purpose of support more explicit, quality should be maximized and greater choice allowed over the use of scarce support resources. For example, a person may find it preferable to have a short period of intensive support for their interest rather than longer hours of support to participate in mediocre activities that hold little meaning for them. A broader understanding of day support reflecting the new emergent paradigm of lifestyle support is:

> Provision of support of varying intensities provided to individuals, during their waking hours, that facilitates access to activities and pastimes of choice, that are meaningful to them, which increases their quality of life and that may also ensure their personal safety. (Bigby *et al.* 2001, p.16)

Day support of this nature is fundamental in supporting the individual's chosen lifestyle, 'giving people a reason to get up in the morning'. It is not however just about providing intensive periods of activity or engagement in order to be away from home. Day support may fulfil a variety of purposes and a range of factors mediate the type of day support required by an individual, its purpose, intensity, frequency and timing. These relate to both the micro context of the individual, their characteristics and immediate social context as well as macro factors such as community attitudes, location, development of the service system and levels of funding. One of the most common dimensions that affects the purposes and quantity of day support needed is the nature of accommodation and whether or not 24-hour staffing is provided.

The overriding factor however that should drive the nature of day support for every individual is his or her individual choice of lifestyle. This is the key element that lies behind activities and gives similar activities different meanings and satisfactions for each individual.

Processes and structures for lifestyle support

Key criteria for effective support

Following an extensive literature review, Bigby et al. (2001) propose key criteria for effective lifestyle support to older people with intellectual disabilities that combine aims, objectives and program characteristics as:

- provision of choice and individualized planning
- maintenance and strengthening of social networks
- support for participation in the community
- maintenance of skills
- opportunities for self-expression and sense of self
- promotion of health and a healthy lifestyle.

Research in Australia that evaluated six quite different program types suggests that, contrary to expectations, performance on these criteria is not related to program type. Rather it is the manner in which the key concepts are understood and operationalized that is important in determining performance (Bigby et al. 2001). This suggests that processes are more important than structure. The following sections are based on this study. The six types of program evaluated were:

- brokerage

- age-integrated day centre for people with intellectual disability

- specialist centre for older people with intellectual disability

- specialist non-centre based outreach program to older people with disabilities living in supported accommodation

- specialist intellectual disability program incorporating accommodation and day support

- a jointly sponsored centred-based program that integrates older people with intellectual disability into a generic aged day centre.

No one type of program demonstrated a unique or exclusive capacity to excel on all key criteria for effective support. Indeed, the two programs judged as meeting the key criteria most effectively were a traditional age integrated centre-based program and a newer style brokerage program.

Few programs performed well on criteria of skill maintenance, opportunities for self-expression and sense of self and promotion of health and a healthy life-style. Effective operationalization of all the criteria, but particularly these latter three, depended first on an acknowledgment of their importance in respect of older people and second on appropriate strategies. Both of these require positive attitudes towards ageing and a good knowledge of the biopsychosocial processes of ageing.

Particular program types were not associated with staff knowledge or attitudes towards ageing. Somewhat surprisingly, age specialist programs did not necessarily perform any better than non-specialist, age-integrated programs. It was the expertise of individual managers and staff and the articulated philosophy and associated program monitoring that determined how systematically programs attended to enhancing physical and mental health, maintenance of skills and self-expression and sense of self. Very few initiatives related to healthy ageing were found.

One explanation for the failure of age specialist programs to perform better than age-integrated ones may be the inbuilt assumption of these program designs that reaching a certain age should be the basis for grouping people together – even before individualized planning is considered. This approach runs the risk of stereotyping people by their age. The analysis showed that grouping people in the first instance according to age may actually introduce some impediments to quality by reducing the range of options available and increasing the risk of referring people to programs (such as day centres for older people) on the basis of age rather than individual preference or interest.

Although programs evaluated used similar concepts in their documentation, the way these were operationalized differed substantially and it was the manner of operationalization that differentiated effective programs.

Individualized planning and choice

The notion of individualized planning and choice were common to all programs but the scope and breadth of these dimensions varied. In some services choice was from a pre-set menu of activities and planning limited to one small part of the person's life. Individualized planning is constrained when a program is already committed to delivering particular activities. While such programs emphasize individual planning and choice, it is only within predetermined parameters. programs that plan in this style do not typically link their activities to the overall lifestyle of the individual and do not have (or take on) responsibility for planning across all of the person's life circumstances. The constraints of such planning are illustrated in one program where 'a program booklet is developed each year and the client and/or carers get to choose what programs they will do each day'.

In contrast, some programs, such as the brokerage models planned more comprehensively across all aspects of a persons life, doing so collaboratively with the person, their informal network and other services involved in their life and took account of all their waking hours. The starting point for this sort of planning is the individual's circumstances and interests rather than what the available program can offer. Decisions about specific activities flow from the planning process rather than driving it. This type of planning considers all possible options, formal and informal support, disability, community and aged care activities, varied delivery modes, such as episodic, intermittent and ongoing delivery, and reviews the outcomes. Such planning abandons notions of full and part-time day services and builds a pattern of support to an individual over the entire week. Opportunities offered extend beyond the specific activities conducted by the program directly. The starting point for all activities is individual. Groups are only formed based on common interests – if at all. As one staff member said, 'Life has not been reduced to a series of program slots.'

An example of the outcome of an individualized planning process for one older man who used the age-integrated day centre is summarized below.

> Joe was referred to the disability day centre when he moved to a local group home after living a very secluded life for many years with his family. He was 65 and wanted to be with other people and access to the community but had very little experience of participating in any structured activities. Initially he partici-

pated in the orientation programme for six weeks, observing various activities offered both in the centre and the community with one-to-one staff support.

He now attends the disability day centre on Mondays, when he goes out into the local community with one-to-one support of a staff member. He is starting to use this time to go swimming. During the rest of his day at the centre he is supported to compile a personal interest book that is helping him to put together his life.

On Tuesdays he stays at home. On Wednesdays and Thursdays the centre has negotiated and supported him to attend an older person's day centre. This setting offers him some structure physically – as he can wander and be safe when he does this, and a very safe environment for socializing with some same aged peers. On Fridays he attends the local day hospital where additional staffing is funded by the disability service to enable one-to-one support to help him participate in activities.

Whilst it is true to say the staff and management have made these decisions, they have been based on very thoughtful assessment – both of the person, his skills and needs, his background and his environments. His age was only significant in relation to his activity levels as he is slow and a bit frail, and his access socially to people of his age. The day programme has assisted in the development of a social network, access to the community, safety and stimulation.

Building social networks

Programs that are effective in building or maintaining social networks specifically plan support and activities around this goal. In programs where people are grouped on a basis other than friendship or common interest, for example, on the basis of age alone, opportunities for building social networks are fewer. Such programs are more likely to increase a person's social proximity to others rather than their social networks.

One service that worked with very socially isolated older people had an explicit aim to develop a 'circle of acquaintances – staff, people with disabilities and community people, around each person'. Most commonly programs emphasized the social networks developing through participation in various group activities. These included individuals supported to be part of pre-existing community or aged care groups and the establishment of groups of people with disabilities. One service stressed the essential role of the program to 'build connectedness' with the staff and then with other community members.

Participation in the community

Participation in the community is more than community presence; it involves the person experiencing themselves as a contributing member of the community and being perceived in this way by others. As with social networks, effective programs actively facilitate opportunities for older people to become and remain contributing members of the community. Services varied in their interpretation of this characteristic. Most notably the difference was between the 'person experiencing themselves as a contributing member of the community' versus being 'physically present in community settings', a very similar issue to that found in relation to the social network criteria.

Community participation was most usually understood as providing at least physical access to disability specific and other aged care or community activities. For example:

> On Mondays Ethel, who is 63 years old, does Literacy and Numeracy at the community education centre. Tuesdays she goes to Elderly Citizens with others from the house and dancing at night with others from the house. Wednesday mornings she has a one-to-one session at the YMCA gym and a social club at the community centre in the afternoon with Fiona. Thursdays she has no planned activities and Fridays a friendship club from the church, which she attends on a Sunday.

Programs with a broader perspective on individualized planning were more likely to identify opportunities for people to participate actively in the community through avenues such as volunteer work and typical leisure pursuits. For some services, due to the previously restricted lifestyle of some of their participants, creating opportunities for people to be in community settings was a prerequisite to more active participation.

Only one service had an explicit commitment to community development, typified by the following example:

> I met with Mary on the day that she has morning tea with another woman and they are both supported to go to the Embroidery Guild group. Here her support worker helps her do the embroidery that the coordinator of this group sets up for her. Mary was very happy with the glasses case she had embroidered. It is planned that in the future someone from the group will pick Mary up and take her to the group and drop her off afterwards. The coordinator of this group spoke to me about how good it is to have Mary in the group. It is a very serious embroidery group. It is a truly valued activity for Mary.

Maintenance of skills

The criteria of maintenance of skills was not well met by any program types. Programs generally had few ambitious individual program goals in regard to skills development or maintenance, and program goals often reflected a sense of a gradual decline to passive rather than active pursuits. In some programs, resistance was found to any individual planning around skills or activities as it was seen as irrelevant because people were older.

Programs that did meet these criteria were focused on maintaining an active schedule of interests and physical activity to maintain people's independence within their homes and in the community. For example, 'the program aims to ensure that the residents of this supported accommodation have the opportunity to engage in enjoyable and interesting activities at home and in the community which enhance their abilities and quality of life'.

Opportunities for self-expression and sense of self

Self-expression and sense of self are fundamental to a sense of purpose, engagement and enjoyment. For many people, their chosen activities provide avenues for self-expression and reflection. In programs that met this criteria staff had an understanding of psychological tasks associated with ageing and provided opportunities for individuals to express how they felt about themselves and what was happening in their world. For example, by drama, telling your story, reminiscence, photo albums and art. Where people had lost contact with families, lived in institutions or moved many times, the impact of earlier life history may be of particular significance. Examples of the provision of such opportunities were:

> The worker takes things to prompt discussion – for example, shells brought back many memories and discussion about going to the sea – many of the people would not have been to the sea for years and this was a great way of talking about memories.

> The worker has a record of events, incidents and observations that are used to 'recount' with people what they have done, and this assists in the revision of programmes but also provides a history for the person.

Promotion of health and a healthy lifestyle

All services were sensitive to decline in physical health issues and many assumed a strong association between people aged over 50 years and declining health and fitness. In some instances, age-related decline was accepted without accurate assessment, for example, in relation to the onset of dementia, and meant failure to implement preventative health measures: 'One staff member commented that she thought there was too much emphasis on the women's health as much of what they experienced was either just old age or common ailments.'

A minority of services made explicit mention of emotional health and well-being or enhancement of health. For example, an exceptional program expressed the view:

> People need to be kept active as they get older, even though age-related health problems may modify the kind or level of activity possible. It is considered essential to build on people's strengths and to facilitate positive experiences which will enhance the individual's self-esteem.

The interrelationship of social networks, maintenance of skills and health issues is described by the following program description:

> The support worker also picks up on many other health and general 'well-being' needs and has connected many people with their families to maintain contact or re-establish contact. She takes people out to the hairdresser, provides opportunities for exercise, entertainment, celebrations, in one case support for an overseas holiday and the use of communication to encourage expression of feelings and emotions. Some other secondary outcomes are stimulation of the senses, maintenance of dexterity, muscle flexibility and fine motor skills, enhancement of self-esteem, self-awareness, self-fulfilment and maintenance of cognitive functioning, lack of isolation and increased feelings of value.

In summary, the service evaluations in this research highlighted that structural arrangements or program types alone do not guarantee that the criteria for effective services are satisfied; also that some programs operationalize standard concepts more effectively and with better outcomes than others. It is the micro-operationalization of concepts such as participation and the building of networks that are fundamentally important in determining effective programs. This highlights the need for program advocates, funders and evaluators to delve below glossy program documentation and address the values and means that are driving and sustaining the delivery of support.

Summary: retirement or adaptation?

This chapter has demonstrated that there are no simple answers to whether people should retire from their existing day occupation as they get older. It depends on the nature of their occupation and the ability of existing supports to adapt to their changing needs.

This chapter has suggested that retirement has limited applicability to older people with disabilities who have utilized day support services for significant periods during their younger years. As they age, people with intellectual disabilities themselves want to remain active and engaged. Nevertheless, flexibility and a change of pace and adaptation of activities as people age are important. This reflects the view that ageing is a process that impacts on each individual quite differently rather than a sudden event with similar outcomes for everybody.

The primary issue for those people using intellectual disability day programs as they age is the provision of continuing support adapted to their changing needs rather than transition to a fundamentally different sort of day support. In this context it must be noted that the aims of day support services at earlier stages in the life course are very similar to those proposed for older people, involving elements such as choice, community access, community participation and skill development and maintenance. The most commonly identified issues in relation to older people were the necessity to reduce the intensity of programs, hours of active programming and altering the environment in which programs occurred.

The approach of adaptation rather than transition potentially disadvantages those people ageing with a disability who are outside the disability day support system. Those people who work in open or supported employment must be given the choice to retire when they wish. Retirement and transition are issues that affect this group and they are likely to need some form of flexible day support to pursue their chosen lifestyle. In addition some people may have survived outside the day support system for much of their lives and will only seek support in later life when they loose parental or other family support. For both groups the common but often unofficial practice of an upper age limit for entry into disability support is discriminatory and few other alternatives that provide the level of support they may require to pursue a chosen lifestyle are accessible without additional sources of support.

Although a range of formal and informal community leisure programs are found in different communities and many have inclusion of people with disabilities as a key operating principle, significant barriers to access still exist. Both organizations and individual people with intellectual disabilities require an array of different resources to support access. Such resources range from staff training, effective transport systems and attendant care to individual support to select and participate in activities. Utilizing the aged care system also presents significant barriers for older people with disabilities in terms of both appropriateness and accessibility. However, the primary targets of the aged care system are the frail aged and people living with informal carers in the community, neither of which are sizeable subgroups amongst people ageing with intellectual disability. Some people will acquire additional age-related health conditions or disabilities, which will mean that services for the frail aged might be more appropriate for them.

A key conclusion is that as people with intellectual disabilities age there is a potential for day support or activities to be available to them from generic community leisure or aged care services as well as the disability day support service system. However, in many instances to gain access to such services requires additional supports from the disability day support system. This suggests a continuing role for the disability day support service system as people age, its adaptation and entry into that system for people who have spent their younger years in supported employment or without any day support.

Further reading

Bigby, C., Fyffe, C., Balandin, S., Gordon, M. and McCubbery, J. (2001) *Day Support Services Options for Older Adults with a Disability*. Melbourne: National Disability Administrators Group. Available on disability and research pages at www.dhs.vic.gov.au

Hogg, J. (1994) 'Leisure and intellectual disability: The perspective of ageing.' *Journal of Practical Approaches to Developmental Handicap 18*, 13–16.

Simmons, K. and Watson, D. (1999) *New Directions: Day Services for People with Learning Disabilities in the 1990s. A Review of Research*. Exeter: University of Exeter. www.ex.ac.uk/cebss/

Chapter 7

Achieving a Sense of Continuity and Security

Housing and Support Options to Enable Ageing in Place

Most older people in the general community have a strong desire to remain in their own home for as long as possible, and as a group they are much less likely to move than the rest of the population. For some, however, changes such as retirement, widowhood, poor health or increased disabilities mean they do move home. In Australia, small but significant numbers of older people relocate to coastal or other non-urban areas when they retire. For example, 32 per cent of all older people live within 5 km of the coast compared to 25 per cent of the rest of the population (AIHW 2002a). The very old are the subgroup most likely to move, and they do so in order to find more appropriate housing to be closer to family, or to accommodation with support commensurate with their increased needs. However, most only move within their local area and the majority remain living in a private home until well into old age. For example, only 8 per cent of older people live in any type of non-private dwellings, including hospitals and aged care facilities.

Moving requires considerable adaptation to new physical surroundings, changed social and community connections and possibly to a person's independence and the nature of supports provided. It is not generally until people reach the 'fourth age' and require substantial support with activities of daily living and healthcare that they are likely to move to an aged care facility. The proportion of older people in aged care facilities is 5.2 per cent, although for those aged over 65 years, women have a 48 per cent chance and men a 28 per cent of entering such an aged care facility (AIHW 2002a). The majority of residents in such facilities are aged over 80 years and have high dependency levels. Aged care facilities, particularly those that were formerly known as nursing homes, are generally regarded as an option of last resort for older people, where support is provided for the end of life.

Ageing in place

The broad theme of deinstitutionalization has shaped aged care polices in Australia and the UK since the mid-1980s. Policies are directed towards supporting older people to remain in the community rather than placing them in institutions (AIHW 2001; DH 2001). This has been achieved largely through programs to support the informal provision of care, predominantly by spouses and female relatives, and provision of individually tailored in home support services. In Australia, for instance, respite care, information services and mutual support groups have been developed to support carers. In addition a range of programs provide individualized flexible packages of support to older people in their own home. These range from basic home and community care packages that may include home help, domiciliary nursing, home maintenance or personal care to those that combine intensive case management and substantial brokerage funds. These programs seek to break the nexus between a person's residence and the type of support available, providing, for example, support in their own home to older people who are eligible for entry to aged care facilities.

A key concept of aged care policy is 'ageing in place'. This was originally used by urban geographers to describe the ageing of neighbourhoods that occurred as older people remained in the same area while younger people had higher residential mobility. It drew attention to the need to develop support services and more diverse housing, so older people could move to more suitable housing but remain in their local community and thus be enabled to age in place (Howe 1999, cited in Ecumenical Housing and Bigby 2000).

Ageing in place has developed as a concept that attempts to maximize choice for an older person, by allowing them to remain in the living situation of their choice for as long as they wish and are able to. It means coordinated effort is required to adapt the physical and social environment to the person by providing flexible supports as needs change rather than moving the person to a new environment where the required level of support is already in place – adapting the environment to the person rather than moving the person to new environment. The concept of 'ageing in place' is applicable to all older people, whether they live in their own homes, in public and private rental housing or in supported accommodation.

As people's physical capacity and available social supports change with age, the nature of their home – its physical and social environment – can be modified to achieve a better fit between their capacity and environmental demands or 'press' in order to maintain their quality of life. For example, physical changes such as grab rails or lighting can increase physical safety and enable continued engagement in day-to-day activities, by reducing the risk of falls and compensating for vision impairment. The introduction of in-home supports such as delivered meals, cleaning services, or personal care can complement the person's own capacity. Such supports compensate for reduced capacity and at the same time provide the opportunity for selective optimization, allowing an older person to concentrate on the tasks or activities that provide most satisfaction. Social support programs that provide transport, access to social groups or day centres, or facilitate contact through use of telephone trees, the internet or volunteer visitors, can provide opportunities to meet new or existing friends, participate in meaningful activities and reduce feelings of isolation. Programs of this nature compensate for increased social isolation that can result from mobility difficulties, or incapacity and death of spouse or friends. Relocation to a new environment that makes fewer demands, such as supported accommodation, where many instrumental activities of daily living such as cooking, shopping are provided, is often a last resort.

Achieving a good fit between an older person and their physical and social environment is crucial to aspects of their quality of life, such as safety, ensuring an optimal level of social engagement and participation as well as their ability to learn new skills and continue exercising existing ones (Lawton and Nahemow 1973). An environment that is too unstimulating or undemanding may lead to sensory deprivation, boredom, loss of skills and unnecessary dependence. In contrast if an environment is too demanding, they may be overwhelmed. Ideally a person's living situation should compensate for reduced capacity but provide sufficient challenge to enable the person to optimize their lifestyle, maintain skills and activities and prevent boredom and decline.

This chapter examines the application of the concept of ageing in place for people with intellectual disabilities and the range of possible housing and support trajectories that can occur as they age. While the focus is on the breadth of possible options for all older people with intellectual disabilities, particular attention is paid to two critical subgroups: middle-aged people living with parents who will be confronted sooner or later with making the transition from parental care; and middle-aged or older people living in shared supported accommodation whose need for support with tasks of everyday life and healthcare may increase as they age.

Key issues

Younger and middle-aged people with intellectual disabilities live in various different types of housing, and for most their support with tasks of everyday living is closely connected with their housing situation. Despite policies of deinstitutionalization, legislative and philosophical thrusts towards equal citizenship and participation, the patterns of their living situations are quite different from those of the general population. The majority of adults with intellectual disability remain at home with their parents well into middle age (Emerson *et al.* 2001). The key issue for this group is the inevitable loss of the day-to-day support provided by older parents and consequent threat to their lifestyle that will occur in middle age with the death or incapacity of their parents. Finding support with tasks of everyday living from sources other than parents, and sometimes also housing options other than the family home, will be pressing issues for a large proportion of middle-aged or younger old adults with intellectual disability.

The majority of adults with intellectual disability not resident in private homes live in shared supported accommodation, which combines housing and support (Emerson *et al.* 2001; Hogg and Lambe 2000; Simmons and Watson 1999). This large group will confront the critical issue of whether they are enabled to age in place in their home, which for them is shared supported accommodation. Key issues that arise are:

- the capacity of shared supported accommodation services to adapt the environment, type and level of support as an individual's needs change
- the stage at which relocation to an aged care or other specialist facility might occur
- the decision-making processes to make and review relocation decisions
- support available for the process of relocation.

Current trends

Although some middle-aged adults find ways to continue living in their family home after parents die, a strong trend towards relocation to shared, supported accommodation is found as people with intellectual disabilities age. For example, the balance between people living in private homes in the community and in supported accommodation shifts from 70:30 in the 20 to 24 age group to 30:70 for the over-55 age group (Emerson *et al.* 2001). Indeed some research suggests that the proportion of older people with intellectual disabilities living in private homes may be even smaller. For example, May and Hogg (1997, cited in Hogg and Lambe 2000, p.203) found only 6 per cent of people in the 58 to 63 age group lived in a private home and McGrother *et al.* (1996) found only 0.86 per cent aged over 60 years did so.

The absence of a policy framework on ageing with intellectual disability means that the nature of their housing and support is adventitious, determined largely by serendipity and the interplay of local factors (Hogg and Lambe 2000). For most older people with intellectual disability, however, the situation is less than satisfactory. For example, Grant suggests 'there is still a long way to go before it can be claimed that these older people experience a sense of place, control their home and the support necessary to live there, and hold the valued role of tenant or home owner' (Grant 2001, p.163).

Despite the lack of policy several trends are experienced as people age;

- high rates of moving home
- a likelihood of losing support from specialist disability services
- high rates of moving to aged care facilities at a relatively young age
- strong concerns regarding the inappropriateness of support provided by aged care facilities.

People with intellectual disabilities are very susceptible to unstable housing conditions as they age and experience considerable mobility. For example, in their sample of adults with intellectual disability aged over 50 years, Hogg and Moss (1993) found that 37 per cent had moved home in the previous five years. An Australian study (Bigby 2000) found that although half the group of 62 older people did not move house when their parents died, when their average age was 52 years, but by the time their average age was 65 years, only 9 out of 62 people had not moved at all. By this time half the group had moved twice and one person six times. Moving house meant that older people lost connections with friends, neighbours and acquaintances in their local areas.

Moving was precipitated by inability of replacement of informal carers to continue in that role, pressure from services, increased support needs, choice and concerns about the quality of service. Underlying causes were connected to death of parents, uncertainty or a lack of tenure rights for those in shared supported accommodation and issues relating to policies, operation, resources and staff knowledge of ageing in shared supported accommodation services.

In Bigby's study just under half the group of 62 people did not move from the parental home when they lost the support of parents. For this group supported living situations were established, where informal support, provided by siblings or other relatives and neighbours, was supplemented by formal in-home support services from either aged care or disability sectors. Such arrangements were often ad hoc, pieced together by relatives rather than occurring in the context of a comprehensive person-centred plan. A few people moved into private homes with other family members or shared the family home with a co-resident. Overall, at the time when parental support was lost, 61 per cent remained in a private home in the community, 21 per cent moved to an aged care facility and 18 per cent to disability shared supported accommodation. Even after the transition from parental care, as people aged their housing situations were not stable. Many of those who remained in a private home eventually moved to shared supported accommodation and in turn many of those who moved to shared supported accommodation moved out again to aged care facilities. Of 22 people who eventually moved into shared supported accommodation, 16 moved out again. Thus, by the age of 65 years over two-thirds of adults who had lived with their parents for most of their lives were living in an aged care facility.

Although figures are only indicative, it would appear that in both the UK and Australia disproportionately high numbers of older people with intellectual disabilities live in aged care facilities. For example, in Scotland it is estimated that one in ten of people with an intellectual disability living in all forms of supported accommodation are in an aged care facility (Scottish Executive 2002). Thompson and Wright (2001) estimate that older people with intellectual disabilities make up between 0.15 per cent and 13 per cent of residents in aged care facilities and, in the relevant administrative areas represented between 0.5 per cent and 73 per cent of people with intellectual disability receiving some form of residential provision.

Various studies and indicators suggest significant concerns exist as to the appropriateness and quality of support available to people with intellectual disabilities in aged care facilities. For example, the UK White Paper *Valuing People* suggested that some older people are 'misplaced in older persons homes living alongside much older and more incapacitated people' (DH 2001, p.104). Several studies in both the UK and Australia support this view, demonstrating that people with intellectual disabilities in aged care accommodation are significantly younger than other residents (Bigby 2000; Thompson and Wright 2001). For example, a UK study found the average age of residents with intellectual disability to be 71 years, and only 38 per cent to be over 75 years compared to an average age of 80 to 85 years for other residents. Reasons for such inappropriate placement include a lack of alternatives, stereotypical attitudes, misplaced ideas about normalization, inflexibility of shared supported accommodation or a joint placement with an older parent who moves to an aged care facility.

A comparative study of older people with intellectual disability in disability and aged care facilities concluded that the residents in aged care received poorer quality services, less indivualized programs and were less involved in leisure pursuits than their peers in disability accommodation (Moss and Hogg 1989). Bigby's (2000) research in Australia found that moves to aged care facilities were often contested by family members who considered such services to be of inferior quality, and lacked staff with the knowledge and skills to respond to the needs of older people with intellectual disabilities.

Housing and support options for older people with intellectual disability

Table 7.1 is a schematic summary of the various housing and support options that may be available to people with intellectual disability as they age. The sections below discuss the various options and consider ways in which they could be adapted to optimize quality of life or enhance possibilities of ageing in place. Particular attention is focused on options for those who have lived at home with parents and who in middle age lose their support, and those living in disability supported accommodation as they age. The discussion is in terms of general models, rather than the detailed specifics of programs as these vary considerably over time and across different jurisdictions. Models of housing and support provide only a partial picture, as important are the micro processes of day-to-day implementation – operationalization sophistication. In the UK this has come to be associated with the active support model (Simmons and Watson 1999), the importance of which is captured by both Mansell and Felce:

> The key determinant of quality of residential care is the way staff provide support to individual service users; therefore the improvement of services

Table 7.1 Existing housing and support options for people ageing with intellectual disability

	Semi-independent or supported living: separation of housing and support		Communal living: partial integration housing and support		Group Living: integration of housing and support	
Housing/ living arrangements	**Independent housing in the community** i.e. have own front door and address **With informal carer/s, usually parents or could be siblings or other family**	**Independent housing in the community** i.e. have own front door and address **Alone or with partner or friends** • choice of co-residents if at all	**Living in a room in a building with others with some communal facilities** • uncommitted/ unconnected to each other • no choice of other residents	**Living in a room in a building with others – some communal facilities and support provided** • uncommitted to other residents • may try to connect residents • usually less than 20 residents • with paid family carer	**Small group congregate living (3–10 people)** • living with others • no choice over fellow residents • access is based on care, rather than housing needs • no tenancy rights (exception is shared equity ownership)	**Large group congregate institutional living (10–60+ people)** • living with others • no choice over fellow residents • access is based on care, rather than housing needs
Examples	• own home • private rental flat unit or house • public housing • community housing • (all likely to be in name of the carer)	• own home or joint ownership • private rental • public housing • community housing • shared equity housing	• boarding/ rooming house (private or public) • shared housing with: strangers, friends, people with similar needs	• Abbeyfield housing • boarding house with some services, e.g. meals • serviced apartments (private) • adult home board	Shared accommodation with variation in regard to: • proximity to other services • physical design • mix of residents age and support needs • support models • hours of staffing • tenure/ownership	• nursing homes • hostels • supported residential services (usually private) • disability institutions • design, management and approach to provision of care can increase or reduce institutional feel

Possible supports and age-related adaptations	• informal co-resident carer • other family or friends • flexible in-home support from disability, aged care or health domiciliary servcies with or without long-term case management • targetted at carer or person with disability • replacement of parents by other informal carer • transfer of ownership/tenure to person with disability	• from family or friends • flexible in-home support from disability, aged care or health domiciliary services with or without long-term case management • local mutual supportive network • local community support worker available to call on if necessary	• from family or friends • flexible in-home support from disability and/or aged and/or domiciliary with or without long-term case management • potential for sharing support services	• some support with meals, domestic chores or personal care are built into the housing model • can be supplemented by external flexible in-home support from disability, aged or domiciliary health services with or without long-term case management • potential for sharing support services	• support services predominantly provided by service itself • possibility of supplementation by external in-home support from age care, domiciliary health services, targeted to a particular individual • possibility of resources and consultancy re ageing from external or internal sources	• support predominantly provided by service itself • may be supplemented by external programs predominantly in area of recreation and social support
Location	• scattered through community • in a retirement village	• scattered through community • in retirement village • clustered together in walking distances of others in supported living e.g. Key Ring.	• scattered through community • in retirement village	• scattered through community • in retirement village • e.g. sheltered housing	• scattered through community • in retirement village • near a hostel/nursing home or SRS	• scattered through community • in retirement village • near other congregate care services

Source: Adapted from Ecumenical Housing and Bigby (2000)

requires management focus on staff training, leadership and practice instead of building and location. (Mansell 1998, cited in Simmons and Watson 1999)

If as the research seems to show, supporting people with learning disabilities is not an intuitive skill, it will be the adoption of effective working methods, backed by good management and staff training, which will result in the delivery of support, not further appeal to ordinariness. (Felce 1999, cited in Simmons and Watson 1999)

Possible options for those living with older parents: supported living

The alternatives for people living at home with parents are limited only by visions of what is possible. In the last decade, both the aged care and disability sectors have focused considerable attention on developing models and technologies that enable people to be supported in their own home in the community. The core of this approach is the separation of housing from support and the provision of planned, coordinated support tailored to individual needs. The aim is that a person should not have to move home to acquire the type of support they require. In seeking access to supported living, older people with intellectual disabilities can potentially draw on both the aged care and disability sectors.

In Australia relatively low levels of in-home support are provided by generic home and community care services that have both the aged and younger people with disabilities as their clients. Although this program covers a range of service types, support is restricted to a few hours a week. In the aged care sector flexible 'care packages' are the most common model of supporting people with more intensive needs. Such packages combine case management with flexible funds to broker support services. The primary focus is on practical support and 'care'. Attention to social supports and maintenance of social networks is not as well developed. The value of packages varies with program and target group. It is clear, however, that agencies which administer packages operate with considerable creativity, mixing and matching packages, blending components of each to attain the degree of support required by an individual. Of necessity, costs are averaged across the entire agency caseload rather than each client being allocated a predetermined amount.

In the disability sector the notion of flexible care packages is encompassed by the concept of supported living. In this model, although similar to that found in the aged care sector, the focus is more strongly on support and participation rather than simply care, with the twin aims being support for people to live in their own homes and enabling participation in the community. Ideally supported living encompasses a combination of person-centred planning, individualized support and community development activities to build bridges to the community and achieve systems change. Advantages of the approach are:

- it opens up to people with disabilities the full range of housing options and tenure, e.g. private rental, community or public housing, private ownership or shared equity arrangements

- greater choice can be exercised with whom, if anyone, a person lives

- supports are designed around a person's existing community connections and informal supports

- as needs change support can be reconfigured without having to move home

- security and status as tenants or home owners is gained

- increased possibilities exist for people to control their own lifestyles (Simmons and Watson 1999).

It is impossible to define clearly the characteristics of people who can be supported to live at home and those who need support in a more highly supervised and supported environment. In fact, as evidence from field of ageing suggests, it is often the nature and availability of informal support rather than an individual's characteristics that determined whether they are able to remain in a private home (Fine and Thompson 1995).

The boundaries are shifting as more diverse models of community support develop, expertise of support workers increases and attitudes of families and the community change. Management of the tensions that exist between supporting independence, allowing people to choose to take informed risks and professional, community and family concerns about duty of care and fears about safety is a key challenge for case managers. These tensions too have a significant influence on who is regarded as able to stay at home, how such decisions are made and by whom. However, the philosophy, although not always the practice, behind supported living in the disability sector is that no one is too disabled to live in their own home. Many people who in the past would have been in institutional care are now being effectively supported to live at home.

Considerable overlap exists in the dependency and care characteristics of older people with intellectual disabilities who are supported to live in the community, who live in shared supported accommodation and who live in aged care facilities. For example, a NSW study that contrasted residents with mild or moderate intellectual disabilities in group homes with those living in supported living situations found people with similar characteristics in both settings (Stancliffe and Keane 2000). On most indicators the outcomes for the two groups were similar, although less support hours were provided to those in supported living. Outcomes for those in supported living were better in regard to use of community facilities and participation in domestic tasks.

The concept of supported living has broken the nexus between assessed level of dependency and formal support options, substantially adding choice into the equation for those with high support needs but few informal supports.

Features of supported living

Individualized packages are the most common model of supported living and although models vary they have key features in common that are central to their success including:

- individualized assessment of capacities and needs of the person with a disability that take into account their informal support system, preferred lifestyle, life stage and aspirations

- a collaborative approach to support planning with the person and those in their informal network that covers all aspects of a persons life

- a case manager who ensures that appropriate and coordinated services are provided and available and monitors their provision

- flexible funding for purchasing services that are needed but not available from other sources.

Some supported living models blend such packages with other types of support such as mutual, informal, ad hoc, or on call. One of the most well-known examples are the Key Ring networks that aim to build a network of mutual and informal community support for a small cluster of people with disabilities living within walking distance of each other in single or shared rental accommodation. In addition to facilitating such support a community worker lives within each network providing back-up or on-call advice or support when necessary (Simmons 1998).

In Queensland, lifestyle packages have combined funding for accommodation and day program support, removing program boundaries that have segmented people's lives. This approach allows flexible 24-hour support to be built around an individual to optimize both housing and lifestyle support. If accompanied by effective planning and monitoring, the advantages of integrated support may outweigh fears implicit in a whole of life service approach to support. The Western Australian local area coordination model takes a similar approach, combining various sources of funding, together with informal supports and community development strategies, to build a lifestyle around an individual.

Ensuring success

For middle-aged people with intellectual disabilities living at home who lose the support of parents, supported living, remaining in a private home in the community with a blend of informal and formal support, is a more viable and acceptable option than it was a decade ago. Clearly, decisions must take into account factors such as individual choice, competence and support needs, risk, nature of available informal support, access to secure housing, and access to packages of support from disability or aged care programs. Ability to access support packages in a climate of unmet demand is a major obstacle but sometimes protective attitudes, lack of vision and coordination can be just as obstructive. In the absence of formal support packages, ad hoc arrangements are often made. For example, Bigby (2000) found examples where small amounts of aged care and disability supports were blended together with neighbourhood and family support to enable people to remain either in the family home or to move to rental accommodation. Availability of a key informal network member or proactive case manager to oversee the organization and quality of support was in many instances the lynchpin of continued residence in a private home. Situations that fail often do so through lack of thorough assessment of support needs, which means some needs are not adequately addressed, poor communication between support workers or lack of regular monitoring and oversight to identify difficulties before they develop into major problems. An ongoing challenge for case managers and informal network members in supporting independent living is achieving a balance between choice and risk and the use of directive support.

Secure housing is a prerequisite for supported living. For people with intellectual disabilities this can range from simple home ownership, trust arrangements that enable the person to remain at home, shared equity schemes, or rental in the private, public or community housing sector. Using the family home or its value to maximize the long-term housing choices of a person with intellectual disability has been explored both in Australia and the UK (King and Harker 2000). Various models of trusts or shared equity arrangement are proposed. A key principle to such arrangements however is flexibility, to ensure an person is not locked into housing that may become inappropriate as they age because of size, location, physical design, or maintenance costs. Evaluations of supported housing have not focused on age, as Hogg and Lambe suggest:

> It is however in the very nature of the community living philosophy that there has been no need to focus specifically on the fact of people's ages in making provision for them. Since the development of support begins with the individual's needs, then age related needs will be taken into account as part of the needs assessment, and change functions and abilities responded to accordingly. (Hogg and Lambe 2000, p.209)

Communal living: partial integration housing and support

As Table 7.1 suggests, some models combine housing with limited inbuilt support but also rely on flexible individualized external supports. These models include sheltered housing or clusters of older persons' units where residents each have their own unit, often linked to a resident warden by an alarm system. There may also be communal facilities such as a common room, laundry or guest room.

Another approach is the Abbeyfield model which accommodates up to ten residents in one house, each with their own bedroom and ensuite bathroom. The kitchen, laundry, house bathroom, spare bedroom, sitting and dining rooms are common areas. A key feature of this model is the employment of a housekeeper who lives rent free in a self-contained unit on the site. The housekeeper prepares two meals five days a week, cleans the common areas and provides limited support, but not personal care assistance, and is available to be called upon during the night in the event of an emergency. An important part of this model is to encourage residents to participate in the ongoing management of the house through participating with daily household chores (cleaning their own rooms), assisting with shopping and cooking, participating in house meetings and the selection of new residents. Residents are expected to manage their own lives but can access external packages of care from aged care or disability services. This model has similarities to some types of boarding houses, although it is on a smaller scale and residents are more likely to share similar characteristics.

Compared to living in their own unit, people in the Abbeyfield model may have less control over some of their living arrangements because of shared facilities and expectations of communal eating. However, these restrictions may be compensated for by the greater sense of security and support available.

Group living: integration of housing and support

Difficulties of ageing in place in shared supported accommodation

Most older people in the general community who live in private homes have both the choice and opportunity to remain at home as they age and their need for support increases. The key issue is whether this same opportunity can be afforded to people with intellectual disabilities whose home is shared, supported accommodation.

The available evidence suggests that shared supported accommodation is as effective for older as for younger people, that age is not an indictor of quality and that the benefits of small group living compared to institutions are equally applicable to older as younger people (Hogg and Lambe 2000). However, as discussed in an earlier section, the trend exists whereby ageing people are moved out of shared supported accommodation. This indicates that these services have difficulty adapting to changing needs as people age. Key areas of difficulty are:

- accommodation funding models based on full-time attendance at a day program for residents

- lack of resources or flexibility to respond to changed support and care requirements

- concerns about the safety and well-being of frail residents in mixed age houses

- poor design and adaptability of houses

- lack of expertise and skilled assessment capacity

- inability to access external specialist resources

- misconceptions about ageing.

In Australia the dominant funding arrangement for shared supported accommodation assumes that residents attend a day program on a full-time basis. Most day services are programmatically and organizationally separate from accommodation services. Few incentives and many obstacles to collaboration and creative use of resources across services exist. Rigidity in accommodation and day service funding models often means therefore that when older residents spend more time just at home, out of choice or due to chronic health problems, the accommodation service must provide additional unfunded support during the day.

The notion of 'double dipping' means that accommodation services may find it difficult to access home and community care services such as domiciliary nursing, as it is assumed they are already funded to meet all the personal care and support needs of residents. Where frail older residents who live in accommodation with more active younger people, this may pose potential physical dangers and risks for an older person. The ageing of some residents may result in greater diversity among residents, leading to incompatibility or difficulties in adapting routines to take into account diverse needs. The design of some shared supported accommodation means it cannot easily be adapted to age-related needs, increasing the costs of modifications and limiting the potential to make required modifications to facilitate the continued independence and safety of an older person.

Accommodation services find it difficult to respond to the changes in health, personal care and support required by residents as they age. Staff may lack knowledge and understanding of the ageing process or health issues and be unsure how adapt types of assistance and the manner in which they are provided. As most residents in shared supported accommodation do not have an active case manager, accommodation services fill the gap by taking responsibility for coordinating healthcare and monitoring overall well-being. As people age these tasks can become more complex and may place demands beyond the financial and professional resources of accommodation services.

The absence of skilled case managers may also exacerbate difficulties in accessing comprehensive assessment of health and related care issues, central to effective planning. Aged care assessment services and general practitioners, who should play a key role in assessment, often have limited experience or understanding of people with intellectual disability. Their existing assessment approaches and tools may be inappropriate for this group. The consequence is that accommodation services may be unable to access good information on which to undertake sound planning as to how best to meet a person's needs. This can also lead to decisions to relocate a person with less than optimal outcomes. The absence of transparent processes to make and review decisions to move a resident to an aged care facility mean that families and advocates cannot be satisfied all options have been considered and have no real avenue to seek review.

Strategies for ageing in place

Various strategies should be used to adapt shared supported accommodation to the needs of older people and ensure, in the longer term, service systems are designed to take account of ageing residents. However the adoption and implementation of such strategies must occur in the context of overarching policy that acknowledges the rights of people with intellectual disabilities to age in place and the responsibility of the disability service system, ideally in collaboration with the aged care sector, to provide the resources to support this. Flowing from this, as suggested in Chapter 4 in regard to dementia, accommodation services must develop clear statements on their position in regard to ageing in place that articulate the levels of support they can sustain for older residents and provide indicators as to when continuing care may no be longer viable. This will help ensure that long-term planning can occur for older residents and any moving that is necessary occurs in predictable, planned, timely manner in accordance with clear policies and transparent decision-making processes.

Adaptation of shared supported accommodation to the needs of older residents must be supported by access to person-centred planning, coordination and implementation of plans, and is also likely to require change to other systems, particularly day programs. Possible strategies are:

- design and building modifications
- staff training and education processes
- changes to staff mix and resourcing
- use of external services to provide specialist assistance
- changed resident selection practices
- strategic location close to aged care facilities
- designation of specific houses within a service for older people.

Identifying and undertaking required building modifications is an approach that adapts housing to a person's changing needs. In the longer term adoption of adaptable housing designs means that required modifications can be carried out more cheaply and easily. For example, installation of benches with adjustable heights may be a high cost initially but could effect substantial savings in the long run and ensure an older person who becomes wheelchair dependent is able to remain engaged in domestic activities.

Staff training to increase understanding of ageing processes and counteract stereotypical images of ageing is an important way to enhance the ability of support staff to respond to the changing needs and be sensitive to age and capacity. For many organizations, due to staff turnover and use of casuals, this must be a continuous process. A model adopted by some organizations is the employment of a registered nurse or ageing specialist who trains and supervises support workers to undertake specific nursing-related procedures for individual clients.

Other staffing strategies relate to the skill mix and quantum of resources available. As suggested earlier, as older residents alter their lifestyle, staffing across the day may be necessary. However, not all people require constant monitoring and daytime support could be organized on a drop-in, shared basis between several houses. On-call rather than constant staffing may be another possibility.

The skill mix of support staff could be changed over time to ensure the organization has staff with experience and qualifications in nursing or gerontology. A possible approach is a consultancy/resource model, where an aged care or nursing professional is employed to resource a cluster of shared supported houses. Their role could include staff training, assessment and monitoring clients' health-related needs, coordination of responses to health and medical needs of older residents and liaison with general practitioners and aged care assessment services. This approach may be viable where an organization has a critical mass of older people to sustain the employment of an ageing professional to resource the organization. Alternatively a regional resource of a similar nature could be established and available to be shared between a number of organizations.

Residents in shared supported accommodation should be able to access specialist domiciliary nursing. One approach is to purchase such support externally rather than relying on internal organizational resources. This may be more appropriate for small organizations or those in rural areas without the volume demand necessary to sustain their own internal resources.

In the longer term housing design and resident selection practices could support the better adaptation of shared supported accommodation to older residents. However, diversity of individual ageing processes means that selecting residents of similar ages will not necessarily ensure their health and support needs are aligned. Designs other than communal houses may however facilitate the accommodation of differential support needs and ageing processes. For example, designs such as bedsits, or separate units on one site, can facilitate co-location of people of different ages or support needs. This approach has the potential to enhance the ability more effectively to respond to some needs of older people in mixed age houses, as well as the potential to provide more flexibility and choice about degree of interaction with others. It would require careful planning and selection of residents and development of an effective model for providing support to people with varying types and levels of need.

A final strategy is that of designating specific shared supported accommodation for older people. In some services this occurs naturally when an existing household of residents all start to age about the same time. In other instances a household may be developed where some of the residents in a house are already ageing and vacancies are filled with older clients from mixed age houses. One advantage of this approach is its cost effectiveness, if for example three older people can be supported at home together rather than one. This approach will also increase the viability of employing staff with specific skills and expertise in working with older people. It may facilitate the development of household routines that reflect age-appropriate needs and can take account of changing capacities without disadvantaging some residents.

However, developing special houses for older people could also be viewed as a threat to ageing in place, as potentially older people may be encouraged to move to fill vacancies. Unless very carefully implemented, such an approach could result in discrimination on the basis of age. There is also the potential problem that healthier older clients may be confronted with a procession of frail older residents who come to the house and then die relatively quickly.

One example that takes this strategy further was developed in a rural region in Victoria, where a house was designed for ten people ageing with an intellectual disability. The team of staff who work at the house is carefully selected to ensure they have the skills and knowledge required to provide appropriate support and care and includes a qualified nurse. This model falls between the more traditional shared supported accommodation model developed for people with intellectual disabilities and a specialist aged care facility. It involves segregation of older people in groups larger than that commonly accepted for younger people. The creation of larger specialist facilities creates a new model that poses difficult issues. The advantages of such a model must be juxtaposed with those of integrating older people with disabilities into already existing congregate care facilities for older people in the community. Such an option that may involve clustering people with intellectual disabilities within an aged care facility is probably less discriminatory and more commensurate with current policy directions.

If an older person is to move from shared, supported accommodation, their most likely destination is an aged care facility. The next section examines the nature of these facilities and possible adaptations to increase responsiveness to people with intellectual disabilities. The last section discusses assessment, decision-making and moving processes that are fundamental in considering relocation for an older person.

Larger congregate care facilities

Large congregate care facilities include government subsidised aged care facilities that in Australia now incorporate hostels as well as nursing homes, and private non-subsidied facilities that cater for younger people with disabilities as well as the frail aged. In Victoria these latter facilities, known as supported residential services, are divided into the pension-only sector that serves low income groups and those that charge well in excess of the pension and serve the more affluent. Although different terms are used and they are subject to differing licensing requirements, many jurisdictions have similar private sector congregate care facilities.

The majority of residents in aged care facilities are over 80 years with high levels of dependency. Facilities provide assistance with all activities of daily living and personal care. Support must include staff continuously on call, meals, accommodation, furnishing, linen, laundry, bedding, cleaning and maintenance of buildings and grounds. These facilities cater for the frail aged, many of whom have severe mobility limitations, or well-developed dementia with significant levels of confusion or behaviour difficulties. The median length of stay in nursing homes is 395 days and in hostels 758 days. In 1996–7 43 per cent of nursing home residents stayed for less than two months and 78 per cent of residents left aged care facilities because of death (AIHW 1999). Aged care facilities are essentially places where people with very high support and medical needs go to be supported at the end of life.

The main difference between hostels and nursing homes is the level of care. Hostel level care includes accommodation, personal care and some nursing care, whilst nursing home level care has 24-hour nursing care. The majority of aged care facilities are larger than 20 beds, with 10 per cent having over 60 beds. Although at any one time a very small proportion of older people live in aged care facilities, the chances of residence increase substantially with age. For example, at age 65 an older person has a one in three chance of entering a nursing home, whilst by age 80 this has increased to a one in two chance.

The private pension only congregate care facilities increasingly support younger people with disabilities, who cannot gain access into more suitable state-subsided forms of supported accommodation. The proportion of residents with intellectual disabilities has decreased and been replaced by those with psychiatric or dual disabilities. The dependency levels of residents are less than those in aged care facilities. Support provided can include assistance with personal care, physical assistance for people with mobility problems, supervision, assistance or supervision of medication and emotional support. Major concerns have been expressed about the level of care and degree of social isolation experienced by people in these facilities and the continued viability of this sector (Green 2001).

Quality of care issues

As suggested earlier in this chapter, people with intellectual disabilities are often regarded as misplaced in aged care facilities where they tend to be much younger than other residents and stay for longer. Concerns about the quality and appropriateness of aged care accommodation include:

- lack of staff understanding, experience and training about people with intellectual disability
- poorer quality of service compared to disability services evidenced by larger facilities with lower costs and inputs
- a milieu of care which is dependency enhancing rather one of active support and competency enhancing found in disability services
- lack of input from or contact with specialist disability services, or staff knowledgeable in this field
- restricted access to activities and relationships outside the home (Hogg and Lambe 2000; Thompson and Wright 2001).

Thompson and Wright suggest that not only are older people in aged care accommodation misplaced, but they are also forgotten. Responses to these issues have been to advocate avoidance of such placements, development of specialist aged care facilities for people with intellectual disabilities and the adaptation of existing facilities to make them more appropriate.

Relocation to an aged care facility is usually the option of last resort for the frail aged and should also be so for older people with disabilities. These facilities are conceivably the most appropriate option only for older people with intellectual disabilities who require constant nursing care, particularly those with advanced stages of dementia. Some have argued, however, that because of the poor quality of aged care facilities and lack of responsiveness, specialist aged care facilities for people with intellectual disability should be established. One such facility with 52 beds has been built on the grounds of one of the few remaining large-scale institutions for people with intellectual disability in Australia. Services such as social work, speech pathology, physiotherapy and recreation and leisure support staff are shared with the larger institution. The staff represent a mix of expertise, including registered nurses, care workers with a background in intellectual disability, a developmental educator and a clinical nurse consultant. Funding is provided through the standard subsidy for aged care beds, complemented by some disability funding and internal organizational funds.

Issues arise regarding the viability, necessity and advisability of constructing specialist facilities. It is not clear whether there is a sufficiently high, stable and predictable demand to ensure the viability of facilities of this nature. Older people with intellectual disability are still a very small group relative to the aged population in general. A danger is that the catchments of such facilities would have to be so large that older people would be moved a great distance from their locality, effectively dislocating continuing connections with family and friends. Alternatively, if demand is low a downward pressure may be exerted on the level of support required for admittance, opening facilities up to people do not require intensive support in order to maintain viability. It has not been clearly established that such facilities are necessary. As a concept such developments contradict policy thrusts towards inclusion and appear to perpetuate segregation of people with intellectual disabilities. Insufficient evidence exists to suggest the quality of specialist facilities is better than found in the mainstream. Neither have strategies, such as those discussed below, to increase the responsiveness of mainstream aged care facilities been fully explored or evaluated. The absence of demonstration projects testing adaptive strategies and comparative data leaves the case for specialist facilities unproven at this point.

Increasing quality and responsiveness

A number of strategies to resource or restructure aged care facilities can be used to ensure they are more responsive to older people with intellectual disability. They are premised on the understanding that older people with intellectual disabilities are a very small group and aged care facilities will be appropriate for only a very small proportion of them. Thus facilities will have very limited exposure to this group. Strategies include:

- clustering older people with intellectual disability within facilities to allow employment of staff with expertise in disability as well as aged care or nursing, which may involve regional specialization where one facility within a region builds up its expertise and responsiveness

- establishment of a regional resource to offer staff training or consultation to facilities when they have residents with intellectual disability

- continuing case management from disability services, proactive support to maintain links with family and friends and ongoing contact with familiar staff from previous accommodation situation for people with intellectual disability who move to aged care facilities.

As well as the importance of increasing responsiveness, additional input to aged care facilities in respect of people with intellectual disabilities may be justified on the grounds that they are one of the most vulnerable aged groups. As suggested in Chapter 5, they are unlikely to have strong informal connections or advocates available to monitor the type of care provided.

Relocation, assessment, decisions and review

Given the high probability of entry to an aged care facility for the old old in the general community, it is conceivable that such facilities could provide the most appropriate nursing care for some older people with intellectual disability with very high health or dementia-related needs. Major questions however surround the assessment and decision-making process associated with relocation. The absence of skilled assessment and transparent processes at present means relocation is often sudden, controversial and poorly implemented.

In Australia access to aged care facilities is restricted to those assessed as eligible by an aged care assessment team. As suggested earlier, the expertise of these teams lies in the assessment of needs arising from age-associated disabilities and health problems and they have limited understanding of intellectual disability. Assessment must take account of lifelong skills, starting points and loss of skills rather than simply assessing current functioning. The danger is that a high proportion of people with intellectual disability will be assessed as eligible for aged care facilities by using global assessment of function.

Only after attaining a comprehensive assessment and a full consideration of less restrictive options should the decision be considered to relocate an older person to an aged care facility. The guiding questions must be as follows:

- Is the proposed relocation commensurate with organizational and broader disability policies?

- Are the person's support needs so great that they can no longer be optimally met in their existing situation?

- Have all possible adaptations to their current situation been considered?

- Is a move to an aged care facility the least restrictive for the older person?

Decision making of this nature must seek the views of the person where possible, and involve informal network members and staff who know the person well. They should never be made by the current accommodation service alone. Clear processes must be in place to ensure decisions reflect the best interests of the person rather than merely cost considerations. For example, in Victoria decisions should be made within the context of a general service plan, which will ensure involvement of a case manager and informal network members and can be subject to appeal process if any party is dissatisfied. Realistically cost will always be part of the equation in such decisions, but transparent decision-making processes can at least ensure that all perspectives are heard and all options considered.

Once a decision is made, its implementation must be planned and purposeful rather than haphard and crisis driven. A period of familiarization and adjustment to a new environment must be built in if feasible. A major consideration for this group is to ensure lasting mechanisms are in place to retain social connections to friends that may be left behind in previous accommodation and to family members and friends in the community.

Summary

Solutions to meeting the housing and support needs of older people with intellectual disability lie in broadening visions of what is possible when parental support is lost, adaptation of shared supported accommodation to changed support needs and the flexible, creative use of available funding. Support provided by shared supported disability accommodation must be melded to be more responsive and adapted to the needs of older residents just as that provided by aged care facilities must be fashioned to be more responsive to older people with lifelong disabilities. Relocation to an aged care facility may be inevitable at some stage, particularly for those with dementia. However, if comprehensive assessments and transparent decision-making processes are a sine qua non of such relocations, less contested and inappropriate placements are likely to occur. It is in the arena of housing and support more than any other aspect of their lives that older people with intellectual disabilities are subject to age discrimination and the inappropriate application of stereotypical responses. If these can be broken down, then a better chance of ageing in place in an optimal environment of choice will occur.

Further reading

King, N. (2001) *Family Home: Using Parental Property to Provide Future Housing for People with Learning Disabilities. Guidance for Families and Advisers.* London: Foundation for People with Learning Disabilities. www.learningdisabilities.org.uk

Simmons, K. and Watson, D. (1999) *The View from Arthur's Seat: A Literature Review of Housing and Support Options 'Beyond Scotland'*. Edinburgh: Scottish Office Central Research Unit. www.scotland.gov.uk/publications/ or www.bris.ac.uk/Depts /NorahFry

Thompson, D. and Wright, S. (2001) *Misplaced and Forgotten: People with Learning Disabilities in Residential Services for Older People*. London: Mental Health Foundation.

Part 3

Vignettes

Henry Parkes

Henry is 67 years old. For the past seven years he has been living in a hostel for older people run by a church organization. Henry has very poor vision and wears thick glasses to see things close up. He is a heavy smoker. He participates in regular outings with groups from the hostel but doesn't really like going out much. He really enjoys looking at picturebooks of places around the world and would love to be able to write. Henry has always needed quite a lot of help with personal care and his failing sight means it is increasingly difficult to shave without assistance. He spent his younger years at home, where he and his twin brother did everything with their mother.

Henry is good friends with Bessie, another resident of the hostel, who also has an intellectual disability. They often sit together in the lounge watching television and share a table at dinnertime. He used to have another friend, Jim, but he hasn't seen him since he moved to another aged care facility. Jim rings every couple of weeks. Henry goes home with his niece, Maddy, for tea one night during the week and he sees her another night when she brings his washing back. Maddy takes him to medical appointments when necessary and to family events such as her son's wedding or her granddaughter's christening. The minister from Harry's old local church visits once every couple of months.

Both Henry's parents are dead, as are his twin brother and elder brother. Maddy is his only close relative. When Henry's parents died, he and his twin lived with their elder brother until he too died. They stayed in the house for a while alone, but found it quite difficult to look after themselves as neither had domestic or household management skills. The local minister used to keep an eye on them and organized meals on wheels and home help. Every now and again Maddy would get a phone call from the neighbours complaining about the state of the house or their fighting. Maddy had a young family and though she stayed in touch she really couldn't help much. Eventually, the minister persuaded Henry and his brother to move to a private supported accommodation facility in a converted motel. They shared a room, but there was nothing to do all day and very little assistance with personal care or health needs. Henry's brother got pneumonia and died, which Maddy felt was due to poor care and neglect. She spent a long time persuading Henry to move, and then in finding somewhere that would accept him. Many of the private accommodation facilities she looked at didn't seem to offer the kind of assistance or health monitoring that Henry needs. A lot seemed reluctant to accept someone with an intellectual disability and a few suggested that Henry was a bit young. She approached the regional disability team who indicated there was a long waiting list and unless Henry was actually homeless or at severe risk he would be unlikely ever to get a place in a shared, supported accommodation house funded by disability services.

Eventually through her family's longstanding connection with the church Maddy managed to secure Henry's current accommodation to which he moved five years ago. It is a medium sized hostel that accommodates a maximum of 75, people most of whom are in their late seventies or early eighties. Although the hostel is mainly for older people, there is a small group of younger older people with intellectual disabilities. Henry has his own small room with a few of his possessions from home, such as the clock his brother was presented with for 30 years service on the trams. Henry thinks it is OK here but said, 'I'm not always happy here. I don't like the way I am treated sometimes. I often feel like packing my bags and going. Sometimes it's lonely and I would like someone to talk to.'

Questions

1. How would you describe Henry's informal social network?

2. What are the strengths and weaknesses of his informal network?

3. In what ways could his informal network be strengthened?

4. How could Henry's sense of purpose and achievement be increased?

5. Does Henry have a strong sense of significance and continuity?

Michael Handy

Michael is a 55-year-old man who has lived in a nursing home for the past five years. His sister says that until he was 50 he was bright and active, although he struggled with academic tasks. His social skills were such that he could go anywhere and he had perfect table manners. Michael has few words but communicates well through sign and gesture to those who know him well. When he was born in 1944 his mother was told that the best thing she could do with her baby was to take it home and let it die. Later she was told he wouldn't live past 16 years. Michael lived at home with his two brothers and elder sister, who says he was adored by all of them. When Michael reached his early twenties his parents worked hard with a group of other parents to establish a sheltered workshop and then to build a number of group homes. Most of the money was raised by the parents association and the work done on a voluntary basis. Michael attended the workshop and built up a group of close friends there. His sister commented, 'He was so much a home body, he was just at home. Mother was very caring, there was a circle at the workshop, he didn't need anything else.'

In his early thirties Michael moved to one of the group homes with five other residents but went home every weekend to stay with parents. He continued to do this after his mother died, and then alternated between his father and his sister when Parkinson's disease affected his father's capacity. When his mother died, he was extremely distressed and cried on and off for many months. He settled in the house very well and enjoyed going out with the other residents to eat or to the local bowling alley.

When Michael was 50 his skills began to deteriorate and he forgot what he was doing sometimes. He started waking in the night and wandering around the house, looking for the staff to get breakfast. The house supervisor rang his sister saying that Michael was in the early stages of Alzheimer's and he couldn't stay there much longer. At this time his sister had two teenage children and was trying to look after her father whose Parkinson's was getting worse. She ignored the demands for a while, although it seems the manager put Michael's name on various waiting lists for nursing homes. The decision was made when his sister was told Michael had been offered a place and had to take it as he couldn't stay at the house.

Since the move to a nursing home, his sister has been very concerned about the quality of care that Michael has received. She has become heavily involved in monitoring what happens to him and advocating for better treatment. One occasion she visited and the staff member told her Michael's behaviour had been very difficult and as punishment he had been made to stay in his bedroom all day.

She said, 'He was sitting on the bed with his head in his hand. I went and put my arms around him and he said my head hurts and I held his hand. He was showing signs of cerebral irritation…she should have picked that up.' She went on to say:

> Since he's been there the deterioration has been so great, there's no stimulation, he is just left to sit, left to rot. There are no activities for him. When he first went in they didn't watch his bowels and he got grossly constipated. He was crying all the time but they didn't take any notice of him, they weren't really listening to him. I know Michael very well and I knew there was something wrong with him. I told them he had a pain in his tummy. I forced the issue and demanded treatment. I can't really blame them. I know Michael well. I can pick up on things and they just don't realize. I don't think there are many people that do know him well.

Michael still recognizes familiar faces and his sister is concerned that since he moved he has not seen any of his friends, either from the workshop or the house. She had expected the staff to bring them to visit and regrets that she didn't think to do this herself.

His sister also described a situation where Michael had become increasingly reluctant to walk and complained of a sore back. She had to take the iniatiative to organize a physiotherapy assessement, which recommended a different type of mattress and an insert in his chair. After these changes his pain slowly disappeared and he was more willing to walk. Michael's sister regularly takes him to see his father who is in a nearby nursing home and drops in to see him at least once every two days. She said, 'Every time I go I try and walk him. They weren't walking him. They were just letting him sit there, so his walking was getting worse and worse. They weren't keeping him active at all. That's why I go. He's got to do something, but nobody was doing anything about him. I can't complain too much they just don't know.'

His sister manages all his affairs and is down as next of kin with the nursing home. Her brothers ring her to enquire how Michael is and call in to see him when they are in the area. Ever since they were children, however, she has had the closest relationship with him. She said, 'I've never thought I would abandon Michael. Now I wish he would die because his life has no quality. He's miserable when he'd been such a happy person. He is so unhappy his life is so miserable that I wish he was dead. He needs someone who is able to stimulate him, to jolly him along, give him a cuddle.'

Questions

1. How would you describe Michael's informal support network?

2. What roles does Michael's sister play?

3. What might have made it possible for Michael to stay at the group home for longer?

4. What are the arguments for and against ageing in place in group homes?

5. What should be the process for making decisions about moving?

6. How might the quality of his care in the nursing home be improved?

Martin Holmes

Martin is a 59-year-old man who for the last four years has lived in a group home with four other residents. Martin is very independent in many respects and able to travel around the city by public transport. He loves watching cricket and football and going to the free concerts in the town hall. Martin has rudimentary literacy and numeracy skills but has never been really interested in developing his domestic skills. When he lived with his mother she did all the household management. Martin's health is generally good, although some problems have developed in the last four years that his brother thinks may be due to stress. He takes regular medication for an ulcer and had a hernia operation last year.

Martin has always got himself around the city to concerts, football matches and the cricket and has continued to do this since he moved to the group home. He goes to church on Sundays, and loves to watch sport on the television. He has attended the day centre since was 19, although then it was a sheltered workshop. Martin loves the centre and he has a couple of close friends there. The centre has organized volunteer work for him. One day he helps at the local council delivering meals on wheels and another day he takes care of all the water vases at the local hospital. The other three days he participates in various activities at the centre including cooking. The centre has a retirement policy that concerns Martin. He said, 'I'll be 65 soon. Then I'll only be coming here one or two days a week. What am I going to do with the rest of my time? I haven't got any hobbies at the house. There isn't room for them.' The policy of semi-retirement also concerns his brother who said, 'He is a very regular ritualistic person who thrives on routine. His only troubles will come if those rituals are changed and he is asked to leave the centre. I can't see there is any need to retire. It's a social program not work.'

The last few years have been particularly stressful for Martin: living with mother who developed Alzheimer's disease; coping with her sudden hospitalization when she fell and broke her leg; having to pack up all his belongings and move out of the family home, first to a temporary hostel and then to a group home. About living with his mother he said, 'I couldn't cope looking after her in the house. It got to the stage where she couldn't do the shopping by herself. I took every Thursday off from the centre and stayed home with her and helped with the shopping. We managed together quite well until she broke her leg, but I couldn't have carried on. It wasn't easy, but I did what I could to help her, but now that she's in a nursing home it's off my shoulders.' From his brother's perspective, Martin and his mother were dependent on each other. He said, 'It was a knife-edge situation. Martin got sick and went to hospital. Mum was on her own and needed help. Then she went to hospital and he needed help. Together they could manage but on their own they couldn't.'

The plan to move Martin and his mother together into an aged care facility unravelled when his mother fell and broke her leg and it was clear she would need a much higher level of care than originally thought. When this happened his brother and sister-in-law began to negotiate a place for Martin in a group home. Although Martin wanted to stay at home or move to a flat, they were advised by the day centre staff that he lacked the skills to cope alone and required a more supported situation. His brother and sister-in-law likened the whole process of finding accommodation as traversing a minefield, and felt they had very little support. In particular they were concerned about professionals who had never met Martin before coming out to assess him, making quick judgements and taking what he said at face value. His sister-in-law explained that it had been clear to her that sometimes Martin had misunderstood what had been said or had not given the worker a clear message. She said, 'The worker heard Martin's response and was making an interpretation from it, and I had to say I don't think that's what he meant. He has limited capacity to choose words. I tried to help tease out what he was actually saying by asking further questions. I didn't just tell her what I thought he meant. I just asked a lot more questions so she got a much deeper response. You have to know him well to do this, but she had been willing to take the first thing he said. He doesn't need a spokesperson, he needs someone to tease it out of him.' She was concerned that if she and Martin's brother were not around there would be no one to interpret for Martin. She said, 'What do others do who don't have access to the type of care we provide? It's not physical washing but it's all the paperwork, that minefield of institutions and organizations.'

Martin's brother and sister-in-law saw it as their responsibility to find somewhere for him to live. His brother said, 'We do tend to think that he is our responsibility. There isn't anyone else to do things. I don't see it as a burden. It's always been there. It's not something that's been put on you by your parents.' He said he had talked to his young adult children who were aware that if anything happened to their parents it would be their responsibility to keep an eye on Martin.

Martin was distraught when he had to pack up all his things from the family home, and his brother said it was the first time he had ever seen him cry. Martin understands that his brother has tried to help but is not happy living in the group home. He has much less money to spend than ever before as now he has to pay rent and board costs, which takes up about three-quarters of his pension. His room is very small and he finds it difficult to cope with the constant noise and squabbling that goes on among several other residents. He said, 'I'd just like a little bit more room. I realize he (brother) was only trying to do the right thing and he thought the group home would be best for me. But they are always squabbling there. That gets me down. I would have preferred to go into a flat or unit. My brother says I can't afford it. Where else can I go? The group home was the only place.'

Questions

1. What other possibilities for housing and support might have been feasible for Martin?

2. How could the trauma of the move from his family home have been reduced?

3. What issues are associated with adult children with intellectual disability moving to aged care facilities with their elderly parents?

4. Do you think day centres should have retirement policies, and if so what should they be based on?

5. What roles do Martin's brother and sister-in-law play in his life?

6. What are the characteristics of Martin's informal social network?

Bill Bentham

Bill is 76 years old and lives in a large retirement village run by the church. The village has about 600 residents, split between independent units, a large hostel and a nursing home. Bill generally looks after himself and has little to do with anyone else at the village. He has few words. He can read a bit and enjoys drawing. Some residents are unsure of him as he has a habit of creeping up behind people and startling them. He doesn't attend any of the occupational therapy programs on a regular basis but spends most of his day wandering around the grounds or watching the world go by. No one visits Bill and no one really knows much about his past. He has lived in the village for 15 years since he was aged 61. The manager said he thought Bill had lived with his brother who had then remarried and found his wife couldn't cope with Bill. Bill's brother used to visit once a month but had stopped coming about four years ago. After several months with no contact the manager had made some enquires and found out that his brother had died.

The records of the regional disability team indicate that Bill had lived with his mother and then his sister in the country. When his sister died Bill had moved to the city to live with his brother. His brother had contacted the regional disability team seeking assistance with accommodation in 1987 and his name had been put on the shared, supported accommodation waiting list. The team had had no further contact with Bill.

Questions

1. How would you describe Bill's informal social network?

2. What strategies could be used to improve Bill's quality of life?

3. Would it be helpful for Bill to try and find out more about his life and family?

4. How might this be accomplished?

5. If Bill needs to make any decisions in the future who is in a position to support him to do this?

PART 4

Older Parental Carers of Adults with a Lifelong Disability

Chapter 8

Issues Confronting Older Parents Living with their Adult Children

The increased life expectancy of people with intellectual disability not only means an increasing number live into middle age and beyond but also extends the parenting career of their parents. Many parents continue to live with their adult child with intellectual disability until they are in their eighties or nineties. From a policy perspective these parents are perceived as 'carers', part of a diverse group that includes spouses and adult children. However, their situation and the issues they confront have some unique and very different aspects from those of other carers. Their caring will have lasted much longer and had a greater salience to their life. Unlike other carers, cessation to their caring will be brought about by their own death rather than that of the person for whom they care, which throws up issues of their replacement. Rather than seeing themselves as carers, these older parental carers are more likely to continue their lifelong perception of themselves as parents (Llewellyn in press).

The increased longevity of adults with intellectual disability means that many are likely to outlive their parents. The continued caring roles of older parents, their inevitable incapacity or death and cessation of caring, throw up multiple challenges for professionals: assisting parents to adapt to their own age-related changes and possibly those of their adult child; supporting an optimal lifestyle for both parent and adult child; and facilitating preparation, planning and decision making for the transition from co-residence. In meeting these challenges, many issues arise similar to those encountered earlier in the life course. These include ensuring the voice of the person with intellectual disability is heard, making trade-offs between security, continuity and independence, achieving a balance and reconciling conflicting needs and wishes.

This chapter examines the situation of older parental carers and their co-resident adult children. It explores their relationships and the issues confronting them. This provides a background for the following chapter that focuses more specifically on strategies for working with older parents to support continued family care and plan for the future. The focus of this chapter is older parents living with an adult child with intellectual disability. Almost nothing is known about other older parents; those, for example, whose adult child has moved away from home and lives in supported accommodation. Neither does the chapter include older carers such as grandparents who are more likely to be caring for younger chidren (see McCallion and Janicki 2000).

Characteristics of older parents

Continuing commitments

The demographic bulge of the baby boom generation, together with increased life expectancy of both parents and people with intellectual disability, mean the number of older parents living with a middle-aged or older adult with intellectual disability will continue to increase over the next decade. For example, in Australia the estimated number of parents aged over 65 years caring for an adult child with a disability at home, the majority of whom have intellectual disability, increased from 7700 in 1993 to 9700 in 1998 (AIHW 1997, 2001). UK estimates suggest that approximately 44 per cent of all adults with intellectual disability who live at home, 30,000 to 35,000 people have a parental carer aged over 60 years (Hogg and Lambe 1998; McGrother et al. 1996). In the USA the estimated figure is 676,492 adults living with an older carer, which accounts for 26 per cent of all adults with intellectual disability living in the family home (Janicki 2002).

Older parents are not a homogeneous group. Their experiences and needs are mediated by the cohort to which they belong, culture, access to economic resources and diverse individual biographies, as well as their experience of the formal service system (McCallion, Janicki and Grant-Griffin 1997; Todd et al. 1993; Walden, Pistrang and Joyce 2000). Feelings about their continued caring role may be positive, negative or ambivalent, stemming from their satisfaction and benefits gained, the centrality of the caring role to their own identity, a lifelong commitment to caring, distrust of alternative forms of care, or simply a lack of viable support alternatives for their adult child. For example, in the UK context, Todd and Shearn (1996) found that 29 per cent of older parents were 'captive' and would welcome the opportunity to relinquish their role, whilst over half were captivated and found considerable meaning to their caring role and did not want to relinquish it. Parenting an offspring with an intellectual disability can be considered an active career for up to five decades (Todd *et al.* 1993, p.137). An Australian study found the average age of parents when co-residence with their adult child ceased to be 85 years, with their own death or incapacity being the most common reason for its occurrence (Bigby 1997a).

Cohort effects and service experiences

Policy initiatives to support older parental carers have used a benchmark of 30 years caring to denote this status. This means the minimum age differential between older carers and their offspring is 30 years, thus offspring will range upwards from 30 years of age and are likely to have been born between the 1930s and 1970s, whilst older parents will be aged anywhere from their fifties to nineties (Pierce 1993; Stehlick 1997; Todd *et al.* 1993). Older parents have lived through tremendous changes in community attitudes towards intellectual disability and been subjected to differing ideologies of care.

Their relatively low use of formal support is often explained by reluctance and mistrust stemming from their negative experiences of government polices and service use in the past (McCallion and Tobin 1995; Stehlik 1997) Accounts of the predominantly institutional and paternalistic services available between 1930 and the 1970s, the negativism of professionals towards children with intellectual disability and heartbreaking parental experiences clearly illuminate why some older carers are reluctant to approach formal services for assistance (Llewellyn in press; Pierce 1993; Scholes and Scholes 1992). For example, children with disabilities were denied access to services such as preschool and school during this period and few alternatives to institutional care were available. Services that did exist emphasized relief to hard-pressed families rather than positive developmental intervention and family support.

In Australia the current cohort of elderly parents established the non-government organizations that from the 1950s, for many years with only limited government financial support, provided the backbone of adult day and small group residential services (Cocks *et al.* 1996; Stehlik 1997). Governments have progressively assumed greater control for the funding, regulation and access to these services, meaning that the older carers who 'built' them are no longer guaranteed access. Stehlik documents the changes that have occurred in ideologies and relationships between older carers, their offspring and the state. In the 1950s children with intellectual disability were regarded as slow learners or patients. In the 1980s they became 'clients' and in the 1990s were regarded as consumers (1997). In the twenty-first century their adult children have become citizens.

Older parents began their careers in another era when values and ideologies were quite different from those currently prevailing. Pierce suggests: 'it should not be surprising if ageing carers are protective and cautious, and reluctant to choose new service options. Their life experience has involved successive exclusions from generic community services and facilities' (1993, p.22). Narrative work with older parents conducted by Llewellyn and her colleagues adds further understanding of parental reluctance to have contact with formal services. This work suggests that an enduring feature of parental contact with services over many years has been the disregard by professionals of the knowledge and expertise of parents about their own child. The experience of being devalued by a procession of professionals who only stay involved for short periods will have been more likely to undermine than support parental coping. Echoes of these experiences are found in the current critical and blaming attitudes towards older parents held by some professionals. Several US studies have demonstrated that case managers often feel anger and frustration with older parents, perceiving them as overprotective and having jeopardized the growth and development of their offspring (McCallion and Tobin 1995; Smith and Tobin 1993a).

Unique features of older parental caring

Although in the general community an increasing number of adult children live with their parents into young adulthood, the continued provision of direct care by parents to adult children is less common (Seltzer and Krauss 1994). The family lifespan of older parents is 'off cycle'. The launching stage that involves separation and letting go by parents of responsibility for their children is postponed, as is the occurrence of an 'empty nest'. The lengthy duration of their caregiving and the stability of the psychodynamics of the caregiving relationship differentiate older parents of adult children with intellectual disability from other carers. They do not experience role changes or reversal common to spouse or filial carers. Their own death or incapacity often marks the cessation of caring, whereas for other carer groups the situation is reversed and cessation more often results from death or entry into a nursing home of the care recipient (Seltzer and Krauss 1989; Smith and Tobin 1993a). If they do seek out services, older parents are more likely to fall through service system gaps than other carer groups, as the diversity of household composition means they do not fit neatly into either ageing or disability service systems.

Comparison with younger parents

On various dimensions, older parents differ from their younger peers. Older parents are more likely to live in smaller households, be single parents due to widowhood, have other caring responsibilities, have smaller informal support networks and use less formal support services (Hayden and Heller 1997; Janicki 1996; McGrath and Grant 1993; Smith, Fullmer and Tobin 1994; Todd *et al.* 1993). Older parents are less optimistic about the progress of their offspring than younger parents, although their adult children are less dependent (Todd *et al.* 1993). Due to non-use or drop-out from services, adults with intellectual disability living with older parents are less likely to have a full-time occupation and more likely to have unoccupied days than younger offspring (Todd *et al.* 1993).

Older parents are more resigned to their role than younger parents. They are, however, more adept at reframing their situation and less dependent on information as a coping strategy. They have greater analytical ability and expertise specific to their situation (Grant and Whittell 2000).

Resilience and adaptation

For older parents adaptation to age-related changes that impact on their caring ability occurs within the context of ongoing parental responsibilities (Seltzer and Krauss 1994). Some older parents will be confronted with additional caring tasks due to the illness of a spouse or the advent of grandchildren. They are likely to be confronted by age-related decrements such as reduced stamina, physical capacity and mobility (Hawkins, Eklund and Matz 1993; Heller 1993). Day-to-day tasks may take longer and consume more energy. With the deaths first of their own parents and then of their spouse, and the ageing of friends they will lose valuable sources of support. Like many older people, their capacity to drive may diminish, leading to reliance on public transport that may be difficult to access. This makes attendance at medical and other appointments more difficult and may restrict the community-based recreational and social activities previously undertaken with adult children.

These factors suggest that as carers age their internal and external caregiving resources are reduced, which may increase the stresses and burdens of caregiving. Possible stresses of later life caring are perceived as unending dependency, chronic sorrow, age-associated decrements, lack of formal services, social isolation and financial pressures (Smith 1996). However, the most common stress mentioned in relation to older carers is anxiety about the future care of their offspring.

Despite these factors indicative of greater stress, older carers appear resilient and adapted to rather than worn down by lifelong caring (Grant 2000; Seltzer and Krauss 1994). US and some UK research have found that older carers experience greater satisfaction with caring and less stress than their younger counterparts (Hayden and Heller 1997; Seltzer and Krauss 2001). For example:

> Overall parents of children were more likely to be confronted with more demanding caregiving than parents of adults, because children were likely to be more highly dependent and to have more behaviour problems. (Todd *et al.* 1993, p.141)

> Despite the long duration of their caretaking roles, many of the mothers seemed resilient, optimistic, and able to function well in multiple roles. Specifically the women were healthier than other non caregiving women their age, they had better morale than caregivers of elderly persons and reported no more burden than family caregivers of elderly residents and less stress than parents of young children with retardation. (Seltzer and Krauss 1994, p.7)

The balance between the positive and negative effects of family caregiving is particularly salient for older parents (Seltzer and Krauss 1994, p.6). Compared to other women of their own age and other carers, older mothers of adults with intellectual disability experience less depression and have greater subjective well-being (Seltzer and Krauss 2001). The importance of the cultural context of care is emphasized however by a study that suggests older carers in the UK do not seem to be functioning as well as those in the USA and experience greater stress, less sense of purpose, growth and development (Walden *et al.* 2000).

Although older parental carers had greater subjective well-being than their aged peers, they were less reconciled to the ageing process and death, and their fears of death increase with age (Smith and Tobin 1993a). Indicative of this is the evidence that although anxious about future care for their adult child, older parents across cultures are reluctant to engage in formal or concrete planning (Bigby 2000; Heller and Factor 1991; Prosser 1997; Seltzer and Krauss 2001).

The well-being of older parents of adults with intellectual disability compares favourably with another group of older parental carers – those who care for an adult child with mental health problems (Greenberg, Seltzer and Greenley 1993). Comparison between the two groups suggests that although the mothers of adults with intellectual disability provide higher levels of care, they experience less objective burden, greater gratification and a better relationship with their adult child than mothers of adult children with mental health problems. Some of the differences may be explained by the differential context of caregiving. Mothers of adults with mental health problems had smaller support networks and less cohesive families. The offspring for whom they cared also had a greater range of behavioural problems (Greenberg *et al.* 1993). High levels of stress are a major reason that mothers of adults with mental health problems cease caregiving, whereas reduced caregiver capacity and ill health account for care relinquishment by mothers of adults with intellectual disability (Seltzer *et al.* 1997).

The satisfaction of older parents and their relatively less stressful caring situations may result from greater reciprocity and mutuality in their caregiving relationships, as they age and accommodate to the child's strengths (Grant 1993; Heller, Miller and Factor 1997; Seltzer and Krauss 1994). Seltzer and Krauss suggest that the experiences of older carers conform to a model of adaptation over time rather than one of wear and tear (1994).

Factors affecting well-being

Amongst older carers well-being is strongly related to age, level of education, marital status and income (Grant 1993). The involvement of siblings with the adult with intellectual disability rather than their engagement with parents is also an important factor in maternal well-being (Seltzer *et al.* 1991). This suggests the importance of a supportive family environment to caregiver well-being (Seltzer and Krauss 1989, 1994) and reinforces the salience of the entire family system to caregiving rather being restricted to the carer and care recipient dyad. Some research suggests that linkage to a range of formal support services such as respite care will also affect their well-being (Walsh, Concliffe and Birbeck 1993).

Connections to formal service systems

Australian, US and UK research suggest that many older carers do not make high demands on formal service systems and under-utilize both the ageing and disability support networks (Fullmer, Smith and Tobin 1997; Magrill *et al.* 1997; McCallion and Tobin 1995; McGrath and Grant 1993; Smith 1997; Todd *et al.* 1993). Demonstration service models that have included outreach to older parents have highlighted their disconnection from formal support services. For example, in one US study half of those identified by outreach projects were unknown to formal services systems (Janicki *et al.* 1998).

However, not all older carers are similarly or totally disconnected from services. Several studies in Victoria demonstrate that a high proportion are connected to the disability system through their adult child's continuing attendance at disability day programs, but often wait until their coping capacity is stretched to the limit before seeking support with caring (Bigby 2002c; Bigby, Ozanne and Gordon 1999).

Several studies suggest that parents do not know about supportive services and that a lack of knowledge about possible accommodation options is a major obstacle preventing parents planning adequately for the future (Collinson 1997; Heller and Factor 1988a; Kropf 1994; Magrill *et al.* 1997; Walker and Walker 1998). Low usage may also stem from poor understanding about the operations and applicability of services, particularly more recent and innovative models (Smith 1997; Smith, Tobin and Fullmer 1995). However, it is likely that low use of services may stem from various reasons: a lack of perceived need by parents who do not see caring as a problem; lack of trust or confidence, as discussed in an earlier section, for those who have withdrawn from services in the past; and limited knowledge or fear of intrusion for those who have never used services (Smith 1997).

The relationship between carer characteristics and service use is difficult to untangle. For example, a study that compared adults who used day services with those who did not found the carers of the latter group were more likely to come from lower socio-economic backgrounds, have fewer informal support, distrust services and were likely to have had an unfavourable service experience in the past (Smith *et al.* 1995). In contrast another study found that parents who used accommodation waiting lists had smaller informal networks, higher unmet needs and a greater use of formal services than carers who did not utilize waiting lists (Essex, Seltzer and Krauss 1997).

Networks of informal support for older adults with intellectual disability living with older parents

Mothers generally take sole responsibility for the day-to-day tasks associated with caring for their adult child with intellectual disability and have few expectations of support from outside the immediate family (Prosser and Moss 1996). Attrition of informal support associated with later life is not compensated for by other sources (Grant 1993), although the mother's role may be taken over by the father on widowhood or a mother's incapacity. Other family members have supportive relationships with both parents and the adult with intellectual disability, though these tend to be affective, providing companionship or emotional support rather than being instrumental and assisting with direct care tasks (Grant 1986; Krauss, Seltzer and Goodman 1992; Prosser and Moss 1996).

As suggested in Chapter 5, the informal support networks of adults living at home with parents tend to be dominated by family members and insulated from the community in general. Networks are dense and social activities are shared by the adult and their parents. Friends and neighbours are often connected to the adult with intellectual disability through their parents resulting in a significant overlap between the parents' network and that of their adult child (Grant 1986; Krauss *et al.* 1992).

Seltzer and her colleagues found that the majority of adults with intellectual disability living at home with older parents had siblings with whom they continued to have meaningful relationships. Siblings generally provide emotional rather than instrumental support and sustained rather than extensive contact. They do however have considerable knowledge about their brother or sister with intellectual disability and though not co-resident should be regarded as an integral component of continued family care (Krauss *et al.* 1996; Seltzer *et al.* 1991; Seltzer and Krauss 1994).

Relationships between older parents and their adult child

Parents living with adult children with intellectual disability have been referred to as perpetual parents or experiencing a constant burden of care. While these notions may accurately reflect parental commitment, they should not be interpreted to imply constancy in the relationship between parents and offspring through the life course (Todd *et al.* 1993, p.147). Parental caregiving relationships are dynamic, occurring within the temporal and developmental context of an individual's and their family's life course.

Interdependence and reciprocity are a feature of the later life relationship between parents and their adult child with intellectual disability (Bigby 1997a; Grant 1986; Heller and Factor 1988b; Prosser 1989, 1997; Walmsley 1996). Adults living at home undertake a range of domestic chores and the financial viability of the household may depend on their contribution (Grant 1986). Reciprocity may be critical to the continuation of the family unit for the 'carer' and 'care recipient' as well as a factor in parental satisfaction. Grant suggests:

> It was not just the existence of blood ties, or affinity, that helped to sustain carers in these [caring] roles, often into ripe old age, but the recognition that their own survival was to an important degree dependent on the help, or at times, the mere presence of the mentally handicapped person. (1986, p.337)

Walmsley developed a threefold typology of family relationships: 'supportive', 'dependent' and 'conflict ridden' (1996). She describes a subgroup of mutually supportive relationships that occur when one parent has died and the surviving parent becomes physically frailer. Help is proffered from both sides with tasks such as gardening, cooking, housework and shopping undertaken by the adults with intellectual disability who often take pride in their roles. However, the sometimes restrictive nature of these relationships is also noted. For example, in her study one man said, 'Not being nasty, but when me mum goes I'd like to marry Isabelle' (Walmsley 1996, p.12). Similarly restrictive aspects were found in an Australian study where one women talking about when she lived with her mother said, 'I couldn't get out then like I do now' (Bigby 2000). However, it is clear that trade-offs are involved in these relationships. For example, in the same study one man drew attention to the advantages of living in the family home, where he had been able to keep his vast collection of cricket memorabilia, although his mother's frailty had meant he was unable to leave her alone for long periods of time. When he moved to a hostel, he had to part with many of his treasures as they would not fit into his single room.

However, despite increased interdependency in later life relationships, Walmsley found they continued to be characterized by the parental control over key aspects of their adult child's life (1996). Similarly, another UK study found that despite mutual dependency, the roles and capacities of the adult with intellectual disability in the partnership often go unrecognized by parents who continue to exert considerable control over finances and personal relationships (Willams and Robinson 2001). Such views however reflect the norms of caring developed by parents over many years that often include a fierce sense of independence, reluctance to seek help and the protection of their adult child against a hostile community (Engelhardt, Brubaker and Lutzer 1988; Grant and McGrath 1990; Prosser 1989; Shearn and Todd 1996).

The reduced mobility of parents and their need for the physical presence and support of their adult child may restrict the lifestyle of the adult who may have been reliant on their parent for social outings. The inability of parents to meet inflexible pick-up times or full-time attendance requirements imposed on adults who attend day programs may also lead to some dropping out and further restrictions on their lifestyle. Adults living at home with parents may have had few opportunities to develop lives separately from parents and in some cases may never have spent a night away from home (Bigby *et al.* 1999). Possible conflict of needs between an elderly parent and their adult child are more likely to be perceived by outsiders, such as professionals conducting carer assessments or siblings than identified by parents or adults (Bigby 2000; Williams and Robinson 2001). In the post-parental care phase siblings often express the view that loyalty and understanding of parental life experiences had disempowered them to inter-fere in restrictive relationships, but they had resolved to take counter-measures when parents were no longer around. They express this however in a non-judgemental fashion, understanding the social context and life experiences that informed the perspectives of their parents (Bigby 2000).

Parental control over many aspects of their adult child's life, including medi-ating their contact with the community, is often labelled 'overprotective' by pro-fessionals. As suggested earlier, parental attitudes may be perceived to have jeop-ardized the growth and development of their offspring and provoke feelings of anger and frustration in professional staff (McCallion and Tobin 1995; Smith and Tobin 1993a). Understanding parental perspectives, the dynamics of the caring dyad and engaging creatively to meet the needs of both the parent and the adult, rather than adopting a blaming confronting approach, is the challenge for profes-sionals working with older parents (for further discussion see Chapter 9). The issue of preparation and planning for the transition from parental care further highlights the potentially conflicting needs of parents and their adult children with intellectual disability.

The challenge of planning for the future

It is not a normative expectation that elderly parents will plan for the future care of their adult children (Heller and Factor 1991). However, such planning is increasingly seen as a fundamentally important task (Smith *et al.* 1995). Parental planning has diverse goals and multiple beneficiaries. Adequate planning, it is supposed, can avert the crisis of an ill-prepared transition from parental care for a middle-aged adult with intellectual disability, ensure their longer term security and stability, and forecast future service demands (Heller and Factor 1988; Kaufman, Adams and Campbell 1991). The process of planning has also been suggested as important to elderly parents to allow them to deal with their own psychological tasks of ageing and coming to terms with their own life (Kaufman *et al.* 1991; Heller and Factor 1991; Smith and Tobin 1989, 1993a, 1993b).

Parental planning is usually conceptualized into three areas: *guardianship, financial* and *residential* provisions (Heller and Factor 1991; Seltzer and Seltzer 1985; Smith *et al.* 1995). However, Bigby (2000) suggests that the notion of 'key person succession planning' may be more applicable to Australia and other juris-dictions where the nature of guardianship legislation precludes the anticipatory appointment of a guardian (Carney and Tait 1997). Planning is generally seen as straightforward: 'Proper planning includes making financial and guardianship arrangements and finding appropriate placements' (Heller and Factor 1988b, p.2). However, it is also regarded as a complex dynamic process whereby plans must be sufficiently flexible and adaptable to meet the changing residential, financial and legal requirements of an adult who may survive their parents by 30 or 40 years (Kaufman *et al.* 1991; Seltzer and Seltzer 1985). With this in mind, Seltzer and Seltzer (1985) suggest that planning may not achieve a secure permanent residential situation but may be important to ensure that family members remain involved with the person with intellectual disability and monitor the quality and appropriateness of services. Plans have two major functions: facilitating the transition from parental care; and ensuring in the longer term an optimum quality of life and security for an ageing adult with intellectual disability (Bigby 2000). Parental planning may also be used as a mechanism to promote cost sharing of future care between parents and the state (CSV 1988, 1992b; Sach and Associates 1991).

Extent and nature of planning by parents

Richardson and Ritchie (1989) suggest that parents of adults with intellectual disability hold three attitudes towards planning: affirmative, avoidance, and ambivalent, of which avoidance is the most common:

> With advancing years, carers became preoccupied, and somewhat fearful, about the future. Many carers and their families tended to live life on a day to day basis, preferring to blot out the agonies of contemplating the future when they are no longer able to cope or else themselves deceased. (Grant 1986, p.336)

Most studies show that only between one-third to one-half of parents make concrete plans for future care of an adult with intellectual disability who is living at home (Campbell and Essex 1994; Freedman, Krauss and Seltzer 1997; Heller and Factor 1991; Kaufman *et al.* 1991; Prosser 1997). Financial planning is the most common type undertaken.

Smith *et al.* (1995) suggest that planning is not a simple act occurring at one point but has five stages, ranging from no discussion to definite plans. Some families may not move along the full continuum and plans may remain implicit, comprising informal agreements or understandings between family members (Bigby 2000; Heller and Factor 1991; Kaufman *et al.* 1991). Some are never formalized and may not even be discussed, with the family members expected to be involved in future care (Goodman 1978; Richardson and Ritchie 1989). The formulation of plans may not involve the discussion of alternatives with the person concerned (Gold 1987; Richardson and Ritchie 1989; Wood 1993). These factors can lead to inconsistencies between family members' perceptions and parental plans. For example, Griffith and Unger (1994) found a higher proportion of siblings expressed a willingness to act as carer in the future than was reflected in parental expectations and encapsulated in plans. A further confounding factor is that plans and expectations may also change over time; for example, Grant (1989) found that over a two-year period just over half the parents changed their preference for future care.

Parental expectations of future care

The choices and options that plans contain often emerge from the social context of care, with preferences generally evenly split between continued family care, primarily by siblings, and residential placement (Grant 1989; Heller and Factor 1991; Wood 1993). Parents are more likely to expect a family member to provide indirect care for the adult with intellectual disability by, for example, overseeing their well-being, than to expect a relative to provide hands-on support (Bigby 2000; Goodman 1978; Krauss 1990).

Parental plans value protection and permanency rather than developmental opportunities. Instead of looking towards increased independence for their adult child in the future, parents seek residential accommodation to duplicate the care and protection that they have provided at home. Griffin and Bennett (1994) found when parents discussed planning in a group they generally emphasized security, attaining peace of mind and a safe, secure situation as most important to them. However, Brubaker and Brubaker (1993) suggest that the greatest concern that parents have regarding the future is the adult child's social and emotional well-being.

Factors affecting planning

Most studies have found an association between the use of formal services and both the parental propensity to make plans and an expected reliance of formal services rather than other family members for future care. This suggests that use of services may lead to a greater knowledge of options and more trust in the quality of formal services (Essex et al. 1997; Grant 1989; Heller and Factor 1991; Seltzer et al. 1991; Smith et al. 1995; Wood and Skiles 1992). The decision to plan is multifactorial and has been associated with carer characteristics, stressors and resources (Essex et al. 1997; Heller and Factor 1991; Seltzer and Krauss 1994). For example, behaviour problems of the adult with intellectual disability, high unmet needs and small support networks are positively associated with planning, whereas age of the carer is negatively associated (Essex *et al.* 1997).

Obstacles to planning

Despite the suggested benefits of comprehensive planning, many parents do not undertake this task. The most common reasons proposed are a lack of information about service options and parental distrust or dissatisfaction with formal services (Grant 1989; Heller and Factor 1988a; Kaufman *et al.* 1991; Kropf 1994; Smith *et al.* 1995). Other suggestions are that planning is emotionally challenging for parents, logistically complex and confronts professionals with difficult ethical issues.

Formulating a plan forces parents to come to terms with their own ageing and mortality. They may also have to deal with the tension between a desire to continue caregiving and their anxiety about future care (Kropf 1994; Seltzer and Ryff 1996; Smith *et al.* 1994). The process may also require parents to balance their own needs and desires with the rights and needs of their adult child (Grant 1986). The type of future care parents want for their offspring may conflict with the values and options preferred by professional workers. The resultant clash of values may be an obstacle to effectively working with older parents to develop plans.

The lack of concrete alternatives available to parents and long waiting lists, particularly for supported accommodation, may mean that parents see planning as pointless. With some accuracy they may assume that accommodation is only likely to be forthcoming from the state disability services system in a crisis situation rather than in a more timely manner (AAMR 1998; AIHW 2002c; Walker and Walker 1998).

Planning issues

Despite the focus by professionals on the critical importance of planning, little research is available as to its outcomes, effectiveness and whether or not parental expectations are met. Few writers have raised questions about the appropriateness of parents formulating plans that resemble detailed blueprints for the future of their adult child with intellectual disability. However, Grant (1988) has suggested that contemporary ideologies and values reflected in the service system may challenge previously taken-for-grants rights of parents to decide the future pattern of care.

Adults who make the transition from parental care in their forties and fifties have perhaps 20 or 30 years of their lives ahead of them. Designing and implementing a plan to determine the course of their life in the post-parental care phase is a difficult task. Many contingencies must be dealt with. As this book has considered, this phase of their lives may be characterized by instability and change. Individual characteristics such as health status may vary. Other skills may develop or decline and social and service contexts may alter because of changes in the circumstances of family and friends or organizational policies (Bigby 1997b, 2000). While some changes may be foreseen, their impact cannot be accurately predicted. Attempting to identify a plan, particularly one that involves a suitable and desired residential situation for the rest of their adult child's life, may not be realistic for some parents. It may be argued that it is inappropriate, particularly in view of the lack of consultation that sometimes occurs, the later life development that is yet to be experienced and the risk of locking someone into an environment which may become inappropriate or be more restrictive than warranted.

Bigby's research demonstrates that key person succession plans which centre on the nomination of another person to replace the parental role of oversight of well-being are more effective than those of a more concrete nature (Bigby 2000). Their critical features are flexibility and responsiveness and they provide a mechanism in the form of a key person to organize and plan the detailed provision of primary care and relationships with formal services. Though key person succession plans are unspecific and remain informal, the relatively smooth nature of transition where they do exist suggests their efficacy in this facet of planning. By mandating the intervention of a key person, less emotionally involved than parents, these plans relieve parents from confronting the challenges of making detailed transition arrangements that may involve difficult choices and conflicting values and needs. They avoid a need for more concrete residential plans and perhaps also counter the conservatism of parents by handing decisions to key people with a different and perhaps less protective attitude. They do not tie adults with intellectual disability into the particular visions of their parents and earlier times. Instead, they allow for new opportunities to be created and expectations about potential that parents have not foreseen (see Chapter 7 for a discussion of housing and support options). Key person succession plans also have advantages in the second aspect of parental planning. They rarely go awry. Nominated key people, with their open brief, can be responsive to unexpected changes that occur. These plans do not achieve stability but provide the security of an advocate to negotiate service provision and ensure that the interests of the older person with intellectual disability are foremost in decisions made about aspects of their life. Key person succession plans effectively ensure the continued availability of informal support in the lives of older people with intellectual disability suggested by Seltzer and Seltzer (1985) to be a primary function of planning. The potential roles and relationships of key people are discussed in Chapter 5.

Summary

This chapter has explored the situation of older parents who live with their middle-aged adult children with intellectual disability. The potentially conflicting needs in these situations and the sometimes restrictive lifestyle for an adult that can be a consequence both of parental caring norms and aged associated limitations experienced by parents have been highlighted. Many older parents are out of touch with support services other than day programs, often through distrust, lack of understanding or lack of perceived needs. They do not often actively seek support with caring or the processes of preparation and planning for the transition from parental care. Yet this transition is inevitable and outreach and engagement of older carers in these processes is commonly perceived to be one way to avoid the crisis of unplanned transition. The next chapter discusses the imperatives to bring older parents closer to formal support services, the suggested tasks involved and strategies for working with them and their adult offspring both to optimize current lifestyle and plan for the future.

Further reading

Bigby, C. (2000) 'Models of parental planning.' In M. Janicki and E. Ansello *Community Supports for Ageing Adults with Lifelong Disabilities.* Baltimore: Brookes, pp.81–96.

Seltzer, M. and Krauss, M. (2001) 'Quality of life of adults with mental retardation/developmental disabilities who live with family.' *Mental Retardation and Developmental Disabilities Reviews 7*, 105–114.

Walmsley, J. (1996) 'Doing what mum wants me to do: Looking at family relationships from the point of view of adults with learning disabilities.' *Journal of Applied Research in Intellectual Disabilities 9*, 4, 324–341.

Williams, V. and Robinson, C. (2001) 'More than one wavelength: Identifying, understanding and resolving conflicts of interest between people with intellectual disabilities and their carers.' *Journal of Applied Research in Intellectual Disabilities 14*, 1, 30–46.

Chapter 9

Working with Older Parents

As Chapter 8 suggests, many older parents are resilient and have adapted to an interdependent relationship with their adult son or daughter with intellectual disability. Many are self-reliant, preferring to remain outside a service system that has in the past devalued their role and in which they have little trust. Others do not perceive caring to be a problem and see no need to seek out family support services, although their adult child may utilize a day program. Most however are anxious about the future. A minority will have made formal plans regarding the transition of care, whilst a larger proportion will have made informal arrangements, nominating a key person to succeed them in overseeing the well-being of their adult child with intellectual disability.

Compared to the demands on the disability, community care and aged care systems made by other groups of carers supporting those with high complex needs and struggling with day-to-day caring tasks, the needs of older parents do not appear complex or urgent, indicating no particular attention from service systems is warranted. However, the unique dimension of their caregiving relationship, its vulnerability to breakdown as a result of their own death or incapacity, indicates that unmet though perhaps unexpressed needs of older parents cluster around issues related to future planning and the transfer of care (Brubaker and Brubaker 1993; Heller and Factor 1991, 1993; Smith *et al.* 1995).

Researchers and advocacy groups make a strong case for proactive, preventative intervention with older parents to address preparation and planning for transition. It is argued that such intervention will help avoid future crisis and reduce both financial and emotional costs (Grant 1986; Harris 1998; Magrill *et al.* 1997: Smith and Tobin 1993a; Walker and Walker, 1998; Wood 1993). Proactive support to prepare for the transition from parental care has more chance of being empowering and ensuring decisions reflect the needs and wishes of an adult with

210 / AGEING WITH A LIFELONG DISABILITY

intellectual disability than intervention that occurs in the aftermath of parental death when decisions are made in situations of crisis, grief and loss. For example:

> We strongly believe that when you assist an ageing carer, everyone benefits. The help provided can avert crises and keep the family intact. It can also help adults with a lifelong disability plan their own future and make a planful transition from their family home, if they choose to do so. We found that staff resources can be conserved and monetary resources can be preserved for when they are most needed. Contact now with families will permit timely consideration of more independent and therefore less costly options for services in the future. (Janicki 1996, p.110)

> Just because carers are coping now doesn't mean they don't need help…an investment in preventative partnership work with families is at the core of meeting the needs of this user group and determining accurate, cost effective planning for future years. (Magrill *et al.* 1997, pp.15–16)

However, it is important to consider the nature and quality of support to be offered if professionals are proactively to engage older parents. As Llewellyn's (in press) work discussed in the previous chapter has demonstrated, their past experiences of services are more likely to have been of devaluation rather than empowerment. In the 1980s and 1990s, the orientation of family support services shifted to one of partnership with families rather than that of professional dominance, and the underpinning principles speak of empowerment and respect for cultural and family values. However, the potential to disempower and failure to adapt support to needs and coping styles still exists, particularly amongst services and professionals who work with older parents. For example, the values that professionals hold about the rights of adults with intellectual disability may be very different from those of parents. Some workers are found to judge or blame parents for their parenting style and perceived overprotectiveness (McCallion and Tobin 1995). Such an approach is likely to alienate parents, be perceived as interfering with their relationship with their son or daughter, and may lead to withdrawal from services. Findings from a UK study of parental views on family support services found the manner in which respite was provided was disempowering and failed to support parents to develop additional roles (Todd and Shearn 1996). The lack of choice about the time of day respite was provided meant parents not only lacked control, but often meant it occurred at times not conducive to pursing other interests or was too short a period to do so. Another UK study suggests that care managers have difficulty in understanding and supporting the different modes of coping used by families (Grant and Whittell 2001). The finding that cognitive coping strategies, which are the type most commonly used by older carers, are the ones most likely to be both undervalued and unrecognized by care managers, suggests that older parents are particularly in danger of inappropriate support. Parry-Jones *et al.* (1998) reinforce this proposition, suggesting that because of shortfalls in resources and the current mode of working care managers are forced to adopt, they have a very limited scope to mould support to the needs of families. Workers are dissatisfied with their roles and because of high turnover and the resultant discontinuities in contact are unable to build relationships and knowledge of family coping strategies.

Bringing older carers into touch with formal services is a first step, which if it is to achieve positive outcomes must be followed by good professional practice to support their styles of caring and engagement with issues of the transition from parental care. The quality of formal services varies enormously, mediated by the broader policy context, resources, mandates, skills and continuity of staff. This chapter examines the potential roles of formal support to older parents, their adult children and broader family networks. It argues, however, that if attempts are to be made to engage with older parents, it is crucial this is done through sensitive effective programs and practice, based on respect and understanding for their roles and coping strategies, that support rather than confront or devalue older parents

The first section of the chapter highlights the diversity of older parents and considers aspects of support valued by them. This is followed by an exploration of the key elements of intervention, possible strategies and tools for working with this group. Finally various program models are considered. The chapter draws primarily on Australian evaluative research of both specialist case management programs targetted at older parents and generic disability case management programs, conducted by the author and her colleague Elizabeth Ozanne (Bigby 2002c; Bigby *et al.* 1999, 2002).

Diverse situations and aims of intervention

Older parents of adults with intellectual disability are a diverse group whose involvement and pathways to support services reflect each family's coping style, internal and external resources. Some do use formal services effectively and some manage their own lives and effectively plan for and manage the transition from parental care without the need of formal support. The notion that all transitions occur in crisis mode is a myth, driven by the fact that crisis transitions are the type most commonly seen by services which largely remain unaware of the uneventful, gradual types of transition handled by family and other informal network members. For example, in Bigby's study, the majority of families managed the transition from parental care themselves, and only a quarter had any involvement with formal services during this process. Typically as the health of the remaining parent declined, family members provided more support to both the parent and the adult with intellectual disability living with them. A key person, who had already been nominated in an informal key person succession plan made by a parent, gradually assumed responsibility for planning the transition by investigating and negotiating a place for the adult to live in the future; either organizing continuation of informal support in the family home, a move to co-residence with another family member or to some form of shared supported accommodation. Contact with formal services for this type of family, if it occurs at all, is often confined to the provision of information and support to access alternative accommodation options, or to organize in-home support.

However, as many as 50 per cent of parents are out of touch with support services and some of these will require additional resources to manage the transition from parental care for their adult child or to continue caring (Janicki *et al.* 1998). For this group, if help is sought it is most likely to be from case management services in reaction to a crisis at a time when the caring situation is at risk of breaking down (Bigby 2002c). For these families the aims of intervention are clearly to sustain the current living situation if possible, but otherwise to support both parent and adult to make the transition from parental care. Key tasks are person-centred planning around additional support or alternative options, putting in place mechanisms to ensure continued contact with family and friends, and preserving the life history of the adult with intellectual disability. The danger is that all of these planful responses can be thwarted by the limited resources available, or overtaken by the urgency of the situation and the need to 'find a bed'.

Not all families out of touch with formal services will find themselves in a crisis situation or needing formal support. However, as it is difficult to predict which families will need support in addition to their own resources, the aim must be to locate, engage and offer support to all older parents prior to their reaching the point of relinquishment and perhaps a crisis. The broad objectives of reaching out to older parents are:

- to identify 'hidden' older parents

- to engage and link older parents with formal service systems, if they wish

- to facilitate planning for the future

- to avoid transitions occurring in crisis situations

- to prepare adults with intellectual disability for transition from parental care through, for example, extension of social networks, development of skills

- to support existing care situations for as long as possible

- to assist parents to resolve conflicting demands and psychological issues and to renegotiate their caring role

- to help predict future needs to assist service system planning

- to develop the capacity of the service system to meet the needs of this group.

The type of support valued by older parents

Bigby and Ozanne's Australian studies have demonstrated that older parents value two key aspects of support services: concrete help and emotional support. They value the provision of very practical support that helps with day-to-day tasks, such as transport to appointments, provision of taxi vouchers, pieces of equipment or physical adaptations to their home. Being supported to have a 'break' from caring is also appreciated, particularly so if it can be constructed by a parent as also providing an opportunity for their adult child to get out and partici-pate in a valued activity. Of equal importance to practical help is the relationship between older parents and their case manager, and the emotional support and sense of security they derive from this. In both specialist and generic case manage-ment programs, older parents refer to the importance of the respect they feel given by case managers, of being heard and listened to, and an appreciation of a non-directive approach towards them that allows parents to be self-determining. When asked what they valued most about a service, many older parents said it was the strong sense of 'peace of mind' derived from both their relationship with the case manager and contact with the service. For these parents, the case manager represented someone outside their family who was interested and concerned about the future care of their adult child.

Underpinning approaches to work with older parents

Two key approaches should inform work with older parents. The first is an appre-ciation of the context in which caring occurs, the experiences and coping styles of parents and families to ensure support is matched to these. The second is an informal network/family focused approach that extends beyond the adult with intellectual disability and their parents to their broader family and informal network. This type of approach recognizes the interdependence of family members and maximizes support from informal sources across the generations.

Matching support to coping

Traditionally, an understanding of informal caring has focused on models of stress and adaptation (Grant *et al.* 1998). For example, the double ABCX model suggests that caring demands are mediated by internal family and external formal resources (McCubbin and Patterson 1983). Objective burdens such as the characteristics of the care recipient, poor health of the carer, social isolation or other caregiving responsibilities are mediated by factors such as the provision of formal support, family relationships and the strength of informal support networks (Seltzer and Krauss 1989). The transactional model suggests a carer's perception or appraisal of their situation is more important than objective burdensome factors. In this model stress occurs when there is a perceived mismatch between the nature of the demand and the individual's ability to respond (Lazarus 1966). More complex conceptualizations of transactional models recognize multiple dimensions, suggesting that rewards and gratification coexist with and mediate stress. It is suggested that 'the co-existence of stresses and rewards can be viewed as "pull–push" factors which create tensions for caregivers in everyday life; the very circumstances which generate problems may also create moments or enduring periods of gratifications' (Grant *et al.* 1998, p.59). This perspective helps to explain why it is difficult for families to make major life decisions, such as accepting formal services or deciding an adult child should move out of the parental home. For example, respite offered to reduce parental stress may actually lead to feelings of guilt and result not only in increased stress for a parent but also the loss of day-to-day rewards that stem from caring and sharing the life of their adult child. Grant and his colleagues suggest three sources of caregiving rewards:

- from the interpersonal dynamic between carer and relative, for example, pleasure for the parent derived from seeing their adult child happy

- from the intrapersonal orientation of the carer, for example, a parent seeing their adult child having their needs attended to

- promotion of positive or avoidance of negative outcomes, for example, a parent helping their adult child to reach their full potential.

The main beneficiary of rewards may be either the carer or the care recipient, or both. Rewards are closely linked to the carer's purpose and how they make sense of what they do. This dimension may be quite invisible to outsiders, unless there is a concerted effort to build a relationship and understand how the carer perceives their situation. The art of empathy, being able to place oneself in another's shoes and see the world from their perspective, is therefore fundamental to working with families.

Sources of stress may be: the relationship with the care recipient; reactions to caring; physical demands; social restrictions; lack of family support; lack of professional support; the nature of professional support or financial consequences of caring. The transactional model suggest that understanding the unique factors that contribute to stress and rewards in each caring situation and the interrelationship of these should guide the type of support provided. Support must aim to reduce stress reduction while maintaining and maximizing rewards.

Family-focused/network approaches

A family-focused approach to working is derived from practice with younger families and has the following premises:

- The type of support provided recognizes the interdependence of child and family needs.
- Support is provided in a way that strengthens family functioning.
- The nature of support is driven by the family's choices, lifestyle and values (Allen and Petr 1998).

A logical consequence of these tenets is that decisions about needs identification, prioritization and the provision of formal support to an individual must also take account of the needs of the family system, other family members, lifestyle and values.

Grant (2001) suggests that the helping principles developed by Dunst, Trivette and Deal (1994) from evaluative research on family-orientated case management could form the basis for work with older parents and their adult children. The principles are:

- use of active and reflective listening skills to understand the needs and concerns of families
- help for families to identify, clarify and prioritize aspirations as well as needs

- proactive rather than reactive helping styles

- help that is compatible with the family's own culture

- help compatible with the family's definition of problems and circumstances

- help leading to the acquisition of competences that promote independence

- help carried out in a spirit of cooperation and partnership to meet needs and solve problems

- the locus of decision making resting with the family as a whole.

As these principles suggest, supportive work with older parents must respect the attitudes and values of families and recognize the interdependence of family members, particularly the parent and adult with intellectual disability. Where change is promoted, it should be done in a way that maintains rather than ruptures or challenges family relationships. Other elements that exemplify this approach are supporting families to move at their own pace rather than being expected to conform to professional expectations or values. Involvement of intergenerational family members or friends is particularly important in work with older families to ensure an extended network of informal support is built around the adult with intellectual disability into the future.

However, it can be argued that work with older parents and their adult son or daughter should differ from that of family-focused practice with children, particularly in regard to decision making and outcomes sought. For children, the active promotion of fully informed decision making by parents is appropriate. With adults and their families it is more appropriate to support the adult to make their own choices and decisions. Strategies for doing this are to strengthen the family's capacity to provide support, guidance and/or advocacy for the adult with intellectual disability to make choices and express their views. Where communication or other obstacles make the expression of preferences directly by an adult with intellectual disability difficult, the strategy must be to ascertain from those who know the person well a sense of what those preferences might be. This approach is closely akin to notions of 'substituted judgement', where the focus is clearly attempting to make the decisions the person themselves would make if they could express them. It acknowledges the rights of people with intellectual disability to pursue their own interests and take risks if they wish. This approach contrasts sharply with that based on notions of 'best interest', where others make decisions based on what is considered to be in the best interests of the person. The latter approach can directly disregard the expressed views of the adult with intellectual disability and should only occur in the context of formal alternative decision-making processes triggered by serious concerns about potential harm stemming from a person's own choices, or dispute about informal decisions based on substituted judgement.

Walmsley (1996) suggests that as the views of parents and professionals are more accessible, particular emphasis should be placed on ensuring the voice of the adult with intellectual disability is heard. In older families the conflict of needs and views is likely to be greater than found in younger families. Potential conflicts may include: parental rights versus the rights of the adult; maintenance of interdependence and reciprocity versus the rights of the 'care recipient' to independence; continued nurturance versus letting go; known costs and benefits of informal care versus the unknown world of future services (Grant 1993).

> Some carers recognised that they were treading a kind of emotional tightrope between fulfilling their own personal and social needs, often through the handicapped person, and trying to avoid exploiting their dependant by demanding too much of them, physically and emotionally. (Grant 1986, p.336)

A central task of a family-focused approach to work with older parents is negotiation and reconciliation of differing priorities, needs and perhaps aspirations. This requires a greater emphasis on complementary individual rather than whole-of-family outcomes. Thus a dual approach may be necessary to achieve different outcomes for the adult and the parent, rather than the emphasis on enhancing family functioning relevant to work with younger families. For the reasons discussed earlier, some older parents are reluctant to accept services or pursue actions that are necessary to support the aspirations of their adult child. As a consequence, much of the individual work with older parents revolves around gaining trust, achieving change and building a greater acceptance of support services either for themselves or their adult son or daughter. However, similar to earlier parts of the life course, trade-offs are inevitable for adults living with older parents. Gains will be balanced with losses and failure to acknowledge this may lead to alienation from parents that is unlikely to produce an optimal outcome.

Key elements of supportive work with older parents

Achieving the breadth of objectives for work with older parents suggested earlier in this chapter involves multifaceted tasks and work at multiple levels: individual and family, group, community and service system. The overarching characteristic of work with older parents is a proactive preventative focus orientated to both maintenance and change. A discussion of these characteristics is followed by a consideration of strategies that can be adopted at various levels of intervention.

Proactive preventive approach to maintenance and change

The primary objectives of support to older parents are proactively to assist them to consider and plan for the future, and to prepare both themselves and their adult child for separation and the transition from parental care. The underlying rationales are preventative: avoidance of a crisis of care in the future; easing the emotional trauma involved in the transition from parental care; diminishing the future formal support needs of the adult with intellectual disability.

In addition, a pressing issue for some families may be maintaining the current situation, which will require the provision of solid practical and emotional support. Essentially, maintenance involves reduction of stress, physical or emotional demands on parents by the introduction of additional supports. This can be conceptualized as a reduction in the demands made by the older parents' physical and social environment and partial replacement of roles previously undertaken by parents with formal or other informal supports: for example, replacing the parental role in organizing recreational activities for the adult by providing a support worker to facilitate activities for the adult; supporting regular contact with friends from a day program in the evening; introducing a home help for domestic chores; providing taxi vouchers to avoid having to negotiate traffic or public transport. Such replacement is a form of compensation for an older parent's reduced stamina and 'slowing down' (Baltes and Carstensen 1996; Silverstone and Burack Weiss 1983). To maintain the caring situation in this manner however, change is often required. Some older parents may have to change their stance on acceptance, trust and willingness to use external supports or services. Supporting such change is a key element of work at the individual/family level, discussed below. In addition, assisting older parents to problem solve, confront issues of planning and separation and begin to let go may require a considerable change and shift in the perspective of a parent.

Actions such as those discussed above that aim to reduce the environmental demands on an older parent and replace previous roles with other supports may simultaneously increase or maintain the demands made on the adult with intellectual disability, thus effecting change in their lives and providing vital ingredients for preparation for the future. An orientation towards change in the physical and social environment of both parent and adult are a central element of work with older families.

Implicit in maintenance and change work is the consideration of dual outcomes for parent and the adult with intellectual disability. When support is designed for a parent, the flip side of achieving a positive outcome for the adult with intellectual disability should always be considered. For example, creating a break for parents can be fashioned to provide an opportunity to extend the community access or recreational activities of the adult with intellectual disability, hence the commonly used term 'recreation as respite'. Organizing weekends away for adults with intellectual disability can extend their recreational experiences and often begin the process of separation, as well as providing a break for parents.

In order to tailor an intervention to achieve outcomes for parent and adult, knowledge, experience and understanding of their differing perspectives and communication skills relevant to both are required. This means that ideally workers require knowledge of working with both older people and with adults with intellectual disability.

Individual work with older families
Use of a relationship to effect change

Demonstration programs and the literature emphasize the importance of sustained and long-term involvement with older parents to build a partnership of trust (Bigby *et al.* 2002b; Magrill *et al.* 1997; McCallion and Tobin 1995). Long-term contact, however, is characterized by variation in the intensity and frequency of contact. In terms of a case management model, the relationship cycles between periods of active planning or implementation and longer term, less intensive but still proactive monitoring.

A long-term trusting relationship is the medium for supporting parents and allowing them to problem solve effectively and experiment with change. The importance of relationships and this approach is widely documented in the social work literature and is one of the key principles of social casework (Biestek 1957). This type of relationships is characterized by respect, consistency, reliability, trust and acceptance and can take many months of painstaking work to establish. It has been summed up as 'doing a special middle thing, which is very time consuming, getting into a real space with families to discuss major and sensitive issues' (Bigby *et al.* 1999, 2002b).

Developing trust and achieving change can mean workers must 'hang in with families' and not give up on the possibilities of change. In Bigby's study one of the workers described her program as a 'taxi voucher program' suggesting that this was the only type of support some older parents were initially willing to accept. Vouchers were used to build up the trust and confidence of parents to accept other types of support. While a family's own assessments of their needs are accepted, at the same time by regularly proffering alternatives workers can keep the door open for change and additional support.

Acceptance and establishing trust involve not expecting families to undertake tasks they are not yet ready to do, or to change long-established ways of coping and behaving. 'Working by stealth' was a term coined by one of the workers in Bigby's study. Rather than confronting the conflicting values and attitudes between herself and older parents, she found imaginative ways to resolve them. For example, she accepted parental anxieties and the very protective role that parents often played in their adult child's life, and provided substantial details of the activities each adult undertook on the weekend holidays and other group activities. However, she also used the feedback as an educational tool for parents and an opportunity to illustrate the capabilities of their adult children and alleviate their anxieties about separation.

Accepting and validating the past choices of older parents, such as opting for family care of their child with intellectual disability, their expertise about their adult child and their current fears about the future, are important supportive strategies. Similarly providing emotional support, 'someone to talk to', is an important role in itself and a means of establishing a trusting relationship, particularly for parents who have been recently bereaved or have to implement difficult decisions about future care for their adult child.

Acceptance involves the provision of emotional support, back-up and non-judgemental understanding of parental perspectives. It can mean affirming their parenting style over the years and their negative experiences of services. It is an essential way of providing support to older parents that involves 'starting where the family are at', 'listening and responding to them'. This means taking at face value the parents' assessment of their needs and their views of what support is required. The anxiety often expressed by parents about the use of services is accepted rather than challenged. The contrasting approaches illustrated below demonstrate the value of acceptance:

> When Roy was referred he was about to lose one of his few weekly recreational outings. The service that he was using was withdrawing funding for a support worker to travel with him to the activity because in their view he was able to make this journey by himself in a taxi. Objectively this may have been the case but Roy's parents were not willing to let him travel by himself and Roy's access to the recreation programme would have ceased. The programme accepted the parents' fears and by providing a regular support worker to facilitate outings

with Roy ensured that he continued to have regular out-of-home experiences independent of his parents. By adopting this strategy, the door was left open for change in the future.

Maintaining lifestyle by substitution of parental roles with other support

Strategies to support parents to maintain their current lifestyle are the provision of breaks from caring and the partial replacement of roles previously undertaken by parents with formal services or other informal sources. This can be as simple as assistance with transport, home maintenance or domestic tasks, but it can also extend to replacing support provided by the parent to the adult child such as personal care or recreational and social activities. Where parental support is replaced, it should be done in a manner that ensures positive outcomes for the adult with intellectual disability and if possible develops their skills or demonstrates their capacity for activity and relationships outside the realm of the family. A common strategy to replace parental roles is the direct employment or contracting of support workers. Such workers should be seen as part of the team working with the family and be included as strategic partners of case managers or social workers. They have the potential to act very much as frontline change agents, delivering concrete services, demonstrating and rehearsing possibilities for change.

When one parent dies the dynamics of the family and caring situation inevitably change, often leaving some roles unfilled. For example, fathers who become sole or primary carers in place of their wives may find tasks such as personal care, clothes buying or packing clothes for their daughters difficult. In such cases support workers can be used to substitute for roles previously played by mothers and provide support to fathers in undertaking tasks such as these.

Demonstrating use of services and ensuring high quality positive experiences

Various strategies can be used to build parental trust and acceptance of services. A key strategy that flows from accepting parental anxiety and reluctance to use services is ensuring that when support is accepted it is of a high quality and appropriate to their needs or that of the adult with intellectual disability. This can be fundamental to the continued and perhaps expanded use of services. Older families have often withdrawn from services in the past due to their dissatisfaction with service quality. A particular concern is often the lack of consistency of support workers, and casual workers whom parents consider do not know their adult child's circumstance and have not built a relationship with them.

One way to achieve high quality is careful matching and monitoring of contracted support workers and care to ensure they are fully acceptable to families.
One way of doing this is for families to be involved in the selection of workers
and be given a veto if they are not happy with them. A useful strategy is to seek
support workers from within the adult's existing informal or formal support
network. For example, employing someone from the family's existing community such as a church or a worker from a day program already known to the adult.
Recruitment of support workers from existing networks can ensure consistency
and continuity across the adult's life and facilitate the development of trusting
relationships with these workers.

Modelling and rehearsing change

If support workers are included as part of a team working with the family they can
play an important role in modelling and rehearsing the possibilities for change to
parents, demonstrating change issues rather than directly confronting at a more
cognitive level. For example, the use of one-to-one support workers to facilitate
time away from home in group activities will not only extend an adult's
out-of-home activities but also rehearse separation for parents and demonstrate
new possibilities to them. Support workers can also model behaviour to parents
such as encouraging adults to make choices or do things for themselves rather
than rely on parents.

Using formal programs or support workers to extend out-of-home experiences for the adult can also provide parents with time away from caring responsibilities and periods of reduced stress. For some parents, this may be a new experience that assists them to realize how stressed they have been, to appreciate breaks
or to begin to separate and develop activities independent from their adult offspring. Supporting parents to deal with 'free time' is also an important task.

Working through existing supportive networks

The active recognition and involvement by case managers of other family
members or friends in existing supportive networks must be a core strategy for
providing ongoing support and planning for the future. In this way maximum
levels of consistent support can be mobilized for older carers. The importance of
involvement of broader support network members and identification of a key
person for the future has been discussed in the section on planning in Chapter 9.
Those nominated in future plans may find their discussion less emotionally challenging than parents, and drawing them in may also facilitate the involvement of

the adult with intellectual disability in future care arrangements. Involvement of potential key people may begin to equip them with knowledge of formal service systems, later life opportunities and the developmental potential of adults with intellectual disability in the pre-transition planning stage.

A case manager can be an important resource to other family members in supporting their involvement with an elderly parent. Conversely, other family members may be supported to try and effect change to parental attitudes, or to present a consistent approach to a situation. Involving other family member can ensure consistency and issues can sometimes be tackled by them that cannot be dealt with by workers.

Protective support

As suggested earlier, negotiating and balancing conflicting needs are features of work with older families. One of the most difficult challenges for workers can be in situations where physical or emotional harm may be occurring to a family member; for example, where the behaviour of an adult child is placing their parent in physical danger, or neglect of an adult's needs is putting their health at risk. In situations such as this respect for self-determination must be balanced with a duty of care to prevent harm. Protection is the most fundamental type of support, and may take the form of a worker being assertive, or suggesting that the wishes of a family member should be overridden to ensure their well-being. However, the most appropriate strategies in situations where the potential for harm to occur is identified are recourse to independent advocacy for the party concerned or instigation of alternative decision-making processes to facilitate the appointment of a guardian, or similar, whose role is to make decisions in the best interests of the person.

Education and information

Another type of support is the provision of education and information about service provision, future planning issues and housing and support options. Again it is important to start where parents are and gauge their level of knowledge, which may be quite rudimentary about the service system. Various strategies can be adopted to inform and educate older parents. These include verbal information, printed literature, assistance to attend more formal community education sessions and accompanying the carer on visits to look over potential services, particularly shared supported accommodation facilities, group homes or respite care facilities.

Community education targetted at parents of all ages is an important component of a more systemic and preventative approach to older parents. Various rationales lie behind the conduct of community education sessions that focus on issues
of future planning, early intervention, reaching a wide audience, an outreach
strategy, addressing the more complex issues of wills and financial planning
about which a case manager may not posses expertise, and providing a safe forum
for parents to discuss future planning and raise issues they may not feel comfort-
able talking about in other contexts. The evaluation by Bigby and her colleagues
demonstrated the value of community education and in particular those sessions
that focused on the area of legal and financial planning.

Advocacy, linkage and collaboration with other service networks

Aspects of work with older parents such as advocacy and linkage to other service
networks are similar to those with families of any age and are not explored in any
depth here. Advocacy in situations of scarce resources and unmet need may be the
only way of obtaining accommodation in the absence of a crisis. Other areas of
advocacy and linkage are likely to revolve around access to relevant services in
other sectors of the system such as health, aged care or rehabilitation, and ensure
their responsiveness to disability issues and their ongoing parenting/caring role.
The current cohort of older parents is exposing this type of service to issues of
lifelong disability and the caring tasks involved for the first time.

Tools for planning

Issues related to planning are discussed in the previous chapter, where it was
argued that drawing up detailed blueprints for their adult child's future lifestyle
may not be a reasonable, viable or desirable expectation of parents. Informally
based plans that nominate a key person and nurturance of a broader supportive
network which can provide flexibility and decisions tailored to changing needs
are a preferable alternative or complement to more formal residential plans.

Various guides are available that aim to assist both the parent and their adult
child express their views about the future and document key information about
the life history and aspirations of the adult. Compilation of a life book can be a
valuable mechanism of life review for both parent and adult, as well as a vital
means of preserving a person's life history to inform those who may become
involved in that person's life in the future. A list of various guides is included in
the resource list. *My Life Book* was developed by Sharing the Caring Project
(1999) in Sheffield and includes the following sections: About Me, Things I Do,

Looking After Myself, About My Health, and other information, leaving space for visual as well as written records.

The range and availability of possible options for housing and support in the absence of parents or the family home vary across jurisdictions. Broad models, however, are discussed in Chapter 8. Financial planning is one area where parents will require expert advice relevant to their own circumstances and the legal framework and regulations that govern their state or country. A range of guides to financial planning is available, but care must be taken to ensure they are up to date, reflect current laws and apply to the jurisdiction in which the parent resides.

Community outreach

In an early model for work with older parents, Kaufman and his colleagues suggested the primary role of community outreach was to locate adults with intellectual disabilities living in abusive care situations (1989). Subsequently, the prime task of outreach has been to locate 'hidden families' and establish linkages with formal service systems if this is needed (McCallion and Tobin 1995; Smith and Tobin 1993b). Janicki suggests that by doing so a mechanism is established to assist with planning and maintaining the caregiving situation intact and viable for as long as possible (1996).

Demonstration projects have had considerable success in locating such parents by adopting strategies that are relevant to and reflect the nature of the community in question. For example, using community gatekeepers such as postmen or chemists is a strategy used in small rural communities (Lagay 1973). Consideration must also be given to the extent to which parents are hidden, from whom and whether they wish to remain so. The possibility of negative past experiences with disability services suggests that outreach may be more successful if it is conducted by generic agencies, such as those from the aged care system (Janicki 1996; Seltzer and Krauss 1994; Smith and Tobin 1993b). A US demonstration project evaluated by Janicki and his colleagues utilized the aged care sector to locate older parents and co-resident adults with intellectual disability (Janicki *et al.* 1998). In this project outreach methods included advertising workshops for families, use of radio, TV and public service announcements, stories in the local press, posting notices in key community centres and meeting places, and more directly through contacts with clergy, police and postal workers.

Registers or regularly updated databases of people born with intellectual disability or those who have previously used services exist in various jurisdictions and can form the basis for inviting those who have lost touch to re-establish their connection to the service system. This strategy was used by Sharing the Caring project in Sheffied (Foundation for People with Learning Disabilities 2002). Utilizing agencies such as day programs or income support services that many older carers are already known to in order to disseminate information and reach parents is another possible strategy (Smith 1997). Clarity of what is being offered is an important consideration in community outreach, as a risk of this type of undertaking is raising expectations that fail to be met. Potential models are discussed further in the section below.

Mutual support and group work

Mutual support groups for older parents can have aims involving both educational and emotional support. The literature reports the success of groups with outcomes, including increased use of services, taking steps towards future planning, being heard and understood by others and receipt of mutual support (Mengel, Marcus and Dunkle 1996; O'Malley 1996; Smith, Majeski and McClenny 1996). In the UK support groups for older carers have been auspiced by local divisions of the national advocacy group, Mencap and local government authorities. Heller (1997) however notes that a drawback of groups may be issues around transport and their time-limited nature. She considers they may also undermine parents' own sense of control and problem-solving capacity. Mutual support groups will only be attractive to some older carers. Others will have their own supportive networks that stem from other parts of their life or reject the notion that listening to and sharing other people's troubles may be helpful.

A concurrent group for parents and their adult children with intellectual disability is reported by O'Malley (1996). This group provided an example of supportive intervention for adults to assist them to deal with their own issues around the future transfer of care, the death of their parents and their own ageing. Examples are also found of successful implementation of a specialist curriculum designed to educate adults with intellectual disability about future planning and lifestyle options (Heller et al. 2000). However, one unexpected outcome of such programs is a drop in expressed satisfaction as adults became more aware of broader opportunities and the limited nature of their lives. This strongly supports the notion that the earlier part of the life course impacts heavily on issues associated with ageing, and that the person-centred planning process and support for the development of aspirations and a lifestyle of choice must occur earlier in the life course. Other examples of this kind of work are found in pre-retirement or seniors groups programs run by day centres (Laughlin and Cotton 1994).

Various demonstration programs in Australia have used a group work approach as a strategy for providing out-of-home leisure experiences and extending the social networks of adults living with older carers. For example, use has been made of small group holidays and activities such as discos and outings. This use of group work techniques with adults with intellectual disability can be a helpful strategy for extending peer relationships and ensuring that carer respite has positive outcomes for the adult. However, optimally such projects should be part of an overall plan and have clearly specified aims and individual outcomes. This could include, for example, short-term use of a group to provide opportunities for the development of friendships which can then lead to facilitation of regular, less formal contact between new friends.

However, ideally where groups are used they should be based around common interest and choice rather than no more than common clienthood, convenience or cost. A challenge for the positive use of group strategies for programs that have a wide geographic catchment area is bringing together and matching people from locations in reasonable proximity to each other. Group programs drawn from large areas risk removing people from their local communities and facilitating friendships that are difficult to sustain without considerable support.

Broader resource development

Group, family, individual, community education and outreach strategies need to be complemented by the development of program models and resources that support work with older parents (Smith and Tobin 1993a). These should include specialist service models, staff development and training materials, as well as developing an understanding of the issues confronted by older parents within both the aged care and disability sectors. Systemic advocacy in regard to unmet need for alternative housing and support options for middle-aged adults living with older parents is also an important task. However, developing a culture of cooperation and collaboration between sectors where resources and expertise can be shared is an important ongoing task that extends to all work around ageing with a lifelong disability, and is not confined to work with older parents.

Diverse program models for engaging older parents

An argument is often made for specialist programs to be developed that focus specifically on older carers (Harris 1998; Janicki 1996). Findings from an Australian study that compared mainstream case management programs that had older parents amongst their clients with a specialist service targetted at older carers supports this argument (Bigby 2002c). Although mainstream programs can work well with older parents, the support provided is mainly reactive to caring situations at risk of breakdown. Mainstream case management programs do not generally have either the mandate or capacity to undertake community outreach to find 'hidden' parents, nor to undertake community education, or provide proactive support to parents without immediate problems to prepare and plan for the future. It is however this latter type of support that is likely to prevent unplanned or crisis transitions from parental care.

Across jurisdictions various specialist models are found that encompass some or all of the approaches and range of tasks discussed in this chapter. One is long-term case management that incorporates ongoing casework and brokerage of resources to support the caring situation, prepare and plan for the future, and engaging in community outreach, education and information giving. This model is ideal for engaging with and building the trust of older parents who have little faith in the service system as it has the resources to deliver immediate and ongoing support and does not have to rely on referral to other services. It also has the capacity for less intensive support through community education forums widely advertised in local networks. This type of strategy is a means of disseminating key information about the service system, financial and legal planning options, but allowing parents to remain anonymous if they wish, with no pressure to identify themselves or have follow up contact with the service if they did not wish to.

However, a drawback of this type of model is its potential to become 'blocked' and exhaust all its resources in supporting parents with ongoing needs, leaving no capacity for continued outreach to new clients. One solution may be to develop ongoing partnerships between specialist and generic programs with negotiated referral at an appropriate stage of the case management to ensure a continuing emphasis on outreach and effective delivery of a mix of low level inputs around future planning to a larger pool of parents, and ongoing support to a capped number of complex high need carers.

Other models were piloted in a US demonstration program that utilized area agencies on ageing to target old parents (Janicki *et al.* 1998). These programs provided additional funds to generic ageing services to undertake outreach, provide linkage and assistance to older parents. Whilst outreach strategies were successful, with 50 per cent of older parents identified being previously unknown to formal services, an issue that arose was the lack of resources available within the host generic programs to meet the identified needs for support to enable caring to continue. This left host agencies in the difficult position of not being able to deliver support, potentially undermining efforts to engage older carers. This raises questions of the ethics of outreach strategies in the absence of a service to offer. A similar type of model was adopted by one demonstration program in the UK where outreach, education, information and low level ongoing monitoring was offered by a specialist program and referral to mainstream disability services relied upon to support families with ongoing high support needs (Foundation for People with Learning Disabilities 2002).

Summary

This chapter has discussed the importance and rationale for working with older parents around issues of preparation and planning for the future. The broad aims and key elements of work with this group have been explored. Clearly not all parents are disengaged from supportive services or need to be transformed into clients. However some will benefit from proactive services. The tasks of engagement, maintenance and change are complex and time consuming. Evaluation of demonstration projects and comparison with mainstream disability programs suggest that the need for specialist programs targetted at older carers to ensure a proactive preventative approach that can incorporate community education and long-term support with planning for parents who do not have immediate difficulties in caring. However, no reasons exist why mainstream services that work with older people or families of people with intellectual disability cannot work with older parents and utilize the practice wisdom developed by specialist programs to work effectively with older parents. The crucial factor is that somewhere in the service system the proposed orientation, levels of intervention and strategies for working with older parents are incorporated. The place where this is done, specialist targetted program or mainstream program, will clearly depend on the nature and resourcing of the existing service system.

Further reading

Foundation for People with Learning Disabilities *Older Carers Initiative*. London: Foundation for People with Learning Disabilities. www.learningdisabilities. org.uk

Grant, G. and Whittell, B. (2001) 'Do families and care managers have a similar view of family coping?' *Journal of Learning Difficulties* 5, 2, 111–120.

Harris, J. (1998) *Working with Older Carers: Guidance for Service Providers in Learning Disability*. Kidderminster: British Institute of Learning Disabilities.

Llewellyn, G. (in press) 'Family care decision-making in later life: The future is now.' In M. Nolan, U. Lundh, G. Grant and J. Keady (eds) *Partnerships across the Caregiving Career.* Buckingham: Open University Press.

Sharing Caring Project (1999) *My Life Book.* Sheffield: Sharing Caring Project.

Todd, S. and Shearn, J. (1996) 'Time and the person: The impact of support services on the lives of parents of adults with intellectual disabilities.' *Journal of Applied Research in Intellectual Disabilities 9,* 40–60.

Part 4

Vignettes

Mrs Parker and Maggie Parker

Maggie is 41 years old, she lives at home with her mother who is 75. Her mother is still sprightly but is anxious about what will happen to Maggie in the future. Her anxiety has increased since her husband died and her other daughter was diagnosed with multiple sclerosis. Maggie attends a day centre five days a week, but seldom goes out in the evenings or at weekends. They used to go out as a family on the weekends when her father was alive. Maggie is very independent and takes care of all her personal needs. She can cook basic meals and looks after her own bedroom. She doesn't help much in the house and rarely cooks as her mother sees this as her role.

Mrs Parker always had a vague idea that she could split her house in two and establish a self-contained flat for Maggie. However she did put Maggie's name on the regional waiting list for a group home several years ago. Maggie is happy living at home and doesn't want to move anywhere else. Although she is out of home a lot, she has only ever spent two nights away from home, when she went on a weekend holiday with the day centre a few years ago. Mrs Parker has little else in her life except looking after Maggie. She used to play golf with her husband, but her arthritis and lack of stamina means she finds this difficult nowadays. She has always been involved in the day centre parents' committee but since her husband died she has found it hard to get to meetings as she doesn't drive. She has a network of friends mainly associated with the centre but they like her find it hard to get out and visit each other as they used to.

Mrs Parker heard about the carers' program from the centre and contacted them in the hope that they might help her think about the future. She got on really well with the case manager, who organized a support worker to take

Maggie to the gym one night a week and helped her with transport to various hospital appointments. The case manager seemed willing to listen to her concerns about the future and unlike others in the past didn't seem to blame her for the sheltered life that Maggie had led. After the first six months she was beginning to feel a real sense of security, that someone cared about Maggie and would be there if anything happened. The case manager offered Maggie the chance to stay over-night in their respite house, but Mrs Parker wasn't sure about this as she felt she didn't need a break and might be lonely without Maggie at home.

The case manager and the support worker left the service after 12 months, leaving Mrs Parker with the sense that she had been let down. She felt very vul-nerable and wasn't at all sure what to expect from the service. A new support worker was appointed but she decided that Maggie was able to travel to the gym in a taxi by herself and gradually withdrew her support. But after a while Maggie stopped going to the gym as she didn't enjoy going on her own. A new case manager contacted Mrs Parker about three months later and began to talk about supporting Maggie to make the transition from home. She helped upgrade Maggie's application for a group home and acted as an advocate for her when vacancies arose. She also persuaded Mrs Parker to let Maggie stay one night a week at the respite house so she could get used to being away from home. Mrs Parker was never really happy with this arrangement as Maggie often came home missing various items of clothing and looking quite dishevelled. Mrs Parker saw little of the case manager, who only rang every couple of months to ask her if she wanted anything. About a year later Maggie was allocated a place in a group home, which Mrs Parker accepted with great reluctance. She phones Maggie every week but can only afford the taxi fare to visit her once a fortnight. She com-mented that she felt she had done the right thing as she knew Maggie was happy, but wondered whether there might an been another alternative where Maggie could have stayed at home longer, as she missed her terribly and felt very depressed.

Questions

1. How did the two case managers differ in their approach to working with Mrs Parker and Maggie? What were the strengths and weaknesses of each?

2. What other ways might Mrs Parker have been supported to help Maggie prepare for the future?

3. Who else might the case manager have involved in discussions about the future?

4. What might have been other housing and support options for Maggie?

5. What alternative approaches might the support worker have tried that would have eventually allowed her to withdraw, but that would support Maggie to continue to attend the gym?

6. How could Mrs Parker's reluctance to let Maggie stay at the respite house have been addressed?

Mr Firman and Harry Firman

Mr Firman is 75 and lives with his son Harry who is aged 47. Mr Firman is very fit and continues to swim at least three times a weeks. He sold his own business about five years ago and since then has enjoyed having more time to do all the things in the house and garden that were neglected while he worked. He also enjoys the freedom to get out to visit his friends and relatives. He and Harry spent most of their days together and regularly go out to eat and have a drink at the local RSL in the evenings. Mrs Firman died after a sudden heart attack two years go. Harry is not as fit as his father and has recently taken a redundancy package from the warehouse where he worked as a packer for 31 years. Harry knows the local area really well and always used public transport to get to work. He has never really done much around the house, as this was his mother's job. He takes care of all his personal needs but sometimes needs reminding to change his clothes. Harry had couple of mates at work but hasn't seen them since he left work.

Harry has two siblings, a sister who lives interstate and a brother who lives in a country town. They both have their own families, stay in touch regularly by phone and visit at Christmas and birthdays.

After the unexpected death of his wife, Mr Firman began to think more seriously about the future. He sought the advice of the family doctor who has known Harry since he was born. The doctor suggested Mr Firman get in touch with the regional disability services team who in turn referred him to the carers' program. The family have never used disability services and Mr Firman was not sure what to expect. Primarily he wanted to ensure that his son would be all right in the future. He has spent a long time talking to the case manager about all sorts of options for the future. Mr Firman was reluctant to have a support worker come into their home to help Harry with cooking and has started to do this himself. However, he isn't sure about the new microwave they bought recently or some of the new types of recipes in the easy cookbook the case manager left for Harry. He is much more at ease with traditional meals of meat and two veg. At the suggestion of the case manager, Mr Firman is also encouraging Harry to do more jobs around the house, but he is finding it hard to explain to him how to use some of the older appliances, such as the old twin tub, which are a bit temperamental. The case manager sorted out a disability support pension for Harry when he was made redundant. She has also helped enrol Harry in the gut busters program to lose a bit of weight. Mr Firman said he 'feels that he can ask the case manager for things and to fix things, as she is a person with clout. She shakes people up and it's great having her at his fingertips to ring up, she always rings back, never fails and always has the answers to questions'. She had suggested that Mr Firman could attend the older carers' group to meet other parents, but he preferred not to do this as he didn't really want to hear about other people's problems.

Mr Firman is now pretty sure that Harry will be able to remain at home. They have talked about who should manage his money and whether he might get lonely. Harry has never spent a night at home on his own and Mr Firman jokingly suggested perhaps he should go away for the weekend to give him a trial run. For Mr Firman the most important thing about the carer program has been Harry's relationship with the case manager. Harry trusts her and he knows that he could turn to her in an emergency.

The case manager has found out about various courses and activities that Harry could go to in the local area at the leisure and community centre, but it has always been difficult for Harry to get to them regularly as he and his father are always off visiting one of the relatives and Mr Firman doesn't like to be tied down to a routine.

Questions

1. What other strategies might the case manager use to help prepare Harry to remain in the family home?

2. What strategies might be used to begin a process of separation between Mr Firman and Harry?

3. Does Harry need to develop his own network of friends? How might he be supported to do this?

4.   What type of support might Harry need to remain in the family home after the death of his father? What might some of the problems be for Harry with this option?

Mrs Walters and Edna Walters

Mrs Walters is 84 years old. She is partially blind, very frail and has had three strokes. She is in a lot of pain in her left arm and just manages to get around the house with the aid of walking frame. She has been assessed as eligible for a nursing home but wants to stay at home as long as she can, although she says, 'I know I should go to a home but I can't last much longer.' She has not been out of the house for the last two years, other than a 12-week stay in hospital. Edna is 55 and lives with her mother in a small unit set in a court of ten other units.

Mrs Walters is totally dependent on Edna to assist her around the house, getting to the toilet and getting into bed. Despite this her mother is still very much in charge of the household and tends to speak for Edna. A home help comes three times a week and does most of the domestic chores and meals on wheels are delivered every day. One of Mrs Walters's friends comes over every week and takes Edna shopping. Edna appears very outgoing and confident, but can sometimes become very agitated and worried about very minor issues. She has been on medication on and off over the years but no one has ever given a clear picture of what her problem might be.

Edna can cook toast and make tea, but has never been able to master more complex cooking and has never been interested in learning domestic tasks. Her great passion is knitting which occupies much of her time when she is at home. Edna goes to the senior citizens' centre that she used to attend with her mother, but now just goes to the special group they have for people with intellectual disability and to the knitting group. She has also been going to a social club for people with disabilities organized by Legacy for many years. Mrs Walters said she used to take Edna everywhere but now she can't go as she has nobody to go with. Mrs Walters said that Edna knew everybody at these clubs but didn't have any friends. Edna however talked of two particular friends; one she sees regularly but the other she has not seen for a while as she stopped going to the club all of sudden.

Mrs Walters is a widow and has thought a lot about the future. Twenty years ago she sold the family home, which was a large old house, and bought a small unit in a new development. She hoped this would provide a supportive community where relationships could be built with neighbours and eventually Edna would be safe to live on her own. The development did not develop in the way she hoped. Disputes arose about car access, a lot of the original occupants have sold up and the neighbours have very little to do with each other. Mrs Walters has a group of six friends who drop in regularly, but she says they are all old like her and she can't expect them to look after Edna.

She has made a will leaving all her assets in a trust for Edna to be managed by a trustee company and hopes that Edna will be able to stay in the unit. Although Edna managed whilst she was in hospital, she is not sure that she will cope alone. She is very concerned that she cannot cook and that she will get lonely. In her view Edna needs to find some good clubs where there are some younger people. Although she gets on all right with the older people, she needs to be with people her own age. She suggested that sharing the house with someone else might be one option. She said, 'I really don't know what to do you know. This would be a nice place for her if she had somebody to live with. It would be a nice home for somebody else, but how long would it last?'

Mrs Walters has found it difficult to talk to Edna about the future and wonders if she really has a conception of what the future is. She says that Edna just gets very upset when they talk about it. Edna said that she would like to stay at home but wasn't sure if she could manage, but she didn't like the idea of living in a hostel with a lot of other people.

Mrs Walters was put in touch with the regional disability team by the social worker at the senior citizens' centre several years ago. A worker had been out to make a plan about the future but as everything was going OK did not stay in touch. Mrs Walters said, 'It isn't that I don't like them [disability services] I don't know them. They have been here and they made arrangements and so on if anything happens to me, but I'm still here. I don't know what they can do, who can help, it's one of those things, who can, what can they do, you just have to live from day to day don't you?'

Questions

1. What could be done to help in this situation?

2. How could Mrs Walters's fears be alleviated?

3. What might be lifestyle options for Edna in the future?

4. What might be housing and support options for Edna in the future?

Mrs Pointer and Len Pointer

Mrs Pointer is 85 years old. She has had a major operation for bowel cancer and has angina. She refuses to have any help in the house and does all her own shopping, although she has to get a taxi home from the bus stop as the hill up to her house is too steep to manage. Her husband died 14 years ago and most of her friends are dead. Her sister is terminally ill in hospital but she has three nieces with whom she is in regular contact; one she knows she can phone at any time if she needs help. In an emergency she can call on either of her neighbours. Mrs Pointer lives with Len, her only son, who is 56 years old. She and Len have a very close relationship. She says he has a great sense of humour and she enjoys his company. When Mrs Pointer was well they used to go out together quite often, and she felt that really most of his friends were her friends too.

Len is a large man with few teeth, which makes communication difficult. He takes medication for high blood pressure. Len does very little around the house but will do anything Mrs Pointer asks of him. He showers and dresses himself, but Mrs Pointer said he has a very slap-happy approach and often misses details like tucking in his shirt. Len has been going to the same day centre for the last 25 years. He has a group of friends there. He enjoys the activities he does which include gardening, making sandwiches and playing the drums in a band. The centre has a dance every week in the evening that he never misses. Len's greatest passion is listening to music.

For the last few years Len has stayed for the occasional weekend at a respite house or in the hostel attached to the day centre. Sometimes however he has walked home on his own from these places. His parents were very involved in building the hostel, but when it opened his father was adamant that Len should stay at home rather than moving. Len's name remained on a waiting list however and three years ago he was offered a place in a group home. Mrs Pointer accepted the place. She said, 'I was very pleased when he got this place at Oxford Road, because I knew then that he would be settled in and when anything happens to me, you know.'

Len moved in but every time his mother visited he asked when he was coming home. One morning he arrived on his doorstep at 5.30 am and said he had come home. Mrs Pointer didn't know what to do and eventually decided to let him stay at home as that was clearly where he wanted to be. She says that she would happily find him another place tomorrow if he would go willingly. Since he has been home Len has had a few violent outbursts, sweeping things off the table and getting very angry. At other times he can be quite weepy and frightened. He has told his mother that he doesn't want to die before her and if she dies he does want to live. He was referred to a psychiatrist who has placed him on tranquillizers.

Mrs Pointer has made a will leaving all her money to Len and has subscribed to the Orphan's Trust which was established to ensure some one would stay in touch with adults with an intellectual disability when their parents died. She has been assured by day program that Len can stay at the respite house should anything happen to her. She doesn't think that any of her relatives could look after Len but knows her nieces will stay in touch with him. Mrs Pointer is not sure whether she has a case manager as she has not seen anyone from disability services for a while. Mrs Pointer said, 'I miss him when he's gone, but I'd be happier to know that he was in a permanent place and he was happy to be there, because I know that he will walk home from anywhere.'

Questions

1. How could Len be supported to deal with the emotional issues that he is confronting?

2. What issues would you take into account in supporting Mrs Pointer make the decision whether or not to let Len return home? Were there any other options open at this time?

3. What strategies could have been tried to ease Len's transition into the group home?

PART 5

Service Developments and Policies
for Successful Ageing

Chapter 10

Policies and Programs for Successful Ageing

At its very broadest policy is conceived as 'the principles that govern actions towards given ends' (Able-Smith and Titmus 1974, p.23) that provide a framework for action (Graycar and Jamrozic 1989). Policy not only signals desired ends but also, through the processes of implementation, the manner in which these will be achieved. Policy and its implementation therefore inform decisions and choices about the level and allocation of resources and types of programs developed. This final chapter considers the types of policies and programs necessary to realize the aspirations for ageing people with intellectual disabilities and overcome the factors that hinder successful ageing, discussed in earlier chapters.

This book has argued that realizing the principles of equal rights, citizenship, community inclusion, participation, choice and self-determination are the markers of successful ageing for older people with lifelong disabilities. Whilst these principles capture desired ends, providing general parameters for action, they are at a high level of generality that requires interpretation and translation into more specific directions. However, moving from the general to the specific is a complex task that cannot occur in a vacuum and must take into account the existing context, policies and programs, culture and values within which ageing people with lifelong disabilities are situated. Ideally at the level of state, local government or region, precise policy and programs will reflect local priorities and the existing social and service configurations.

With the proviso therefore that specific policies and programs must reflect the local contexts, the latter part of this chapter provides ideas for translating general policies into specific actions. However, consideration is first given to the responsibilities of the aged care or disability sectors since both have an important role to play in supporting older people with intellectual disability. Disadvantages of an 'either or approach' and the importance of reframing the debate beyond this narrow conception are discussed. A brief overview of the existing state of policy development in the UK, USA and Australia is presented and finally strategic directions and ideas for development of specific policies and programs are discussed.

Is aged care or disability the right question?

The potential intersection of the two policy sectors, aged care and disability, has set the context of policy debates. As a result the parameters of debate are often narrowed to issues around the intersection and interrelationship of the sectors and which should be responsible. Potentially, either, neither or both sectors could take responsibility. A closer examination of these sectors suggests however that the issues are rather more complex.

Common themes in aged care and disability policy

Over the last 20 years, disability and aged care sectors have followed similar macro policy directions, primarily attempting to move the balance of care from institution to community. Baldock and Evers (1991), writing about the two sectors in the EEC, characterize these directions as moves from:

- standardized to flexible services
- implicit to explicit interaction with informal care systems
- bureaucratic centralism to regulated pluralism
- separate to integrated social and economic criteria in service development.

Personal care services have moved from institutional to community or home-based care and have become more client centred and flexible with a greater focus on coordination between services. Fundamental to this new paradigm are mechanisms such as service brokerage or case management to support individuals to articulate their needs and develop individualized packages of care. Institutions have been closed and restrictions on growth of the residential sector and the tighter gatekeeping on admission to such care have occurred (Baldock and Evers 1991).

The role of families and informal care have been explicitly recognized in a trend towards incorporation of families into the care equation. The emphasis of funding programs has been on support to carers in the form of direct payments via social security systems, and through provision of respite care and other supportive services. The practice of case management has also shifted to a more family centred approach away from a sole focus on the needs of the individual and, in the UK, separate community care assessments are made available for carers.

The shift from bureaucratic centralism to regulated pluralism is characterized by the replacement of monopolistic public provision, state responsibility for dependent groups and a commitment to universalism with a pluralist mix of welfare providers, coordinated services, division of responsibility between the state, family and voluntary organizations and greater selectivity and targeting. Increased reliance on the market to develop services, provide choice and respond to demand and a move away from a planned and community development approach have accompanied these changes to service development. Central to these shifts is greater rationing of public services and targeting of those with the highest level of need. This final shift identified by Baldock and Evers (1991) as a move from providing services where the volume is based on need to one where the volume is limited by cost with inbuilt cost limitations. This move is also characterized by the cost shifting from governments to consumers with expansion of charges and a 'user pays' approach to services. Common to both sectors also has been an underlying ideology of reliance on markets and individual and family rather than collective responsibility (Esping-Andersen 1996; Ife 1997).

Key current issues in aged care policy in both the UK and Australia are broadly: financing and cost containment aimed at ensuring quality; regulation and user rights; access and equity and maximizing capacity to meet demand (Gibson and Means 2000). However, some of the policy options being pursued in aged care are not commensurate with the needs and circumstances of people ageing with a disability. For example, the economically disadvantaged position and low workforce participation of the majority of people with lifelong disabilities means that options, particularly those around financing such as increased means testing and long-term care insurance, will have little impact on costs in relation to long-term care for this group.

The loss of their parents as primary carers by adults with disability in middle age and the absence of other informal network members willing to undertake direct care tasks means too that the emphasis on supporting informal care will have little impact on the demand for long-term housing and support by people with disabilities as they age. As suggested in Chapter 7, many people with lifelong disability will experience a high need for housing and support during middle age when parents die. It is the loss of parents rather than increased support needs due to ageing or fragility that initially leads to their increased need for housing and support. The number of people with lifelong disabilities living in shared supported accommodation increases significantly with age, meaning they are likely to experience increased needs associated with ageing whilst already in receipt of housing and support services. Thus in contrast with most older people, many of those with a lifelong disability are ageing whilst part of a service system rather than external to it. Gibson and Grew (2002) suggest however that both sectors are searching for models that combine housing and support for people with high needs on a scale sufficient for cost-effective service delivery.

Different expectations and perspectives on disability

Despite the commonality of broad directions in the two sectors some significant differences exist. The aged care and disability sectors have developed separate paths and traditions, with different constructions of their constituents and of issues around disability. Disability policy has focused on younger people with disabilities and aged policies on the frail aged. This is something of conundrum as the majority of people with a disability are older. For example, in Australia the rate of disability increases from 4 per cent for children aged 0 to 4 years to 84 per cent for those aged 85 and over (ABS 1998). Though structural issues, such as discrimination, access to public transport or adaptation of the physical environment are common to both younger and older people with disabilities, those affecting the older disabled people are often framed differently. For example, it is suggested that whilst aged policies seek 'a society for all ages', the disability lobby seeks 'an enabling society' (Priestley and Rabiee 2002). Gibson and Grew (2002) suggest the tendency for issues associated with ageing to be perceived at a much more personal and individual level, compared to disability that has a much stronger focus on broader social structural factors. Reaching a similar conclusion from the UK context, Drake (1999) suggests that provision of welfare is central to aged care policies compared to disability where the fabric of community infrastructure is more central. Despite the inherent commonalities, few alliances and little common ground exist between organizations of older people and those of people with disabilities (Priestley 2002).

Commentators suggest that until recently aged care has been constructed around notions of decline, loss and dependency (Kennedy and Minkler 1998; Walker 2000). They argue that although the situation may now be changing, the visions for aged care policies are much more limited than those of the disability sector. The avoidance of institutionalization has become a central theme within aged care policy, whilst disability has adopted greater expectations based on rights to participation, inclusion and autonomy.

As discussed in Chapter 1, the very construction of some notions of successful ageing specifically excludes those with disabilities (Rowe and Kahn 1998). Putnam (2002) suggests this has been one strategy to disassociate ageing from the negative paradigm of decline and loss. However, it has effectively divided the aged into the 'healthy aged' and 'disabled aged'. Whilst it is argued that a more positive paradigm of ageing is emerging that has a growing appreciation of the potential for the aged to reach goals of autonomy, access and participation, the recalibration of goals has not extended to the disabled aged (Kennedy and Minkler 1998; Putnam 2002; Walker 2000). The distinction between the healthy and disabled aged, and associated lesser expectations for the latter group, has potentially negative implications for those ageing with a disability whom, although it can be argued do not fit into either category (healthy or disabled aged), are likely simply to be perceived as the disabled aged.

It is argued that the disability movement has much to offer the aged sector; in particular the ideas that stem from the independent living movement, the social model of disability and the moral economy of interdependence (Kennedy and Minkler 1998). Given the infancy of such conceptions within the aged care sector, it would seem a backward step for those ageing with a disability to move in this direction.

Different needs and characteristics

Aged care is focused on the frail aged, with the bulk of programs and expenditure directed at those over 80 years. It is in this age group where the largest growth has occurred in the past decade. Unlike the disability sector, in aged care chronological age is a useful indicator of need (Gibson and Grew 2002), with the most substantial resources required in the last two years of life. Despite shifts from institutional to community care, in both the UK and Australia 11 per cent of people aged over 75 years are in some form of residential care, which in Australia absorbs 75 per cent of aged care funding (Howe 2001).

As discussed in Chapter 2, despite increased life expectancy of people with intellectual disability, little growth has occurred in the 'old old' age group, and the largest group is the younger old, for whom the age care sector has little to offer. In fact the two sectors have quite different conceptions of what constitutes an older person. In aged care it is clearly someone over 75 years, whilst in the disability sector anyone over 50 years and sometimes younger is likely to be perceived as being older. Whilst some of these differences are due to lack of experience of ageing in the disability sector and stereotypical views of ageing, they also reflect the reality of premature ageing for some groups of people with disabilities, particularly those with Down's syndrome.

Aged care is predominantly concerned with provision of long-term care, either in private homes in the community or in congregate residential care. In Australia, at least, a larger scale of congregate care is considered acceptable for the aged compared to younger people with disabilities. The intensity of in-home support to older people to remain in the community is relatively low with most receiving less than 14 hours in Australia, through the home and community care program (Howe 2001). This level of community care is significantly less than that required by many people with lifelong disabilities who are ageing. For example, a Victorian program such as 'Home First', targetted to support people with disabilities living with older parents to remain at home after their death, provides up to 35 hours of support a week.

The major point is that although the aged care and disability sectors have some commonalities, the pertinent issues in aged care are largely irrelevant to people ageing with a disability. The construction of disability within aged care is much more restrictive than that found in the disability sector and neither the intensity and nature of aged care programs, or the age group at which they are targetted, reflect the needs or characteristics of many people ageing with a lifelong disability. This signifies substantial difficulties in adopting a policy position that advocates solely the inclusion of people with lifelong disabilities in aged care systems.

Accessibility and appropriateness of existing mainstream programs

At the more specific program level, indicators suggest that health and aged care programs may be limited in their responsiveness, accessibility and appropriateness to people ageing with a disability. This section summarizes some of these issues, most of which have been discussed in more depth in earlier chapters.

Aged care programs targetted at the frail aged or those who suffer from dementia, primarily nursing homes and structured day programs, are potentially appropriate for people ageing with a disability with these characteristics. Some of the third age type retirement activities offered to the general community may also be appropriate for younger older people ageing with a disability. Preventative healthcare and other aspects of the healthcare system also have potential to meet the needs of those ageing with an intellectual disability.

However, questions are raised in regard to the capacity of both health and aged care services to respond effectively to older people with intellectual disability. Such questions revolve particularly around the overarching ideology of aged care services as well as the skills of staff and attitudes of participants. Older people with intellectual disability are a small minority in health and aged care programs about whom staff have little experience or training, and this raises concern about the quality of care. For example, the quality of care and support provided in nursing homes has been unfavourably contrasted with that in disability funded accommodation (Walker *et al.* 1996). Negative attitudes of other participants towards people with disabilities and poor staffing resources have hampered inclusion in day programs (Bigby *et al.* 2001).

Gaps exist where the aged care systems does not have programs tailored to the support needs of people ageing with an intellectual disability. For example, although a plethora of activities exist in which older people can participate, there are few mechanisms to support choice, facilitate access or package them into coherent programs for those who lack the skills to undertake this task for themselves. Gaps exist in terms of transport to and from activities for older adults who cannot drive or access public transport. Missing from the aged care system too is an independent system of individualized planning for older people who do not live in a private home in the community. Some form of individualized planning, as suggested in Chapter 2, is crucial to identifying and attaining the aspirations of people with intellectual disabilities.

Finally, obstacles to the use of the aged care system by older people with intellectual disability and drivers towards its use inappropriately stem from programmatic and funding issues. For example, funding issues and rigid program boundaries often make it impossible for people who live in a disability funded 'home' to access specialist in-home support services available to other older people. The split of funding responsibility between levels of government in Australia, whereby the federal government bears the cost for residential aged care and state government that of disability supported accommodation, can lead to cost shifting and inappropriate admission of younger older people with intellectual disability to aged care accommodation. With current policy arrangements, it makes little sense for state-funded disability accommodation services to buy in additional services to support an older person with intellectual disabilities at 'home' when the entire cost can be shifted to the federally funded aged care system by moving the person into a nursing home. However, such logic ignores the high social and emotional cost for the older persons and higher overall cost

for government as people are moved to a more restrictive level of care than necessary.

Accessibility and appropriateness of intellectual disability programs

This review would not be complete without a brief summary of the capacity of
existing disability service systems to respond appropriately to the needs of people
ageing with a disability. Examples are found where access and linkage to third age
retirement activities has been filled by the reconfiguration of disability day
services and the development of specialist programs dedicated to older people
with intellectual disability. However, a primary characteristic of these developments has been its innovative but ad hoc nature and limited accessibility to those
older people who are not existing day service users. The largest group for whom
this is an issue is those who have worked in open or sheltered employment and are
seeking to retire, but would prefer support to access day activity and leisure
opportunities.

In regard to supported accommodation, various factors have obstructed the
capacity of disability services flexibly to adapt to changing needs and facilitate
ageing in place. Access to resources from the aged care sector is one major
obstruction as well as the availability of additional resources from the disability
sector. In many respects, though it is often considered inappropriate by informal
advocates, the disability sector has responded to changing support needs by
shifting older people to the aged care residential sector. The disability sector has
tackled the perceived inappropriateness of such moves by either complementing
aged care services with specialist disability inputs or bypassing them completely
and building dedicated nursing homes for people with intellectual disability with
aged care resources. However, such responses are isolated examples and within
Australia and the UK no systematic response has been made by disability systems
to the issues of quality and appropriateness of aged care services.

Indicators such as waiting lists suggest that it is difficult for middle-aged
people with intellectual disability to access funded housing and supported
options after the death of their parents, as demand currently outstrips supply. In
addition the disability sector has identified a lack of training and expertise in
regard to ageing with intellectual disability but has not developed systematic
partnerships with aged care services to make use of their expertise, nor promoted
specialized training in this area (Bigby *et al.* 2001). Access to individualized
planning and case management services by older people already within the
service system and even more so those who may attempt to enter it in later life
appears problematic. As at other stages in the life course, few mechanisms exist for

resourcing either generic health practitioners or disability staff regarding health needs. Nor has any specific attention been paid to addressing the significant deficits of older people's informal support networks or the crucial role they play in monitoring overall well-being and service quality.

Generally, the disability sector has responded in an ad hoc manner to the needs of older people. Its ad hoc developments have excluded some groups and it has been unable to compensate for the difficulties of accessibility and responsiveness to older people with intellectual disability found in the health and aged care sectors. Neither has it been able to attract additional resources to develop flexibility in support as people age or implement staff development programs around ageing issues. Although considerable innovation has occurred, it has led to uneven service responses and sometimes older people's lives being artificially segmented by service provision.

Development of policies on ageing with a disability

The summative report on 'Healthy Ageing – Adults with Intellectual Disabilities' (WHO 2001) highlights the absence of policies and programs that address the needs of adults ageing with intellectual disabilities, particularly those related to health. An extensive review conducted in 1998 concluded that 'community services and programs to support employment, retirement leisure and activities for older adults with intellectual disability are lacking' (Salvatori *et al.* 1998). Whilst the needs of older people with intellectual disability have been placed firmly on the policy agendas in both the UK and Australia, these countries are still in the early stages of policy and program development. The USA is further ahead with a firmer policy framework and a more substantial record of planning and development, although here significant differences exist between states. The following sections briefly summarize the state of policy development in each of these three countries.

US developments

In the USA service development for people ageing with disabilities has occurred in the context of a clear policy framework. Legislative amendments in 1987 to the Older Americans Act and the Developmental Disabilities Act mandated access to generic aged services for older people with disabilities and collaboration between the two service systems. This policy was supported by the establishment of several University Affiliated Programs for Developmental Disabilities and the Rehabilitation Research and Training Centre Consortium on Ageing and Developmental Disabilities, with briefs to develop public education, provide training and technical assistance to the field and conduct demonstration programs. Sutton *et al.* (1993a) suggest however that considerable disparity in service development exists across and within states.

In New York state, the Office of Mental Retardation and Development Disabilities in collaboration with the State Office on Ageing has, over the last 15 years, funded a range of demonstration projects, research and training publications in this area that have provided valuable resources (Janicki 1991, 1992; LePore and Janicki 1997). The general approach taken in New York and other states has been to foster integration of people with disabilities into mainstream programs, such as luncheon clubs or senior citizen centres, by the provision of specialist support and resourcing. In the mid 1980s, over half of the generic day programs surveyed in Massachusetts were serving an older person with intellectual disability and a sense of shared responsibility for this group existed between disability and aged care service providers. A third of all older people with disabilities in Massachusetts were provided with services by the ageing network (Seltzer 1988; Seltzer and Krauss 1987). Similarly, a survey by Lakin found that specialist day programs were available to less than 10 per cent of older people with disabilities, and that most attended a generic program (Lakin *et al.* 1991). Moss (1993), commenting on developments in the USA, suggests that the strict programming requirements and the vocational orientation of day services available to younger and middle-aged adults with developmental disabilities have driven the need to establish alternatives for older age groups.

Since the 1987 survey undertaken by Seltzer and Krauss, considerable service development has occurred in the USA to develop senior citizen type programs and integrate older people with disabilities into mainstream activities for older people without lifelong disabilities. An excellent overview of these initiatives is found in Janicki's *Integration Experiences Casebook* (1992) which brings together diverse examples of community integration strategies and projects, including systemic as well as individual program level initiatives. Characteristic of US developments has been the development of statewide planning initiatives, bringing together aged care and disability sectors, and more local developments of specialist services such as geriatric assessment or specialist dementia care support. Various examples of these initiatives written by both practitioners and researchers are found in edited texts and in unpublished reports (see for example, Janicki and Ansello 2000; Janicki and Dalton 2000; Sutton *et al.* 1993a).

UK service development

Moss (1993) suggests that in the UK service development has followed a path of age integrated programs, whereby older people have largely been accommodated within existing programs by changes such as part-time attendance, age-appropriate activities, provision of quiet rooms and multidisciplinary screening. He argues that the existing framework of day service provision for adults is sufficiently flexible to adapt to the needs of people as they age. In contrast, Walker and Walker (1998) suggest that the needs of older people with disabilities are not adequately addressed and they fall in a gap between services for older people and those for younger people with disabilities. Comments in *Valuing People* suggest that many older people with intellectual disability are misplaced in facilities for older people (DH 2001). A Scottish report on services for older people with intellectual disabilities suggests that the official policy view is that this group are older people first and should be integrated in generic aged services (Lambe and Hogg 1995). It goes on to demonstrate, however, that in practice they continue to be treated as people with disabilities first and attend specialist age-integrated disability services.

Surveys in the UK suggest that few policy initiatives and little comprehensive service development have occurred. For example, in an analysis of local government community care plans for 1993–4, Robertson *et al.* (1996) found that 82 per cent of authorities had no policies in relation to older people with disabilities. Where specific services for this group were established, they had evolved as service users had grown older in place. This survey found that no consensus or guiding principles are in place regarding the service needs of older people with intellectual disabilities. A 1990 survey demonstrated that a range of innovative programs had been developed (Hogg 1994) although, as in the USA, evidence of poor quality services for older people is found in the UK and considerable variation exists in the nature of service provision across different regions (DH 1997; Fitzgerald 1998; Robertson *et al.* 1996). The Foundation for People with Learning Disabilities (2002) through its GOLD project funded a range of innovative projects between 1998 and 2002 that provided a series of program exemplars as well as, in some cases, leading to longer term service development. Examples include the Birmingham Psychological Service for Older Adults (Kalsy 2003) and the 'Older Carers Initiative' to support local authorities in meeting the needs of older carers and their families (Foundation for People with Learning Disabilities 2002).

Australian developments

In Australia grass-roots innovation and adaptation have occurred in the design and delivery of support services to people ageing with a disability (Butcher 1998; Donovan, Donovan and Gladwin 1993; Gilley 1999; Treanor 1997). Various states and the commonwealth have initiated policy development initiatives. For example, the commonwealth has commissioned studies of retirement and day program models. The Disability Services Commission of Western Australia has commissioned several studies and sponsored a major conference to consider policy options and current developments and Victoria, as well as commissioning reports on day programs and accommodation support, initiated a one-off funding round to stimulate the development of day programs (DHS 1999a; Gatter 1996). However, in the absence of a clear policy framework these developments have primarily focused on existing service users as they have aged in place and little program evaluation has occurred (Bigby 1999b).

An analysis of the challenges and directions in policy and service development for older people with intellectual disability concluded that a central theme was still similar to that found in 1994 that 'funding and service responsibilities in respect of this population are often vague and inconsistent' (Murphy 1994, cited in Bigby 1999b). However, an important role has been played by providers and advocacy groups in ensuring these issues remain on the public policy agenda.

Considerable differences exist between Australian states in the nature of their programs for people with disabilities of all ages and the types of services used by older people with disabilities. Surveys have produced quite different results that are related both to sample selection and state service system variations. A national survey conducted in 1993 found that a majority of older people used mainly specialist disability program services available to all age groups. Relatively little use was made of community-based leisure facilities or the programs for older people in the general community (Ashman et al. 1993). A survey of generic aged and specialist disability agencies in Brisbane conducted by Buys and Rushworth (1997) concluded that little assistance was provided to older people with disabilities by generic services; that financial or staffing constraints detracted from the ability of specialist disability agencies to develop specialist programming for older participants; and little if any progress had been made towards developing linkages between ageing and disability community service networks. In contrast a study of two metropolitan regions in Victoria, which included in the sample older people unknown to the disability service system, found that 21 of the 34 older people who attended day programs used generic services available to all older people in the community (Bigby 1997b) and a series of consultations also revealed a plethora of programs developed specifically for older people within the sector of disability day service providers (DHS 1999).

Developments in Australia are characterized by the ad hoc reconfiguration of programs, uneven development of initiatives and a lack of program evaluation. All of these have the potential to disadvantage older clients in particular services where, because of the serendipitous age composition, small numbers of older people mean that reconfiguration is not feasible and those who have never previously used services.

Multiple policies and strategies

Earlier parts of this chapter emphasized the shortcomings within both the aged care and disability sectors in responding to people ageing with a disability and some of the fundamental differences between the sectors that are potentially disadvantageous for older people with a disability. A focus on aged care or disability also fails to recognize the fundamental importance of other policy sectors such as health, recreation and leisure to their well-being. Whilst the overriding policy approach must be based on inclusion of people with disabilities in the health and other services available to the rest of the community, such an undertaking is not simple and specialist support is often necessary to achieve such inclusion or to provide support where no programs exist in the mainstream (WHO 2001). The following questions provide a broader basis for consideration of policy directions:

1. Which needs during the ageing process can existing service systems, such as aged care, disability, health, recreation appropriately respond to?

2. What new or different policy directions, programs or developments are needed to ensure that relevant other sectors overcome obstacles to meeting identified needs?

3. What resources does the disability sector have that can facilitate other sectors responding to particular needs more appropriately?

4. In what ways can service systems combine their resources, (knowledge, programs, staff skills) to attain optimum outcomes for older people with intellectual disability?

These questions open possibilities for multiple policies and strategies to achieve desired ends. To answer them requires an understanding of the underpinning goals sought for people ageing with a disability, knowledge in regard to the changing needs with age and local data regarding the current policies, configuration, and performance of the sectors that impact on people ageing with a disability. There is no one blueprint of polices and programs, as these must reflect local conditions and will therefore be different for each jurisdiction. However, building on the discussion in previous chapters, a brief consideration of strategic directions and ideas for obtaining some specific goals are outlined here as a guide to local action. This section draws on work undertaken to develop a strategy plan to respond the needs of ageing people with intellectual disabilities in a region of metropolitan Melbourne (Bigby *et al.* 2001b). Overarching principles, strategic directions and specific goals are summarized in Table 10.1.

Strategic policy directions

Adoption of a leadership role by disability services

In order to ensure the development and implementation of comprehensive policies one sector must take a leading role. This does not infer that one sector must 'own' older people with a disability, merely that one must take the initiative in tackling cross-sectorial boundary issues and ensuring the specific needs of this group are adequately represented in the relevant service systems. Older people with an intellectual disability are a small group and one of many minority groups to whom other service sectors such as health and aged care must respond. Without external advocacy their needs are likely to be overlooked or lost among competing demands. It is logical that the disability sector should take the lead role, given the thrust of much of its policy and service development towards inclusion which is focused on the removal of obstacles and ensuring services available to the general community are accessible, appropriate and sensitive to people with disabilities.

Systematically bridge gaps with specialist services or initiatives

New initiatives are necessary to meet some of the needs of older people with intellectual disability that are not currently covered by any service sector. These may be directed to supporting inclusion of people ageing with an intellectual disability in other service sectors, adapting and resourcing the disability sector or the development of partnerships and joint planning: for example, development of a mechanism such as a regional planning and brokerage service to facilitate choice and plan supported access for an older person with a disability to some of the many mainstream activities available in the community; or specialist health and

Table 10.1 Policy directions for ageing with a disability

Realizing overarching principles of:

- equal rights
- citizenship
- community inclusion
- participation
- choice and self-determination.

Strategic policy directions:

- adoption of a leadership role by disability services
- systematically bridge gaps with specialist services or initiatives by

    (a)   supporting inclusion in mainstream services

    (b)   adapting and resourcing disability services

    (c)   development of partnerships and joint planning.

Key goals and strategies:

- knowledgeable, responsive workforce
- individualized planning, monitoring and review
- active and healthy approach to ageing
- knowledge of ageing for people with intellectual disabilities
- ageing in place
- recognition and maintenance of informal social networks
- exercise choice of lifestyle and availability of flexible supports
- the disability sector's leadership capacity and links with other sectors
- a life course perspective to inform practice and service development
- non-discrimination on basis of age or disability
- independent advocacy and transparent decision-making processes
- mechanisms to support for older parents and their adult sons or daughters to prepare and plan for the future
- provision of support for adults to remain within their local area, within the family home, or alternative housing and support options when they lose support of parents.

monitoring programs to ensure this group has preventative health screening, regular health assessment and access to quality healthcare.

Supporting inclusion in mainstream services

Inclusion of people with intellectual disability in mainstream community programs, health or aged care services requires a proactive stance of providing support and consultancy to ensure such services are attuned and able to adapt to the needs of this group. Thus when older people with intellectual disability use such programs from choice or necessity, their specific needs must be identified, and services appropriately supported, if necessary with additional assistance from the disability service system. For example, consultancy may be provided to a nursing home in regard to a new resident with intellectual disability or support for staff training may be provided to assist the integration of an older person with dementia into a day program.

Adapting and resourcing intellectual disability services

Various parts of the disability service system need to be adapted and resourced to ensure responsiveness to older people to enable ageing in place. Currently, in Australia the most critical area in this regard is the relationship between day support and shared supported accommodation services. It may be necessary, for example, to provide additional resources to enable older residents to remain at home if they choose and ensure staff are available across all waking hours, to change the mix of staff employed to include those with knowledge of dementia, to provide additional training to staff or bring in additional expertise from outside services such as palliative care or district nurses.

Development of partnerships and joint planning

Collaboration and coordination between individuals and their families and all parts of the service system is necessary to ensure appropriate supports are provided as people age. Efforts must be made to break down barriers created by service types that sometimes fragment people's lives and instead build collaboration between services. The clearest example, where collaboration is required, is between residential and day services. As service systems move towards individualized funding such program distinctions may disappear but in the meantime making boundaries more permeable and less rigid is a key task.

Linkages and the development of working partnerships between the disability service system and parts of the aged care or health system that will increasingly be accessed by older people with disabilities is a key strategy. For example, dementia services, aged care assessment teams, community health centres and medical specialists such as geriatricians. Joint initiatives with areas such as these will ensure that health and assessment services work together to draw on the expertise of all sectors.

Key goals and strategies

The following are a set of key policy directions in regard to ageing people with a disability, which are also indicators of the goals to be achieved. The sections below give examples of specific strategies for moving towards these:

- knowledgeable, responsive workforce

- individualized, person-centred planning, monitoring and review

- active and healthy approach to ageing

- knowledge of ageing for people with intellectual disabilities and preservation of their life history

- ageing in place

- recognition and maintenance of informal social networks

- opportunities to exercise choice of lifestyle and availability of flexible supports

- the disability sector's leadership capacity and links with other sectors

- adopting a life course perspective to inform practice and service development

- non-discrimination on basis of age or disability

- independent advocacy and transparent decision-making processes

- mechanisms to support for older parents and their adult sons or daughters to prepare and plan for the future

- support for adults to remain within their local area, within the family home, or alternative housing and support options when they lose support of parents.

Knowledgeable, responsive workforce

Attitudes play a fundamental role in mediating opportunities available to people with intellectual disabilities. As discussed in Chapter 2, older people consistently experience discrimination because of their age and are presented with fewer choices and appropriate services. Training staff in disability services on issues around ageing is a primary strategy to combat discrimination on basis of age, low expectations and to increase awareness of age-related needs.

Direct disability service staff within accommodation and day support, case managers and those responsible for program planning and development require training about the normal processes of ageing as well as particular issues that arise for people with intellectual disabilities. More senior staff in disability services should also have knowledge of health and aged care service systems and policy developments to foster their ability to negotiate access and make appropriate use of programs in other sectors. In parallel staff in the community care, aged care and health sectors should have an understanding of the nature of intellectual disability, particularly around issues of communication, specific health needs and informed consent, if they are to provide responsive support. Strategies could include:

- inclusion of ageing as a core component of pre-service qualifications for direct care staff in disability

- development of training modules on the processes of ageing with an intellectual disability for in-service training

- sponsoring staff to attend generic courses on ageing

- review qualifications held by staff and through the recruitment processes and progressively alter the mix of staff qualifications to better reflect the needs of older clients: for example, actively seek to employ staff with nursing, occupational therapy and other relevant qualifications

- ensure professional courses such as social work, nursing and medicine have content relevant to both ageing and intellectual disability.

Individualized planning, monitoring and review

To ensure optimal attention to health and lifestyle choice, an individualized plan should inform the provision of support. Such a plan should be the result of consultation and information gathering exercises with the people themselves, their informal network members and professionals involved in their lives, and extend to all areas of their lives where support to attain their desired lifestyle and sustain good health is required. Ideally development of such a plan should occur outside the parameters of existing services and before decisions about services are made.

As suggested in Chapter 2, the breadth, depth and intensity of planning and implementation needed will vary for each individual. People with complex and changing needs may require a long case manager to develop a plan, oversee its implementation, coordinate support, monitor outcomes and review strategies. For those with less complex or more stable needs, these tasks may be effectively undertaken by a key worker within a shared supported accommodation or day service, provided they have access to consultation and the mandate to coordinate supports outside their own service.

Implementation, mechanisms for regular monitoring and review of plans are as important as plan formulation. These tasks cannot stand alone but are interdependent. Strategies could include the regional/local policy decision by the funder of disability services that every older person in the region in receipt of any type of funded support will have an individualized plan, prepared and reviewed on an annual basis. This plan will nominate a key worker or case manager to oversee its implementation, coordination, monitoring and review. Plans should cover all life areas and pay particular attention to health needs, lifestyle or day support options and links to family and other informal networks of support. Plans should take a proactive, preventative stance to life issues and not only be actively implemented following a crisis.

Various strategies could be pursued to implement this planning function, including the following:

1. Dedicating one or two case managers from the relevant organization, such as in Victoria the disability client services team, to provide a planning service for older adults.

2. Providing consultancy support and initial training to supervisory staff within the community residential system to undertake a planning service for adults within the shared supported accommodation system.

3. Development of a new initiative or reconfigure existing funding to develop an older persons' regional assessment, planning and brokerage program to undertake the planning function in relation to older adults and possibly to act as a broker. Such a regional planning service would provide a focal point for older adults and service delivery within the region and be the logical place for a regional

consultancy resource (see below) to disability, health, community and aged care services to be located.

Active and healthy approach to ageing

As discussed in Chapter 3, people ageing with intellectual disability often have undiagnosed or untreated health problems and do not utilize preventative health screening to the same extent as other members of the community. Diagnosing health problems in people with intellectual disability is made more difficult by their often restricted ability to communicate and the reliance on staff to observe and report changes of function and behaviour. Additionally, as Chapter 4 suggests, diagnosis of dementia is made more difficult as most clinical diagnostic tools available are based on the general population rather than people with intellectual disability who may never have had literacy skills, good general knowledge or abstract reasoning skills. People with intellectual disability have a tendency to be overweight and lead quite sedentary lives with correspondingly low levels of fitness. Women with intellectual disability experience menopause at an earlier age than other women. Possible strategies to address these health and lifestyle issues include the following:

1. Residential and day support programs should adopt a
    health-conscious approach in relation to diet, menus and
    opportunities for exercise commensurate with each individual's
    physical fitness and choice. This approach can build on the recent
    initiative developed for DHS, Let's Get Active (DHS 2001).

2. People aged over 55 years or those with Down's syndrome who are
    younger and show signs of premature ageing should have an annual
    health review which includes appropriate preventative
    health-screening procedures. UK policy is moving in this direction by
    aiming to develop a health action plan for all adults with intellectual
    disability and offer a minimum annual health check (DH 2001;
    Martin 2003).

3. Conduct an annual review of functional abilities for older residents of
    shared supported accommodation to document changes and assist in
    diagnosis of conditions such as Alzheimer's disease. Tools that may
    be useful for this are the broad screen checklist (Koenig 1995), the
    FIM (Balandin, Alexander and Hoffman 1997) or the
    multidimensional observation scale for elderly subject (MOSES)
    (Dalton et al. 2002).

4. Foster the development of expertise in relation to health needs of people ageing with intellectual disabilities within regions to ensure the receipt of optimal treatment and resourcing from the health service system.

5. Allocation of additional resources to the health system to develop expertise and provide an avenue to trial best practice in relation to people ageing with intellectual disabilities. This could be achieved in a number of ways.

6. Appointment of a community health nurse based in a local health centre or aged care Assessment team. This position would develop expertise around healthcare for older people with intellectual disability, build links and consult with other healthcare professionals and assist older people, their families or disability services staff to navigate the healthcare system and receive optimal services from it.

7. Appointment of clinical nurse specialists within the disability system to work directly with ageing people, to plan their care and liaise with health services.

8. Joint projects undertaken between disability services and regional women's health centres to improve clinical responses and knowledge in regard to menopause and women with intellectual disabilities.

9. Joint projects between disability services and regional palliative and hospice care organizations to improve end of life care and decision making for people with intellectual disability.

Knowledge of ageing for people with intellectual disabilities

People with intellectual disabilities have a right to understand the process of ageing and the changes it may bring to their lives and health. They also need time to consider the options for a different kind of lifestyle. Attaining psychological well-being in later life often requires reflection, reminiscence and review of life history, both alone and with others. Older people with intellectual disability, on the death of parents or relocation from an institution, are at particular risk of losing their life histories and having no one who 'knows them well'. Mechanisms to capture life history as well as current lifestyle preferences are crucial to supporting older people with some of the emotional tasks of ageing, as well as ensuring continuity of support that reflects their own networks and preferences. Strategies might include:

1. Development of education programs that aim to educate and prepare people with intellectual disabilities for later life. Several such curriculums have been developed overseas, especially one on planning for later life (Sutton *et al.* 1993b).

2. Provision of peer education about aged-related health issues such as menopause and opportunities for peer discussion of age-related life changes.

3. Use of mechanisms such as 'life books' (Sharing Caring Project 1999) or 'lifemaps' (Gray and Ridden 1999) to preserve a person's history and current networks and preferences.

Ageing in place

As suggested earlier, many people ageing with intellectual disability will be resident in shared supported accommodation services. Rather than build new and separate facilities for this group, or assume they should be transferred to an aged care facility, they should have the same opportunity as other older people to age in place in their own homes if they choose to do so. A policy of ageing in place requires a well-articulated commitment to maintain older residents at home as long as possible and substantial forward planning to ensure this can occur. Ageing in place requires short-term flexibility to adapt physical environments to ageing clients and reconfigure staff support as necessary when support needs of residents change, in addition to longer term planning of the service system. Short-term measures may include:

1. Development of a policy to minimize the mobility of older residents in shared supported accommodation and establishment of a clear rationale and decision-making process where transfer to an aged care facility is considered.

2. Staff education and training on issues such as normal and pathological ageing, the concept of healthy ageing, understanding and responding to dementia, dealing with grief and loss.

3. Development of a pool of staff interested and trained in working with older people.

4. Availability of expertise and resources to adapt physical environments to accommodate age-related changes; for example, colour schemes

and lighting to maximize poor vision, installation of rails and other changes that may be required in accordance with individual needs.

5.   Development of linkages with specialists in the area of adaptation for ageing to advise on changes required, such as occupational therapists working within the aged care system.

6.   Flexibility of the quantity and nature of staff resources when necessary to accommodate additional support needs and use of staff with relevant skills such as nursing, counselling or palliative care.

7.   Development of linkages between managerial staff and local domiciliary services available to support older people to age within the community. Development of protocols and agreement regarding sources of funding and payment for services between shared supported accommodation services and external domiciliary services they may seek to utilize.

8.   Funding of a regional resource (a regional consultant on ageing) whose role would be to provide consultation and expert advice in relation to older people with intellectual disabilities. This resource would be utilized by shared supported accommodation services, day support services and case management and could work in closely with any initiatives in regard to health or aged care issues.

9.   Information, training and support to staff and residents in relation to death, grief and loss where a resident dies either at home or soon after a move from home.

10. Implement measures that ensure older residents are not forced to leave their home all day every day if they choose not to do so. This requires provision of a minimum of one staff on duty during the day or alternative methods of monitoring resident safety. This may involve development of a new funding model for houses with older clients, and trailing alternative safety arrangements such as a floating daytime staff person shared between several houses and/or personal alarm systems for residents who may be at risk alone.

11. Investigate and trial the use of personal alarms and other strategies to support older people to remain at home for periods of time without staff support or a pooled model with one staff supervising several locations.

Longer term measures

1. Ensure that all new shared supported accommodation is built using an adaptable design to facilitate easy adaptation to the changing needs of ageing residents.

2. Develop a wider range of shared supported accommodation options to provide choice and designs that may be more suited to accommodating clients with dementia or with high physical care needs; e.g. co-located smaller units where staff can be easily shared across several discrete units.

3. Address the high demand for supported accommodation from middle-aged people living with ageing parents when they lose their parents by developing new models of in-home support for this group, or shared accommodation arrangements in private or rented accommodation with visiting support.

4. Pay regard to the mix of residents in newly established shared supported accommodation or when vacancies are filled to ensure minimal age differences and thus potential to maximize sharing of in-home support. However, age should not be the exclusive factor; friendship groups/interest groups must also be taken into account.

Recognition and maintenance of informal social networks

Older people with intellectual disability are particularly vulnerable to shrinkage of their social networks as they alter the pattern of their lifestyle, cease full-time attendance at day programs, outlive their parents and are susceptible to residential mobility. Informal network members can play a significant role in people's lives, providing friendship, affirmation of worth and identity, companionship, advocacy, monitoring the quality of formal services and negotiating with service systems. Strategies could include:

1. In the formulation of individualized plans attention should be paid to the maintenance and development of informal social networks, particularly where changes to routine patterns of life are being considered. In particular friendships with other people with intellectual disabilities should be identified and plans put in place to ensure continued opportunities for joint activities.

2. Adoption of measures to support continued contact with elderly family members in recognition that parents or other family members

may experience age associated restrictions on personal mobility, driving capacity or ability to use public transport.

3. Attention to and proactive support for the succession of key informal network members as older family members die.

4. Voluntary initiatives that aim to foster friendship or companionship between older people with intellectual disabilities and other members of the community should be investigated; for example, adding a focus on older people with intellectual disability to existing friendship schemes for older people.

5. Identification of older residents in shared supported accommodation without regular contact with family or other informal network members and discussion with community visitors or other relevant statutory monitoring schemes to ensure the provision of regular monitoring of the service quality provided to these individuals.

6. Training case managers working with older parental carers around issues of future planning and the importance of engagement of more extended family members in this process.

7. Establishment of regular regional information sessions on issues of planning for the future targetted at parental and wider family members such as siblings to increase their understanding of the disability service system and recognize their likely involvement in the lives of their relative with intellectual disability when parents are no longer able to care.

Exercise choice of lifestyle and availability of flexible supports

The notion of day support services for people ageing with intellectual disability as a 9am to 3.30pm day placement in any type of day centre needs to be reconceptualized. Day support can more usefully be seen as provision of support of varying intensities provided to individuals during the waking hours, which facilitate people with disabilities to access activities and pastimes of their choice that are meaningful to them and which increase their quality of life and may also ensure their personal safety (see Chapter 6). This approach seeks to break down artificial programmatic boundaries between day support and other services such as leisure programs and accommodation support. Older people must have the choice to remain at home during the day and choose the pastimes and activities they wish to pursue either at home or in the community. The nature of an older person's accommodation is a factor in determining whether day support must include safety monitoring. For those who remain at home with older carers, the respite function of day support must be acknowledged and factored into any life-style plan. Key outcomes and characteristics suggested by Bigby *et al.* (2001) for day support for people ageing with intellectual disabilities are:

- choice
- strengthening social networks
- participation in the community
- skill maintenance
- development of self-expression
- a healthy lifestyle.

Strategies for providing flexible lifestyle support to older people include the following:

1. Development of a regional planning and brokerage program of day support for older people. A notional amount would be allocated for daytime support, with the program responsible for the preparation, implementation and monitoring of detailed lifestyle plan and use of brokerage funds. Funds could be used to provide individualized support or pooled to provide support to small groups of older people or a combination of these. The funds could also be used to purchase services from existing centre-based programs, or for support to remain at home. Thus such a model can facilitate continued but part-time attendance at a person's existing day program if this is a choice. The advantage of a regional brokerage service would be the development of expertise and knowledge within a region on options available to older people and the ability to put together small group activities for older people based on their interests and choices rather than age and place of residence.

2. An alternative model for those living in the shared supported accommodation system is to combine the accommodation, day support and leisure funds notionally allocated to an individual and give the mandate to residential staff to develop detailed lifestyle plans and implement these with residents.

3. Alternative models may be required for older people living at home with older carers for whom attendance at a day centre may play an important respite role. In such cases the requirement for out of home respite should be recognized and negotiated with carers. For these older clients day support services may combine choice of activity with some more low-key time spent in a day centre for the purpose of respite.

4. A proportion of people ageing with intellectual disability are out of touch with day support services or do not receive any funding from disability services. Consideration should be given to undertaking assertive outreach followed by provision of day support services in regard to this group who are likely to be found in private sector accommodation such as supported residential services, boarding houses or in private homes. A possible model is the provision of a visiting worker to a cluster of private residential services, which are home to a number of older people with intellectual disabilities.

5. Mechanisms for transition from supported or paid employment to participation in funded day support must be implemented for those workers choosing or who are forced to retire.

6. Workforce and occupational safety issues around using shared supported accommodation as the base from which staff employed to provide support operate should be identified and resolution to any obstacles to the flexible use of staff across community and shared supported accommodation may need to be negotiated between key stakeholders.

Building the disability sector's leadership capacity and links with other sectors

At present staff in disability services have very limited knowledge and expertise in relation to issues that affect older people with intellectual disability. Implicit in many of the strategies suggested are attempts to build the knowledge and understanding that the disability sector and other key sectors have of ageing and intellectual disability. As the strategic directions suggest, the development of partnerships between the various service systems that can potentially be used to improve the quality of life of older people with intellectual disabilities is crucial.

In Australia and the UK the disability sector has not developed a strong leadership stance in relation to ageing. Active research, policy interest and practice expertise are scattered across various universities and service organizations.

Lacking are a central focus and systemic linkages between researchers and key stakeholders such as people with disabilities and their families, service providers, policymakers and advocacy groups. A US strategy for concentrating resources and developing leadership has been funding for University Affiliated Programs in Developmental Disabilities and in particular Rehabilitation and Research Centres on Ageing and Developmental Disabilities (RRTCADD). These initiatives bring together researchers with a mandate to involve other stakeholders into the conduct of research and evaluation as well as the translation of findings into policy, programs and practice. This is achieved through the establishment of demonstration programs, training and technical assistance to the field. For example, the objectives of the RRTCADD at the University of Illinois at Chicago are:

To increase knowledge about:

- ○ The changing needs of older adults with mental retardation and their families as they age.

- ○ The effectiveness of innovative approaches, public policies, and program interventions that provide needed supports and that promote successful ageing of these adults and their families. It examines how age-related changes in physical and psychological health affect a person's ability to function in the community, including their home, work and leisure settings.

To identify best practices and current public policies that seek to support these adults and their families. The special focus is on programs that:

- ○ Promote health and wellness.

- ○ Help individuals and their families make plans for their future needs.

- ○ Provide accommodations for employment and community functioning (including innovative strategies, assistive technology and universal design) for these age-related changes. (http://www.uic.edu/orgs/rrtcamr/)

The establishment of such centres in the UK and Australia could provide leadership to the disability sector and act as a stimulus to joint planning and partnerships with other sectors. They would also be an important springboard for interdisciplinary training, program demonstration and evaluation, and dissemination of research findings to a broad audience. Other specific strategies might include the following:

1. Development and maintenance of a database of older people and their needs based on the information from person-centred plans.

2. Creation of a portfolio of ageing issues for people with intellectual disability, at both state and regional levels.

3. Fund or reconfigure from existing resources a position of a regional consultant on ageing, available to services across the region to provide consultation and expert advice in relation to older people with intellectual disabilities. This resource would be utilized by shared supported accommodation services, day support services and case management and could work in closely with any initiatives with the health or aged care sectors.

4. At both regional and state levels hold annual one-day forums on research and service developments around ageing with an intellectual disability.

5. Develop regional networks on ageing and intellectual disability that provide the opportunity to raise and discuss issues in service delivery and development, share new knowledge and foster collaboration. Networks should include representatives from various aged care programs in the region, non-government disability organizations, local government, state disability services as well as key health and geriatric services.

Non-discrimination on basis of age

The age-related needs of each ageing person with an intellectual disability should be acknowledged and responded to appropriately. However, age should not be regarded as a person's sole or dominant characteristic, but rather one of many factors contributing to their choice of lifestyle and support needs. Many of the strategies discussed above, particularly those relating to knowledge about ageing, will help to combat age discrimination. Avoidance of age-segregated services is another strategy but such services, particularly the type suggested above in respect of planning, can be a form of positive discrimination.

A key question must be whether the use of an age specific program will restrict the choices and opportunities available to the person or impose stereotypical views or responses on them. No upper age limit should apply to disability services in respect of people whose disability is lifelong or acquired in adulthood rather than related to the ageing process. Processes should be considered for making eligibility decisions in respect of older people with intellectual disability seeking services for the first time.

Independent advocacy and transparent decision-making processes

Older people with intellectual disability may not have an informal advocate or family member who can oversee their well-being and speak on their behalf and in some instances disputes can arise between informal advocates and others involved in a person's life. For the former group and in the event of conflict about best interests, people ageing with disability should have access to independent advocacy when necessary or when major life decisions are being considered. For all adults with an intellectual disability, but particularly residents of shared supported accommodation, transparent procedures for major life decisions such as transfer to nursing home care should be in place. Formal mechanisms for independent review of such decisions should be available.

A life course perspective to inform practice and service development

Disability services should adopt a life course perspective to inform the planning and delivery of support. The premise for such a perspective is one of continuity. All individuals develop throughout their lives and opportunities and development in earlier parts of the life course will impact on the types of needs in later years. As suggested in Chapter 1, the principles relevant to realizing the human rights and quality of life of people with disabilities are consistent across their life course. Ageing is a lifelong process and preventative health strategies and healthy lifestyle or development of good social networks in a person's younger years will impact on their state of emotional and physical health and well-being as they begin to age. This approach suggests that preparation for healthy active ageing begins in a person's younger years rather than at some magic moment during adulthood.

Policies and programs for older carers

Adults with intellectual disabilities who remain at home with parents are increasingly likely to outlive them and to make the transition to some form of non-parental care in mid to later life. The issue of supporting older parental carers to continue to care but also to consider transition and planning for the future of their adult son or daughter are inextricably linked to the issues of ageing and intellectual disability. Disability services must take a proactive role in assisting parental future planning; ensuring the smooth transition of adults from parental care and creating a wide range of accessible in-home supports or supported accommodation options are available to these adults, which will enable them to maintain links to their local communities and informal networks. Possible strategies include:

1. Target a proportion of existing family support places to people whose carers are aged over 60 years and encourage programs to undertake an assertive outreach role to locate those parents who are out of touch with the disability service system.

2. Dedicate case manager/s within existing services to work specifically with older carers.

3. Establish a regional stand-alone program to work with older carers and their adult children living at home to support planning and preparation for the future and provide consultancy to others who work with this group.

4. Target a proportion of new housing and support packages to adults living at home with older parental carers.

5. Use new funding for accommodation support to establish a respite/shared care facility for use by adults living with older carers to increase their skills, out of home experiences and begin for parents and adults the processes of separation and letting go.

6. Conduct an annual series of information forums on aspects of planning for the future that are targetted at older parental carers and other family members of adults with intellectual disabilities living at home.

Priorities

Determination of priorities must take account of opportunities that arise within the context of existing program and funding initiatives. Some of the strategies suggested can be achieved fairly quickly with minimal additional resources whilst others will require resources and a longer period of time. Pilot and demonstration programs, if thoroughly evaluated, are useful avenues to test and refine ideas. Conferences and forums, as well as providing the opportunity to share ideas, also provide the context for shared initiatives and linkages between sectors.

In the writer's view the formulation and implementation of individualized plans are the lynchpins to developing a good quality of life for older people with intellectual disability. However, it is imperative that the focus is broader than the individual and that program planning and community development occur in tandem with individual plans. Suggested priorities in this area are the adoption of a leadership role and a sustained focus on older people with intellectual disability with the accompanying development of knowledge and expertise by senior staff in the disability sector. In addition, a foremost priority should be a focus on healthy lifestyles and assurance of quality health and screening services for older people with intellectual disabilities.

As this book has clearly indicated, the voices of people with intellectual disability are seldom heard in debates about successful ageing. A research priority must be understanding the perspectives of people with intellectual disabilities about ageing, their fears and aspirations, and their preferred ways of being supported. In addition, despite the innovation that has occurred in programs for older people, a good understanding of what works well and why is lacking. This must be tackled by shifting from a descriptive to an evaluative research approach focused on the individual and system-wide outcomes of programs and service developments for older people that can inform future developments.

Further reading

Hogg, J., Lucchino, R., Wang, K. and Janicki, M. (2001) 'Healthy ageing – Adults with intellectual disabilities: Ageing and social policy.' *Journal of Applied Research in Intellectual Disabilities 14*, 3, 229–255.

Janicki, M. (1992) *Integration Experiences Casebook: Program Ideas in Ageing and Developmental Disabilities.* Albany, NY: New York State Office of Mental Retardation and Developmental Disabilities.

Janicki, M. and Ansello, E. (2000) *Community Supports for Ageing Adults with Lifelong Disabilities.* Baltimore: Brookes.

APPENDIX

Age-related Biological Changes and Health Risks

Normal ageing

Age-related changes to the structures and organs of the body are referred to as biological ageing or 'senescence'. These changes result in a gradual decline in organ capacity, body functioning and performance. They are universal, natural, gradual and unidirectional. However, age-related changes show tremendous variation between individuals and are greatly influenced by genetic differences, lifestyle, social and environmental factors. For example, it is estimated that as much as half the functional decline associated with ageing is attributable to disuse and lack of exercise rather than illness or biological change (ABS 1999).

Old age does not equate with disease, although older people are more vulnerable to chronic and acute health conditions. The distinction is sometimes made between normal and pathological ageing, the latter being a result of disease. However, the boundaries are often blurred, as for example it is difficult to distinguish when loss of bone density (normal ageing) becomes osteoporosis (pathological ageing disease). The differences are nevertheless important as many diseases can be treated or their symptoms alleviated.

Knowledge of probable age-related change is vital to the mobilization of action to slow its occurrence or minimize its impact through appropriate individual or environmental adaptation and compensation. Differentiation of normal from pathological changes is important to help identify unexpected or disease-related changes that require medical diagnosis and treatment. Evidence suggests that too often general assumptions are made that physical decline or poor health are due to the impact of 'ageing'. As a consequence medical conditions, particularly those that are chronic, may remain unacknowledged, uninvestigated and untreated in older people with intellectual disability (Bigby *et al.* 2001; Cooper 1997a).

It is also important to remember that the ageing process spans many years and the greatest changes to biological and health status occur in the old old, after the age of 75 years. Amongst the general population the prevalence of chronic disease and other disabling health conditions increases dramatically after the age of 75 years but are less marked for the younger old. For example, 44 per cent of people between 60 and 65 have one or more chronic illness. This increases to 54 per cent between the ages of 65 and 75 and to 66 per cent for those aged over 75 (AIHW 1997). It is notable however that, despite age-related physiological changes, two-thirds of older people in the general community are free from any condition that makes them dependent for assistance. Significantly, as Chapter 2 demonstrates, most older people with intellectual disability are the younger old rather than this old old group and therefore are less at risk of chronic health conditions. However, this trend is confounded by the subgroup of people, primarily those with Down's syndrome, who show premature age-related changes and for whom a high risk of chronic health conditions occurs at an earlier age.

People with intellectual disability experience many of the same age-related biological changes and associated health risks as older people in general. However, due to diverse factors directly or indirectly associated with their disability, they generally have poorer health and experience some significant differences in health status and needs compared to older people without disabilities. This appendix gives a brief overview of the biological changes associated with ageing and the major health conditions that affect all older people. It provides the backdrop for Chapter 3 that looks specifically at some of the differences and particular health challenges which confront older people with an intellectual disability.

Body system and functional changes

Ageing results in the 'gradual accumulation of irreversible functional losses' (Hooyman and Kiyak 1999, p.56). Changes include: reduced physical stamina, less efficient circulation, reduced bone density and sensory decline such as loss of hearing and eyesight acuity. As a result older people have an increased risk of chronic disease and medical problems (Minichiello *et al.* 1992). Although body functions are interrelated, the rate of change in an individual is not uniform. For example, an older person may experience significant hearing loss whilst maintaining good eyesight. The rate of change varies significantly between individuals and is clearly affected by gender, current and previous behaviours and lifestyle factors. Neither is the impact of change uniform, as it can be compensated for by adapting behaviour, physical and social environments.

Body composition and connective tissue

As people age their body composition changes and weight tends to reduce. The proportions of water and lean muscle tissue decrease whilst fat increases. In addition to physical appearance, an impact of this is changed body reactions to medication. Drugs may remain in the system longer or be more concentrated relative to water and muscle than previously. This in combination with changes to the urinary system mean the effects of medications may change and become more potent as people age, suggesting that regular review of dosage should occur for older people.

The flexibility of the connective tissue found in all parts of the body is reduced as the collagen that makes it up changes composition and water content reduces. This leads to a loss of elasticity in muscles, tendons, ligaments, the lungs and blood vessels that in turn affect muscle and joint functioning. For example, lung capacity or the ability of the eye muscles to focus as effectively may be reduced. The thinning of cartilage and reduced production of fluid that lubricates joints can result in increased stiffness of joints that may affect mobility. These changes to muscles and joints mean strength and stamina declines.

Respiratory system

The respiratory system involves many different muscles and is thus particularly affected by loss of muscle tone and flexibility. Stiffening of lung tissue and loss of muscle strength results in reduced lung capacity and accompanying decline in the maximum intake of oxygen. This reduces the ability to undertake physical activity for prolonged periods of time and increases physical fatigue.

Cardiovascular system

The heart and blood vessels that make up the cardiovascular system are also affected by changes to connective tissue. Arteries lose their elasticity, have weakened walls and may also have a build-up of fats, all of which make pumping blood through the body more difficult. These changes put increased pressure on the heart and may lead to elevated blood pressure. Changes to the heart reduce the maximum heart rate both after exercise and at resting, which means oxygen is used less effectively. The impact of these changes compounds those from the respiratory system, reducing stamina and capacity for prolonged exercise. However, it must be noted that despite changes substantial reserve capacity still exists in most older people and regular exercise can slow these age-related changes (Hooyman and Kiyak 1999).

Differentiating normal from pathological ageing is particularly difficult in relation to the cardiovascular system. For example, although high blood pressure is not a normal ageing process it is one of the most common conditions experienced by older people.

Skin

Changes to the appearance and texture of skin are one of the most visible changes associated with ageing. These changes result from reduced water content, collagen and elastin and mean the skin has less elasticity and a tougher texture. The skin takes longer to resume its shape and can have a sagging and wrinkly appearance. Skin may also show signs of increased or uneven pigmentation. It may take longer to heal and be more easily bruised or damaged.

The secretions of the sebaceous glands are reduced, meaning that skin becomes drier and sweating is reduced. Thinning of the skin reduces the thermal insulation it provides. Together these changes mean that the role of the skin in regulating body temperature is impaired. As a result older people are more sensitive to hot and cold temperatures, need a slightly warmer environment and longer to adjust to the cold. Their vulnerability to hyperthermia and hypothermia is increased. Higher room temperature and attention to appropriate clothing and changes in temperature can all compensate for these changes.

Hair loss increases with age. It also becomes thinner and as a result of reduced pigmentation changes colour. These changes are related to genetics and by no means affect all older people. The resulting baldness and greyness are characteristic of old age but can nevertheless impact on an older person's self-image. Fingernails and toenails increase in thickness, becoming more dry and brittle. One effect of this is increased difficulty in cutting toenails.

Bones and skeleton

Bone growth and density, determined by nutrition, physical activity and hormones, begin to decline after about the age of 40 years. This is compounded by the cessation of oestrogen production in women after menopause. Bone density loss is three times greater for women than for men (Minichiello *et al.* 1992). Bone changes can mean a gradual reduction in height and decreased shoulder width. Loss of bone density below the normal range can lead to osteoporosis that dramatically increases the risk of fractures from falls and other low impact traumas.

Urinary system

The bladder and kidneys that make up the urinary system experience changes to function with age. The kidneys decrease in volume and weight, reducing the rate at which blood and urine is filtered by as much as half. They also lose their capacity for dilution and absorption of glucose, which can lead to increased problems with dehydration and salt loss. A major impact of changed kidney function that combines with changes to body composition is an altered tolerance and absorption rate of medications in older people. Drugs are likely to remain active in an older person's system for longer and as they are less diluted may have a more potent effect. As suggested earlier, this means that regular review of all medications and dosage is important as people age.

Reduced bladder capacity combined with delayed sensation of needing to empty it, as a result of changes to the nervous system, increases the incidence of urinary incontinence among older people. It is estimated that as many as third of older people living in the community and half of those in nursing homes experience some difficulties with bladder control (Hooyman and Kiyak 1999). These changes also mean that older people may be more affected by alcohol and caffeine, as these substances can increase urine production and place a greater strain on the kidneys and bladder.

Embarrassment stemming from bladder problems may make older people fearful of going out and interfere with their everyday activities. Recognizing this issue and altering daily habits such as reducing fluid intake at certain times and planning of access to toilet facilities when in the community can reduce the impact of such problems.

Digestive system

Changes to various muscles impact on the digestive system by, for example, reducing the strength of swallowing and the efficiency of the small intestine. Eating, as well as the time taken for food to reach the stomach, may take longer. Production of digestive juices diminishes as people age, which combined with decreases in size and efficiency of the small and large intestines may impair digestion. Older people are more likely to suffer from inflammation of the stomach lining and have a greater risk of colon and stomach cancer. Sensory changes such as smell and taste can reduce interest in food and this, combined with teeth loss that affects chewing ability, puts older people at risk of poor diet and inadequate nutrition. The use of herbs and other flavours with strong tastes and smells is one way of compensating for sensory changes and countering loss of appetite.

Hormones

Age affects the endocrine system by reducing the production of some hormones that regulate body functions. Two hormones where reduction has a significant effect are oestrogen and insulin. As noted above, menopause means oestogen production is stopped and can lead to increased loss of bone density and osteoporosis. Reduced insulin affects the absorption of glucose and can lead to high blood sugar levels and the onset of diabetes.

Nervous system

Loss of brain cells and weight begins to occur after the age of 30 but does not affect brain function. However, changes to structure and composition of neurotransmitters that begin in middle age affect cognitive and motor function by reducing response rate and increasing reaction time. For example, from 20 to 60 years of age response time may reduce by as much as a fifth (Hooyman and Kiyak). This has implications for activities such as driving that require quick and accurate responses. The brain has significant reserve capacity and despite reduced speed of information processing intellectual functioning does not decline significantly with age.

The central nervous system controls the kinesthetic mechanism that orientates the body in space. Age-related changes to the central nervous system combined with slower reaction times, reduced visual acuity and muscle weakness make spatial orientation more difficult, increasing the likelihood of falls. Older people may adapt to these changes by walking slower and exercising more caution. The risks association with disorientation and falls can be reduced by adaptation of the environment such as the installation of grab rails, increased lighting and remodelling uneven or slippery surfaces.

Reproductive system

Women experience the most marked change in the reproductive system with the onset of menopause between 45 and 54 years. Menopause marks the end of a woman's period of fertility with the loss of ovarian function, the cessation of menstruation and significant hormonal changes. As well as reduction of bone density, the loss of eostrogen can cause vaginal dryness, reduced sexual hair growth, altered libido, irritability, hot flushes and night sweats. Dealing with the impact of these changes can be both psychologically and physically difficult for many women. Hormone replacement therapy is often the medical response to menopause and while it can reduce many of its symptoms it does have a number of side effects such as slightly increased risk of breast cancer, stroke and deep vein thrombosis.

Contrary to popular myths, older people do not lose their sexual desires or function. However, for men there is a gradual decline in sexual function; for example, erection may take longer to achieve and require more direct stimulation and a longer period may be needed between orgasm and subsequent erections.

Sleep

Minichiello et al. (1992) suggest that ageing is associated with more time in bed but less time sleeping, as sleep patterns change with age. Sleep becomes lighter and more fragmented, as older people have less deep sleep and are aroused more easily. Changes to body rhythms and body temperature mean shorter sleep cycles at night may be accompanied with increased daytime napping. This can interfere with a person's ability to participate in chosen activities and perhaps give incorrect and negative messages to staff regarding declining interest in participation. Many older people complain of sleep problems and adaptations can reduce the impact of changed sleep patterns. These include things such as taking regular exercise, reducing caffeine and alcohol intake and improving the sleep environment by more careful attention to blocking out sound and light sources.

Vision

From about the age of 50 years age-associated changes to the various structures of the eye result in impairments to vision. However, the most significant increases in vision problems occur after the age of 65 years. The surface of the cornea thickens and becomes flatter, while the pupil as well as reducing in size becomes more fixed. As a result the eye responds more slowly and less effectively to changes in light conditions. This means that older people find it harder to see in poor light and to adjust to sudden changes of light intensity. Changes to the lens that make it more opaque mean less light passes through, add to the difficulty of seeing in poor light, increase sensitivity to glare and reduce the ability to discriminate between colours. Perceptions of depth and distance detoriate as the lens becomes more opaque and each eye experiences a different rate of change to the lens. Many older people experience more severe opaqueness or clouding of the lens, which prevents all light from entering and if it affects all parts of the lens can lead to blindness. This condition is known as cataract and can be treated relatively easily by surgery that removes the lens, replacing it with an implant.

As muscles change the field of vision can narrow, reducing the range of gaze, making it difficult to see things above eye level. Reduced elasticity of muscles and changes to the lens also mean the ability of the eye to change shape and focus from near to far deteriorates. As a result older people are likely to have problems with close vision or with situations where a change from far to close vision is required, such as looking up from close work.

Changes to vision affect the ability to carry out tasks of everyday living in the home and community as well as activities such as driving, particularly at night. Reading, pursuing hobbies, cooking and navigating in the home and community may all be made more difficult, although aids exist and environmental changes can be made to compensate for impaired vision. These include simple things such as brighter bulbs, use of large print, removal of clutter, clear demarcation of steps or changes in floor surface, in addition to aids such as glasses and magnifying glasses.

Hearing

Change to the structures of the ear and deterioration of hair cells and membranes in combination with nervous system changes and cumulative environmental effects all reduce hearing capacity after about the age of 65 years. Hearing can be affected in several different ways such as difficulty in distinguishing high frequencies, sound distortion and inability to detect low volumes. Loss of high frequencies in particular affects ability to distinguish speech.

Hearing is vital for communication and social interaction, both of which may be impaired when loss occurs. As with vision, a range of aids and environmental changes can compensate for hearing loss. For example, hearing aids can increase volume; environmental design can dampen or reduce background noise; visual clues can replace auditory ones; and communication strategies such as maintaining close eye level contact when speaking can help.

Touch, taste and smell

Age-related changes to the skin and nervous system combine to reduce an older person's sense of touch, particularly in fingertips, hands and feet. This loss of sensitivity means older people are less quick to discriminate sensations and respond to pain from burns, for example, which may lead to more severe injury.

Smell as well as taste has a key role in the perception and enjoyment of food. Both senses become less acute with age, although smell is generally more affected than taste. The effects may be loss of interest in food with resultant poor nutrition. As suggested earlier, one approach to this is to adapt food preparation practices in order to enhance flavours by using herbs and spices, particularly those with strong aromas.

Major health conditions affecting older people

Older people have a higher risk of disease than younger age groups. For example, an Australian national health survey found that 73 per cent of the population over the age of 15 years had experienced one or more illness in the preceding two weeks, compared to 90 per cent of those aged over 65 years (ABS 1999). In this same survey almost all older Australians reported experiencing some type of long-term condition although these included relatively minor conditions such as short-sightedness.

However, it is important to distinguish between acute or short-term conditions and chronic or long-term conditions. Acute conditions actually decrease with age but when experienced by older people tend to have more severe effects. For example, there is increased risk that a cold will turn into pneumonia or bronchitis in an older person. Chronic conditions are those that last for more than three months and may be permanent. In such conditions, rather than effecting a cure the goal is more likely to be prevention of disabling effects by careful management and monitoring.

Chronic conditions do not necessarily restrict activities of everyday living. It is estimated that almost half of those with long-term health conditions do not experience any restriction. The proportion of the population who experience restriction of everyday activities associated with long-term conditions increases with age, from 4 per cent in those under 5 years, 38 per cent in those aged between 65 and 74 years to

83 per cent in those aged over 85 years. In all the older age groups sex differences are clear with a greater proportion of older women than men experiencing activity restriction. For example, in the 75 to 79 age group 24.9 per cent of women but only 19 per cent of men have activity restrictions (ABS 1999).

Despite evidence of increased chronic health conditions with age, the majority of older Australians in a 1995 national health survey rated their health as good, very good or excellent. Perceptions of health shifts as people get older with 9 per cent of the 65 to 69 age group rating their health as poor compared to 17 per cent in the 85 to 89 age group (AIHW 1997).

The most common causes of death in older people are cancers and diseases of the circulatory or respiratory systems. More specifically these are stroke, prostate cancer, breast cancer, heart disease and emphysema. The most common long-term conditions affecting older people are hypertension, or high blood pressure, arthritis, heart disease in men and osteoporosis in women. For example, 55 per cent of people aged between 65 and 74 and 61 per cent of those aged over 75 had some form of cardiovascular disease (including heart disease, stroke and hypertension). Half of all people aged over 65 years had some form of arthritis. Two-thirds of people aged over 65 years were overweight or obese, which although not a disease is a significant risk factor in many conditions (ABS 1999).

The following sections sketch very briefly some of the common health conditions experienced by older people, highlighting symptoms, risk factors and possible treatments. It is not comprehensive and intended to paint an outline rather than a detailed picture.

Disease of the cardiovascular system

Heart disease is caused by a reduced blood flow to the heart resulting from a narrowing of coronary arteries due to fatty deposits (atherosclerosis). The effect can be angina, heart attack or congestive heart failure. Angina causes shortness of breath and pain in the breast, neck and arm. If the blood flow becomes too deficient portions of heart tissue may die leading to a heart attack (myocardial infarction). More acute heart attack may occur if an artery supplying blood to the heart becomes completely blocked. Heart attacks are difficult to diagnose and symptoms include dizziness, confusion and shortness of breath. Risk factors for heart disease are high blood pressure, high cholesterol, smoking, diabetes, inactivity and family history. High blood pressure is more common in women than men and can be prevented by attention to lifestyle factors in conjunction with medication. All the cardiovascular conditions can be treated with medication, diet and exercise.

Cerebrovascular problems

Cerebrovascular disease, like heart disease, is caused by changes in blood vessels that reduce or disrupt the flow of blood. In this case however it is blood supply to the brain that is affected and causes malfunction or death of brain tissue. When part of the brain is deprived of blood due to reduced blood flow, a clot or a burst vessel, a stroke (cerebrovascular accident) occurs. Strokes can affect speech, sight or cause paralysis of one side of the body depending on the area of the brain affected. Risk factors for stroke are quite similar to those for heart disease. A comprehensive rehabil-itation program is often required to restore impaired function after a stroke. Such programs will assist sufferers to regain much of their lost motor function, although often they are left with residual impairment to vision, speech or balance.

Cancers

It is estimated that half of all cancers are diagnosed in people over the age of 65 years (Hooyman and Kiyak 1999). The most common cancers in older people are those of the stomach, lungs, intestines and pancreas. Sex differences are evident with lung and rectal cancers more common among men and colon and breast cancer more prevalent among women. Diagnosis of cancer is more difficult in older people as symptoms may be masked, replicating those of chronic conditions or being attributed to general ageing. General symptoms might be weight loss, fatigue and weakness. Long-term employment conditions or lifestyle factors such as extended exposure to sun, toxic or dusty environments and smoking increase the risk of some cancers.

Arthritis

Arthritis is the most common chronic condition among older people, although it is not a major cause of death. Almost two-thirds of older people have some form of arthritis, with the risk for those over 65 years being twice that of those in the 45 to 65 year age group (ABS 1999). Arthritis is a varied range of conditions that involve inflammation and chronic degeneration of the bones and joints. The two most common forms are rheumatoid and osteoarthritis. Rheumatoid arthritis is a severe inflammation of the membranes lining the joints that causes pain, swelling and some-times bone dislocation. Episodes are acute and cause severe pain, fever and stiffness. Osteoarthritis is a gradual degeneration of the joints, occurring primarily in hands, knees, hips and shoulders, and often leads to reduced activity. This can be counter-productive as inactivity may result in reduced lubrication of joints and muscle tone that further increases pain. Treatments for both types of arthritis are similar, including medication such as aspirin or anti-inflammatory drugs, rest and exercise.

Osteoporosis

Osteoporosis is abnormal loss of bone density caused by the ageing process and cessation of hormone production, most notably oestrogen, in women. Its onset is normally in middle age and it is four times more likely to affect women than men. The bones become more brittle and reduced in strength, making them more susceptible to fractures, particularly the hip. Older people with osteoporosis may experience reduction in height and because of compressed or collapsed vertebra may have slumped posture and be stooped. Risk factors in addition to menopause in women are sedentary lifestyle, smoking, high alcohol and caffeine intake, poor diet and genetics. Treatment in the form of increased intake of calcium and vitamin D and moderate weight-bearing exercise such as walking or weight training aim to prevent further bone loss. Hormone replacement therapy, which replaces oestrogen, is a common treatment but has some associated risks that are subject to ongoing research.

Respiratory conditions

Respiratory problems include chronic bronchitis, fibrosis, asthma and emphysema that cause damage to the lungs. These conditions are progressive, often causing shortness of breath and making everyday activities exhausting. Risk factors are genetic, smoking and environmental such as long-term exposure to dust and fumes. Conditions can be treated by medication, breathing exercises or assistance such as inhalers or oxygen.

Diabetes

Diabetes is caused by insufficient production of the hormone insulin and leads to excessive amounts of sugar in the blood and urine and an inability to metabolize carbohydrates. If the level of blood sugars is too high a person may go into a coma. The cumulative effects of diabetes are renal disorders, stroke or poor circulation that can lead to gangrene, particularly in feet and toes. Diabetes can be a lifelong condition or have its onset in mid or later life. Late onset diabetes is often diagnosed incidentally through eye or other types of tests. Symptoms are excessive thirst, increased appetite, fatigue and weight loss. The risk factors are poor diet, inactivity and coexistent disease. The condition can be managed through diet, exercise, care of feet and skin or may require administration of insulin.

Kidneys and urinary tract

In this area older people are more susceptible to conditions that arise from acute infections or structural deterioration. Cystitis, an inflammation of the bladder, is common in older women and can be treated by antibiotics. Conditions affecting the prostate are common in older men. As many as 38 per cent of women and 19 per cent

284 / AGEING WITH A LIFELONG DISABILITY

of men over 65 years will have problems associated with incontinence. Three types exist: urge incontinence, where a person is unable to resist the strong urge to urinate; stress incontinence, where leakage occurs during physical exertion such as sneezing or coughing; functional incontinence, which is associated with neurological conditions such as Parkinson's disease. Many older people experience both urge and stress incontinence. Incontinence may be caused by physical conditions such as urinary tract infections, anaemia, cancer or the side effects of some medication drugs, and is therefore be amenable to treatment. In some instances it can be managed by dietary changes, protective products such as pads, exercise or behavioural strategies.

Intestinal system

The slowing down of the digestive system makes older people more susceptible to problems such as inflammation of the intestine (diverticulitis), constipation, hiatus hernia and gall bladder disease. Constipation is caused by lack of exercise, stress and unbalanced diet. It may however be a symptom of an underlying disease or obstruction and should be investigated. Hiatus hernia occurs when a small part of the stomach slides up to the diagonal and can lead to indigestion, difficulty swallowing and chest pain. All these conditions can be managed by diet, exercise and weight reduction.

Teeth and gums

Tooth decay and gum diseases increase with age and as many as a third of older people have no teeth at all. Dental care has improved significantly during the last 50 years and each cohort of older people will reflect these changes. However, access to dental hygiene care is strongly mediated by socio-economic circumstances. Lack of teeth or poorly fitting dentures affect ability to chew food and can impact on nutritional balance.

Fall and accidents

Older people have a high risk of falls and death from physical injuries resulting from accidents. Up to a third of older experience a fall in any one year (Hooyman and Kiyak 1999). Falls can cause cuts, bruises, burns and fractures. Risk factors are inactivity, visual impairments, multiple diseases, gait disorders, mediations and environmental factors such as poor light, loose rugs and undemarcated stairs. Home-based modifications such as installation of hand-rails, non-slip strips on stairs and improved lighting as well as changes to personal behaviours such as use of hip protectors, walking aids, glasses and non-slip footwear can all reduce the risk of falls.

Summary

This appendix has provided an overview of key biological changes associated with ageing and major health risks and conditions that affect older people in the general community. Key factors to note are: the variability in the ageing process; the impact of genetic, lifestyle and environmental factors on functional decline and health risks associated with ageing; and the extent to which individual behavioural, social or environmental adaptations can reduce, compensate for or manage age-related changes.

References

Able-Smith, B. and Titmuss, K. (1974) *Social Policy: An Introduction. Richard M. Titmuss.* London: Allen and Unwin.

Adlin, M. (1993) 'Health care issues.' In E. Sutton, A. Factor, B. Hawkins, T. Heller and G. Seltzer (eds) *Older Adults with Developmental Disabilities: Optimising Choice and Change.* Baltimore: Brookes.

Allen, R. and Petr, C. (1998) 'Rethinking family centred practice.' *American Journal of Orthopsychiatry 68,* 1, 4–15.

Amado, A. (1993) 'Working on friendships.' In A. Amado (ed) *Friendships and Community Connections Between People with and without Developmental Disability.* Baltimore: Brookes.

American Association on Mental Retardation (AAMR) (1998) *News and Notes. Special Issues on Older Carers.* Washington: American Association on Mental Retardation.

Anderson, D. (2002) 'Women aging with intellectual disabilities: What are the health risks?' In P. Noonan Walsh and T. Heller (eds) *Health of Women with Intellectual Disabilities.* Oxford: Blackwell.

Antonucci, T. and Akiyama, H. (1987) 'Social networks in adult life and a preliminary examination of the convoy model.' *Journal of Gerontology 42,* 519–527.

Ashman, A., Suttie, J. and Bramley, J. (1993) *Older Australians with an Intellectual Disability. A Report to the Department of Health, Housing and Community Services, Research and Development Grants Committee.* Fred and Eleanor Schonnell Special Education Research Centre. Queensland: University of Queensland.

Ashman, A., Suttie, J. and Bramley, J. (1995) 'Employment, retirement and elderly persons with developmental disabilities.' *Journal of Intellectual Disability Research 39,* 2, 107–115.

Atchley, R. (1976) *The Sociology of Retirement.* New York: Wiley/Schenkman.

Atchley, R. (1999) *Continuity and Adaptation in Aging: Creating Positive Experiences.* Baltimore: Johns Hopkins University Press.

Auditor General of Victoria (2000) *Services for People with an Intellectual Disability.* Melbourne: Government Printer.

Australian Bureau of Statistics (ABS) (1998) *Disability Aging and Carers.* Canberra: Commonwealth of Australia.

Australian Bureau of Statistics (ABS) (1999) *Older People, Australia: A Social Report.* Canberra: Commonwealth of Australia.

Australian Institute of Health and Welfare (AIHW) (1997) *Australia's Welfare.* Canberra: Australian Institute of Health and Welfare.

Australian Institute of Health and Welfare (AIHW) (1999) *Older Australians at a Glance.* Canberra: Australian Institute of Health and Welfare.

Australian Institute of Health and Welfare (AIHW) (2000) *Disability and Aging: Australian Population Patterns and Implications.* Canberra: Australian Institute of Health and Welfare.

Australian Institute of Health and Welfare (AIHW) (2001) *Australia's Welfare*. Canberra: Australian Institute of Health and Welfare.

Australian Institute of Health and Welfare (AIHW) (2002a) *Older Australians at a Glance*, 3rd edn. Canberra: Australian Institute of Health and Welfare.

Australian Institute of Health and Welfare (AIHW) (2002b) *Australia's Health 2001*. Canberra: Australian Institute of Health and Welfare.

Australian Institute of Health and Welfare (AIHW) (2002c) *Unmet Need for Disability Services. Effectiveness of Funding and Remaining Shortfalls*. Canberra: Australian Institute of Health and Welfare.

Bach, M. (1994) 'Quality of Life: Questioning the vantage points for research.' In M. Rioux and M. Bach (eds) *Disability is not measles: New research paradigms in disability*. New York, Ontario: Rocher Institute.

Bagley, M. (1997) *Hearing Changes in Aging People with Mental Retardation*. Arlington: Arc of the United States.

Balandin, S., Alexander, B. and Hoffman, D. (1997) 'Using functional independence measure to assess adults with cerebral palsy: An exploratory report.' *Journal of Applied Research in Intellectual Disabilities 10*, 4, 323–332.

Balandin, S. and Morgan, J. (1997) 'Adults with cerebral palsy: What's happening?' *Journal of Intellectual and Developmental Disability 22*, 2, 109–124.

Baldock, J. and Evers, A. (1991) 'Innovations and care of the elderly: The frontline of change in social welfare services.' *Aging International*, June, 8–21.

Baltes, P. and Baltes, M. (1990) 'Psychological perspectives on successful aging: The model of selective optimisation with compensation.' In P. Baltes and M. Baltes *Successful Aging: Perspectives from the Behavioural Sciences*. Cambridge: Cambridge University Press.

Baltes, M. and Carstensen, L. (1996) 'The process of successful aging.' *Aging and Society 16*, 397–422.

Bayley, M. (1997) 'Empowering and relationships.' In P. Ramcharan, G. Roberts, G. Grant and J. Borland (eds) *Empowerment in Everyday Life*. London: Jessica Kingsley Publishers.

Beange, H., McElduff, A. and Baker, W. (1995) 'Medical disorders in adults with intellectual disability: A population study.' *American Journal on Mental Retardation 99*, 595–604.

Biestek, F. (1957) *The Casework Relationship*. London: Allen and Unwin.

Bigby, C. (1992) 'Access and linkage: Two critical issues for older people with an intellectual disability.' *Australia and New Zealand Journal of Developmental Disabilities 18*, 95–110.

Bigby, C. (1995) 'Is there a hidden group of older people with intellectual disability and from whom are they hidden? Lessons from a recent case-finding study.' *Australia and New Zealand Journal of Developmental Disabilities 20*, 15–24.

Bigby, C. (1997a) 'When parents relinquish care. The informal support networks of older people with intellectual disability.' *Journal of Applied Intellectual Disability Research 10*, 4, 333–344.

Bigby, C. (1997b) 'Later life for adults with intellectual disability: A time of opportunity and vulnerability.' *Journal of Intellectual and Developmental Disability 22*, 2, 97–108.

Bigby, C. (1998) 'Shifting responsibilities: The patterns of formal service use by older people with intellectual disability in Victoria.' *Journal of Intellectual and Developmental disability 23*, 3, 229–243.

Bigby, C. (1999a) 'International trends in intellectual disability policy in the late 1990s.' In E. Ozanne, C. Bigby, S. Forbes, C. Glennen, M. Gordon and C. Fyffe (eds) *Reframing Opportunities for People with an Intellectual Disability*. Melbourne: University of Melbourne.

Bigby, C. (1999b) 'Policy and programs for older people with an intellectual disability.' In E. Ozanne, C. Bigby, S. Forbes, C. Glennen, M. Gordon and C. Fyffe (eds) *Reframing Opportunities for People with an Intellectual Disability*. Melbourne: University of Melbourne.

Bigby, C. (2000) *Moving on without Parents: Planning, Transitions and Sources of Support for Older Adults with Intellectual Disabilities*. Sydney, Maclennan and Petty.

Bigby, C. (2001) *Not Just Marking Time: A Literature Review of Day Support Service Options for Older Adults with a Disability Unrelated to Aging*. Melbourne: Department of Human Services.

Bigby, C. (2002a) 'Social roles and informal support networks in mid life and beyond.' In P. Noonan Walsh and T. Heller *Health of Women with Intellectual Disabilities*. Oxford: Blackwell.

Bigby, C. (2002b) 'Aging with a life long disability: Challenges for the aged care and disability sectors.' *Journal of Intellectual and Developmental Disabilities 24*, 4, 231 – 421.

Bigby, C. (2002c) 'A comparison of specialist and mainstream services for older carers of adults with intellectual disability: Some lessons for future service development.' Paper presented at the National Conference of the Australian Society of the Study of Intellectual Disability, Hobart, Tasmania.

Bigby, C., Frederico, M. and Cooper, B. (2002) *Not Just a Residential Move But Creating a Better Lifestyle for People with Intellectual Disabilities: Report of the Evaluation of Kew Residential Services Community Relocation Project 1999*. Melbourne: Department of Human Services.

Bigby, C., Fyffe, C., Balandin, S., Gordon, M. and McCubbery, J. (2001a) *Day Support Services Options for Older Adults with a Disability*. Melbourne: National Disability Administrators Group.

Bigby, C., Fyffe, C., McCubbery, G. (2001b) *Formulation of a Strategy Plan for the Development of Services for Older People with Intellectual Disabilities in the Western Region*. Melbourne: Department of Human Services, Western Region.

Bigby, C., and Ozanne, E. (2001) 'Shifts in the model of service delivery in intellectual disability in Victoria.' *Journal of Intellectual and Developmental Disability 26*, 2, 177–190.

Bigby, C., Ozanne, E. and Gordon, M. (1999) *Facilitating Transition: An Evaluation of Pilot Case Management Programs for Older Carers of Adults with Intellectual Disability, Eastern and Northern Metropolitan Regions of the Department of Human Services Victoria*. Melbourne: Department of Human Services.

Bigby, C., Ozanne. E. and Gordon, M. (2002) 'Facilitating transition: Elements of successful case management practice for older parents of adults with intellectual disability.' *Journal of Gerontological Social Work 37*, 3/4, 25–44.

Blackman, N. and McEnhill, E. (2002) *Abstracts of the Inaugural European Conference of the International Association for the Scientific Study of Intellectual Disability*. Dublin, Ireland.

Blaikie, A. (1999) *Aging and Popular Culture*. Cambridge: Cambridge University Press.

Bonell-Pascual, E., Huline-Dickens, S., Hollins, S., Esterhuyzen, A., Sedgwick, P. and Hubert, J. (1999) 'Bereavement and grief in adults with learning disabilities – A follow-up study.' *British Journal of Psychiatry 175*, 348–350.

Botsford, A. (2000) 'Dealing with end of life.' In M. Janicki and E. Ansello (eds) *Community Supports for Aging Adults with Lifelong Disabilities*. Baltimore: Brookes.

Bradley, V. (1996) 'Introduction.' In V. Bradley, J. Ashbaugh and B. Blaney *Creating Individual Supports for People with Developmental Disabilities: A Mandate for Change at Many Levels*. Baltimore: Brookes.

Brown, H., Burns, S. and Flynn, M. (2002) 'Supporting people through terminal illness and death.' In *Today and Tomorrow. The Report of the Growing Older with Learning Disabilities Programme.* London: Foundation for People with Learning Disabilities.

Brubaker, E. and Brubaker, T. (1993) 'Caring for adult children with mental retardation. Concerns of elderly parents.' In K. Roberto (ed) *The Elderly Caregiver. Caring for Adults with Developmental Disabilities.* Newbury Park, CA: Sage.

Budge, M. (1998) *Age Matters: The Art of Keeping Active and Independent.* Sydney, NSW: Maclennan and Petty.

Bulmer, M. (1987) *The Social Basis of Community Care.* London: Allen and Unwin.

Butcher, L. (1998) 'Working towards a healthy retirement.' Paper presented at the 34th Annual Conference of the Australian Society for the Study of Intellectual Disability, Adelaide, South Australia.

Buys, L. and Rushworth, J. (1997) 'Community services available to older adults with intellectual disabilities.' *Journal of Intellectual and Developmental Disabilities 22*, 1, 29–38.

Campbell, J. and Essex, E. (1994) 'Factors affecting parents in their future planning for a son or daughter with developmental disabilities.' *Education and Training in Mental Retardation and Developmental Disabilities*, Sept, 222–238.

Cantor, M. and Little, V. (1985) 'Aging and social care.' In R. Binstock and E. Shanas (eds) *Handbook of Aging and the Social Sciences*, 2nd edn. New York: Van Nostrand-Reinhold.

Carney, T. and Tait, D. (1997) *The Adult Guardianship Experiment: Tribunals and Popular Justice.* Sydney: Federation Press.

Carr, J. and Hollins, S. (1995) 'Menopause in women with learning disabilities.' *Journal of Intellectual Disability Research 39*, 2, 137–139.

Carter, C. and Jancar, J. (1983) 'Mortality in the mentally handicapped: a fifty year survey at the Stoke Park group of hospitals.' *Journal of Mental Deficiency Research 27*, 143–156.

Catapano, P., Levy, J. and Levy, P. (1985) 'Day activity and vocational program services.' In M. Janicki and H. Wisniewski (eds) *Aging and Developmental Disabilities: Issues and Approaches.* Baltimore: Brookes.

Challis, D. (1999) 'Assessment and care management: Developments since the community care reforms.' In M. Henwood and G. Wistow (eds) *Evaluating the Impact of Caring for People with Respect to Older Age. Research Volume 3.* Leeds: Nuffield Institute for Health, University of Leeds.

Chappell, A. (1994) 'A question of friendship: Community care and the relationships of people with learning difficulties.' *Disability and Society 9*, 4, 419–433.

Cocks, E., Fox, C., Brogan, M. and Lee, M. (1996) *Under Blue Skies: The Social Construction of Intellectual Disability in Western Australia.* Perth: Edith Cowan University.

Collinson, W. (1997) *Succession Planning. Providing a Future for People with Intellectual Disabilities, Families and Parents.* Townsville: Endeavour Foundation.

Community Services Victoria (CSV) (1988) 'Interim report: Accommodation for intellectually disabled people who are currently living at home with older parents.' Unpublished. Melbourne: Community Services Victoria.

Community Services Victoria (CSV) (1992a) *Services for Older People with an Intellectual Disability.* Melbourne: Community Services Victoria.

Community Services Victoria (CSV) (1992b) 'The planned care approach: Future partnerships in residential care for people with intellectual disabilities.' Unpublished. Melbourne: Community Services Victoria.

Cooper, M. (1998) 'Sharpening the focus on aging and long term physical disability.' *Australasian Journal of Primary Health Care – Interchange 4*, 1, 87–92.

Cooper, S. (1997a) 'Deficient health and social services for elderly people with learning disabilities.' *Journal of Intellectual Disability Research 41*, 4, 331–338.

Cooper, S. (1997b) 'Epidemiology of psychiatric disorders in elderly compared with younger people with learning disabilities.' *British Journal of Psychiatry 170*, 375–380.

Cooper, S. (1997c) 'Psychiatry of elderly compared to younger adults with intellectual disabilities.' *Journal of Applied Research in Intellectual Disabilities 10*, 4, 303–311.

Cooper, S. (1997d) 'Epidemiology of psychiatric disorders in elderly as compared with young adults with learning disabilities.' *British Journal of Psychiatry 170*, 375–380.

Cooper, S. (1998) 'Clinical study of the effects of age on physical health of adults with mental retardation.' *American Journal on Mental Retardation 102*, 6, 582–589.

Cooper, S. (2000) 'Community orientated assessment of and interventions for mental health needs.' In M. Janicki and E. Ansello (eds) *Community Supports for Aging Adults with Lifelong Disabilities.* Baltimore: Brookes.

Creyke, R. (1995) *Who Decides? Legal Decision Making for Others. Department of Human Services and Health, Aged Care Division, Report no.19.* Canberra: Australian Government Publishing Service.

Crow, L. (1996) 'Including all of our lives: renewing the social model of disability.' In J. Morris (ed) *Encounters with Strangers: Feminism and Disability.* London: Women's Press.

Cummings, E. and Henry, W. (1961) *Growing Old.* New York: Basic Books.

Cummins, R., Baxter, C., Hudson, A. and Jauernig, R. (1996) 'A model system for the evaluation of individual program plans.' *Journal of Intellectual and Developmental Disability 21*, 1, 59–70.

Dalley, G. (1988) *Ideologies of Caring: Rethinking Community and Collectivism.* Basingstoke: Macmillan.

Dalton, A., Fedor, B., Patti, P., Tsiouris, J. and Mehta, P. (2002) 'The multidimensional observation scale for elderly subjects (MOSES): Studies in adults with intellectual disabilities.' *Journal of Intellectual and Developmental Disabilities 27*, 4, 310–324.

Davies, N. and Duff, M. (2001) 'Breast cancer screening for older women with learning disability living in community group homes.' *Journal of Intellectual Disability Research 45*, 3, 253–257.

Day, K. and Jancar, J. (1994) 'Mental and physical health and aging in mental handicap: A review.' *Journal of Intellectual Disability Research 38*, 241–257.

Department of Health (DH) (1997) *Services for Older People with Learning Disabilities.* London: The Stationery Office.

Department of Health (DH) (2001) *Valuing People: A New Strategy for Learning Disability for the 21st Century.* London: The Stationery Office.

Department of Health and Community Services (DHCS) (1995) *Report to the Honorable Michael John, MP. Minister for Community Services from the Intellectual Disability Services Task Force.* Melbourne: Department of Health and Community Services.

Department of Human Services (DHCS) (1999a) *Day Services for People Aging with a Disability.* Melbourne: Department of Human Services.

Department of Human Services (DHS) (1999b) *Day Services for People with Disabilities.* Melbourne: Department of Human Services.

Department of Human Services (DHS) (2001) *Let's Get Active. Physical Activity for People with a Disability.* Melbourne: Department of Human Services.

Department of Human Services (DHS) (2002a) *State Plan for Disability Services.* Melbourne: Department of Human Services.

Department of Human Services (DHS) (2002b) *Community Inclusion – Enhancing Friendship Networks among People with a Cognitive Impairment.* Melbourne: Department of Human Services.

Deutsch, H. (1985) 'Grief counselling with mentally retarded clients.' *Psychiatric Aspects of Mental Retardation Review 4,* 17–20.

Donovan, B., Donovan, B. and Gladwin, T. (1993) 'An aging population and community links.' Paper presented at the Victorian State Conference of the Association for the Study of Intellectual Disability, Melbourne.

Drake, R. (1999) *Understanding Disability Policies.* London: Macmillan.

Dunst, C., Trivette, C. and Deal, A. (1994) *Supporting and Strengthening Families.* Cambridge, MA: Brookline Books.

Ecumenical Housing and Bigby, C. (2000) *Accommodation Options for People with a Disability who are Ageing.* Melbourne: Department of Human Services.

Edgerton, R. (1994) 'Quality of life issues: Some people know how to be old.' In M. Seltzer, M. Krauss and M. Janicki (eds) *Lifecourse Perspectives on Adulthood and Aging.* Washington: American Association on Mental Retardation.

Edgerton, R. and Gaston, M. (1991) *'I've Seen It All': Lives of Older Persons with Mental Retardation in the Community.* Baltimore: Brookes.

Emerson, E. (2002) 'Unhealthy lifestyles.' Paper presented at the inaugural European International Association for the Scientific Study of Intellectual Disability Conference, Dublin, Ireland.

Emerson, E. (2003) 'Developing person centred services and support in the UK.' Keynote address at the Annual Conference of the Council on Intellectual Disability Associations. Melbourne, Victoria.

Emerson, E., Robertson, J., Gregory, N., Hatton, C., Kessissoglou, S., Hallam, A., Knapp, M., Jarbrink, K., Netten, A. and Noonan Walsh, P. (1999) *Quality and Costs of Residential Supports for People with Learning Disabilities: Summary and Implications.* Manchester: University of Manchester.

Emerson, P. (1977) 'Covert grief reaction in mentally retarded clients.' *Mental Retardation 15,* 46–47.

Emerson, E., Hatton, C., Felce, D. and Murphy, G. (2001) *Learning Disabilities: The Fundamental Facts.* London: Foundation for People with Learning Disabilities.

Engelhardt, J., Brubaker, T. and Lutzer, V. (1988) 'Older caregivers of adults with mental retardation service utilisation.' *Mental Retardation 26,* 191.

Erickson, M., Krauss, M. and Seltzer, M. (1989) 'Perceptions of old age among a sample of mentally retarded persons.' *Journal of Applied Gerontology 8,* 251–260.

Erikson, E. (1973) *Childhood and Society.* New York: Norton.

Ericsson, K. and Mansell, J. (1996) 'Introduction: Towards deinstitutionalisation.' In J. Mansell and K. Ericsson *Deinstitutionalisation and Community Living: Intellectual Disability Services in Britain, Scandinavia and United States.* London: Chapman and Hall.

Esping-Andersen, G. (1996) *Welfare States in Transition: National Adaptations to Global Economies.* London: Sage in association with UN Institute for Social Development.

Essex, E., Seltzer, M. and Krauss, M. (1997) 'Residential transitions of adults with mental retardation: Predictors of waiting list use and placement.' *American Journal on Mental Retardation 101,* 6, 613–629.

Etmanski, A. (2000) *A Good Life for You and Your Relative with a Disability.* Burnaby, British Columbia: Orwell Cove and Planned Lifetime Advocacy Network.

Evenhuis, H., Henderson, C., Beange, H., Lennox, N. and Chicoine, B. (2001) 'Health aging – adults with intellectual disabilities: Physical health issues.' *Journal of Applied Research in Intellectual Disabilities 14,* 3, 175–194.

Eyman, R. and Borthwick-Duffy, S. (1994) 'Trends in mortality rates and predictors of mortality.' In M. Seltzer, M. Krauss and M. Janicki (eds) *Lifecourse Perspectives on Adulthood and Old Age.* Washington: American Association on Mental Retardation.

Eyman, R. and Widaman, K (1987) 'Life-span development of institutionalized and community based mentally retarded persons revisited.' *American Journal of Mental Deficiency 91,* 559–569.

Factor, A. (1993) 'Translating policy into practice.' In E. Sutton, A. Factor, B. Hawkins, T. Heller and G. Seltzer (eds) *Older Adults with Developmental Disabilities: Optimising Choice and Change.* Baltimore: Brookes.

Felce, D. (1996) 'Quality support for everyday living.' In J. Mansell and K. Ericsson *Deinstitutionalisation and Community Living: Intellectual Disability Services in Britain, Scandinavia and United States.* London: Chapman and Hall.

Felce, D., Grant, G., Todd, S., Ramcharan, P., Beyer, S., McGrath, M., Perry, J., Shearn, J., Kilsby, M. and Lowe, K. (1998) *Towards a Full Life: Researching Policy Innovation for People with Learning Disabilities.* Oxford: Butterworth Heinemann.

Fernando, L., Cresswell, J. and Barakat, F. (2001) 'Study of the physical health needs of people with learning disabilities living in the community.' *British Journal of Developmental Disabilities 47,* 1, 31–37.

Fine, M. and Thompson, C. (1995) *Three Years at Home. The Final Report of the Longitudinal Study of Community Support Services and Their Use.* Sydney: Social Policy Research Centre.

Fitzgerald, J. (1998) *Time for Freedom? Services for Older People with Learning Difficulties.* London: Values in Action.

Flax, M., Wisconsin Council of the Blind and Luchterhand, C. (1997) *Aging with Developmental Disabilities: Changes in Vision.* Arlington: Arc of the United States.

Flynn, M. and Hollins, S. (2002) 'Approaches for health education and policies in health and social care.' In P. Noonan Walsh and T. Heller (eds) *Health of Women with Intellectual Disabilities.* Oxford: Blackwell.

Foote, K. and Rose, J. (1993) 'A day centre for elderly persons with learning disabilities: The consumers' views.' *Journal of Developmental and Physical Disabilities 5,* 2, 154–166.

Forest, M. and Lusthaus, E. (1989) 'Promoting education equality for all students: Circles and maps.' In S. Stainback and M. Forest (eds) *Educating all Students in the Mainstream of Regular Education.* Baltimore: Brookes.

Foundation for People with Learning Disabilities (2002) *Today and Tomorrow. The Report of the Growing Older with Learning Disabilities Programme.* London: Foundation for People with Learning Disabilities.

Freedman, R., Krauss, M. and Seltzer, M. (1997) 'Aging parents' residential plans for adult children with mental retardation.' *Mental Retardation 35,* 2, 114–123.

French, S. (1993) 'Disability, impairment or something in between?' In J. Swain, V. Finkelstein, S. French and M. Oliver (eds) *Disabling Barriers – Enabling Environments.* London: Sage.

Fullmer, E., Smith, G. and Tobin, S. (1997) 'Older mothers who do not use day programs for their daughters and sons with mental retardation.' *Journal of Developmental and Physical Disabilities 9*, 153–173.

Gatter, B. (1996) *The Service Needs of People with a Disability who are Aging.* Report commissioned by Disability Services Commission. Perth: Disability Services Commission.

Gething, L. (1999) *We're Growing Older, Too: Quality of Life and Service Provision Issues for People with Long Standing Disabilities who are Aging.* Sydney: University of Sydney.

Gibson, D. and Grew, R. (2002) 'New models and approaches to care.' Series of eight commissioned papers prepared for 2020 A Vision for Aged Care in Australia. Melbourne: Myer Foundation.

Gibson, D. and Means, R. (2000) 'Policy convergence: Restructuring long term care in Australia and the UK.' *Policy and Politics 29*, 1, 43–58.

Gibson, J., Rabkin, J. and Munson, R. (1992) 'Critical issues in serving the developmentally disabled elderly.' *Journal of Gerontological Social Work 19*, 35–49.

Gill, C. and Brown, A. (2002) 'Health and aging issues for women in their own voices.' In P. Noonan Walsh and T. Heller (eds) *Health of Women with Intellectual Disabilities.* Oxford: Blackwell.

Gilley, T. (1999) 'Better than it was: Seeking good practice in a community access project for older people with intellectual disabilities.' *Interaction 12*, 2, 9–13.

Glausier, S., Whorton, J. and Knight, H. (1995) 'Recreation and leisure likes/dislikes of senior citizens with mental retardation.' *Activities, Adaptations and Aging 19*, 43–54.

Gleeson, B. (1998) 'Disability and poverty.' In R. Fincher and J. Nieuwenhuysen (eds) *Australian Poverty: Then and Now.* Melbourne: Melbourne University Press.

Gold, M. (1987) *Parents of the Adult Developmentally Disabled.* New York: Brookdale Centre on Aging.

Gold, D. (1994) "We don't call it a Circle": The ethos of a support group.' *Disability and Society 9*, 4, 435–452.

Goodley, D. (2000) *Self-advocacy in the Lives of People With Learning Difficulties: The Politics of Resilience.* Buckingham: Open University Press.

Goodman, D. (1978) 'Parenting an adult mentally retarded offspring.' *Smith College Studies in Social Work 48*, 209–234.

Grant, G. (1986) 'Older carers, interdependence and the care of mentally handicapped adults.' *Aging and Society 6*, 333–351.

Grant, G. (1988) *Stability and Change in the Care Networks of Mentally Handicapped Adults Living at Home: First Report. Centre for Social Policy and Development, University of Wales Bangor.* Bangor: University of Wales.

Grant, G. (1989) 'Letting go: Decision making among family carers of people with mental handicap.' *Australia and New Zealand Journal of Developmental Disabilities 15*, 189–200.

Grant, G. (1993) 'Support networks and transitions over two years among adults with mental handicap.' *Mental Handicap Research 6*, 36–55.

Grant, G. (2000) 'Older family carers: Challenges, coping strategies and support.' In D. May (ed) *Transitions in the Lives of People with Learning Difficulties.* London: Jessica Kingsley Publishers.

Grant, G. (2001) 'Older people with learning disabilities: Health, community inclusion and family caregiving.' In M. Nolan, S. Davies and G. Grant *Working with Older People and their Families.* Buckingham: Open University Press.

Grant, G. and McGrath, M. (1990) 'Need for respite care services for caregivers of persons with mental retardation.' *American Journal on Mental Retardation 94*, 638–648.

Grant, G., McGrath, M. and Ramcharan, P. (1995) 'Community inclusion of older adults with learning disabilities. Care in place.' *International Journal of Network and Community 2*, 1, 29–44.

Grant, G., Ramcharan, P., McGrath, M., Nolan, M. and Keady, J. (1998) 'Rewards and gratifications among family caregivers: Towards a refined model of caring and coping.' *Journal of Intellectual Disability Research 42* (part one), 58–71.

Grant, G. and Whittell, B. (2000) 'Differentiated coping strategies in families with children or adults with intellectual disabilities: The relevance of gender, family composition and the lifespan.' *Journal of Applied Research in Intellectual Disabilities 13*, 4, 256–275.

Grant, G. and Whittell, B. (2001) 'Do families and care managers have a similar view of family coping?' *Journal of Learning Difficulties 5*, 2, 111–120.

Gray, B. and Ridden, G. (1999) *Lifemaps of People with Learning Disabilities.* London: Jessica Kingsley Publishers.

Graycar, A. and Jamrozic, A. (1989) *How Australians Live: Social Policy in Theory and Practice.* Melbourne: Macmillan.

Green, D. (2001) *Advice to the Department of Human Services on Supported Residential Services.* Melbourne: Department of Human Services.

Greenberg, J., Seltzer, M. and Greenley, J. (1993) 'Aging parents of adults with disabilities: The gratification and frustrations of later life caregiving.' *The Gerontologist 33*, 542–550.

Griffin, T. and Bennett, K. (1994) 'Peering into the future: Focus group interviews with parents who have a child with an intellectual disability.' Paper presented at the Australian Society of the Study of Intellectual Disability Conference, Tasmania.

Griffith, D. and Unger, D. (1994) 'Views about planning for the future among parents and siblings of adults with mental retardation.' *Family Relations 43*, 2, 221–227.

Hagestad, G. and Dannefer, D. (2001) 'Concepts and theories of aging: Beyond microfication in social science approaches.' In R. Binstock and L. George *Handbook of Aging and the Social Sciences*, 5th edn. New York: Academic Press.

Hand, J. (1993) 'National survey of older people with mental retardation in New Zealand.' *Mental Retardation 31*, 424–428.

Hand, J. and Reid, P. (1989) 'Views and recollections of older people with intellectual handicaps in New Zealand.' *Australia and New Zealand Journal of Developmental Disabilities 15*, 231–240.

Hareven, T. (2001) 'Historical perspectives on aging and family relations.' In R. Binstock and L. George *Handbook of Aging and the Social Sciences*, 5th edn. New York: Academic Press.

Harlan-Simmons, J., Holtz, P., Todd, J. and Mooney, M. (2001) 'Building social relationships through values roles: Three adults and the community membership project.' *Mental Retardation 39*, 3, 171–180.

Harper, D. and Wadsworth, J. (1993) 'Grief in adults with mental retardation: Preliminary findings.' *Research in Developmental Disabilities 14*, 313–330.

Harris, J. (1998) *Working with Older Carers: Guidance for Service Providers in Learning Disability.* Kidderminster: British Institute of Learning Disabilities.

Hatton, C. (1998) 'Whose quality of life is it anyway? Some problems with the emerging quality of life consensus.' *Mental Retardation 36*, 2, 104–115.

Hawkins, B. (1993) 'Leisure participation and life satisfaction of older adults with mental retardation and Down syndrome.' In E. Sutton, A. Factor, B. Hawkins, T. Heller and G.

Seltzer (eds) *Older Adults with Developmental Disabilities: Optimising Choice and Change.* Baltimore: Brookes.

Hawkins, B. (1999) 'Rights, place of residence and retirement: Lessons from case studies on aging.' In S. Herr and G. Weber (eds) *Aging, Rights and Quality of Life.* Baltimore: Brookes.

Hawkins, B., Eklund, S. and Matz, B. (1993) 'Aging adults with Down syndrome. Biological and psychological considerations for caregivers.' In K. Roberto (ed) *The Elderly Caregiver. Caring for Adults with Developmental Disabilities.* Newbury Park, CA: Sage.

Hawkins, B. and Kultgen, P. (1990) 'Activities and adaptation: A call for innovations to serve aging adults with developmental disabilities.' *Activities, Adaptation and Aging 15,* 5–18.

Hayden, M. and Heller, T. (1997) 'Support, problem-solving/coping ability and personal burden of younger and older caregivers of adults with mental retardation.' *Mental Retardation 35,* 5, 364–372.

Heller, T. (1993) 'Mastery and control strategies throughout the life course among families of persons with mental retardation.' In A. Turnbull and J. Patterson (eds) *Cognitive Coping in Families who have a Member with Developmental Disability.* Baltimore: Brookes.

Heller, T. (1997) 'Current trends in providing support for families of adults with mental retardation.' *Alert 9,* 1, 6–13.

Heller, T. (1999) 'Emerging models.' In S. Herr and G. Weber *Aging, Rights and Quality of Life.* Baltimore: Brookes.

Heller, T. and Factor, A. (1988a) 'Permanency planning among black and white family caregivers of older adults with mental retardation.' *Mental Retardation 26,* 203–208.

Heller, T. and Factor, A. (1988b) *Development of a Transition Plan for Older Adults with Developmental Disabilities Residing in the Natural Home.* Public Policy Monograph Series no.37. Chicago: Illinois University.

Heller, T. and Factor, A. (1991) 'Permanency planning for adults with mental retardation living with family caregivers.' *American Journal on Mental Retardation 96,* 163–176.

Heller, T. and Factor, A. (1993) 'Support systems, placement decision making and well being among older parents and adults with developmental disabilities.' In E. Sutton, B. Hawkins, A. Heller, A. Factor and G. Seltzer (eds) *Older Adults with Developmental Disabilities: Optimising Choice and Change.* Baltimore: Brookes.

Heller, T., Hsieh, K. and Rimmer, J. (2002) 'Barriers and supports for exercise participation among adults with Down syndrome.' *Journal of Gerontological Social Work 38,* 1/2, 161–178.

Heller, T. and Marks, B. (2002) 'Health promotion and women.' In P. Noonan Walsh and T. Heller (eds) *Health of Women with Intellectual Disabilities.* Oxford: Blackwell.

Heller, T., Miller, A. and Factor, A. (1997) 'Adults with mental retardation as supports to their parents: Effects on parental caregiving appraisal.' *Mental Retardation 35,* 5, 338–346.

Heller, T., Miller, A., Hsieh, K. and Sterns, H. (2000) 'Later-life planning: Promotion knowledge of options and choice making.' *Mental Retardation 38,* 5, 395–406.

Henderson, C. and Davidson, P. (2000) 'Comprehensive adult and geriatric assessment.' In M. Janicki and E. Ansello *Community Supports for Aging Adults with Lifelong Disabilities.* Baltimore: Brookes.

Heslop, P., Mallett, R., Simmons, K. and Ward, L. (2002) *Bridging the Divide at Transition.* Kidderminster: British Institute of Learning Disabilities.

Hogg, J. (1993) 'Creative, personal and social engagement in the later years: Realisation through leisure.' *Irish Journal of Psychology 14,* 1, 204–218.

Hogg, J. (1994) 'Leisure and intellectual disability: The perspective of aging.' *Journal of Practical Approaches to Developmental Handicap 18*, 13–16.

Hogg, J. (1996) 'Leisure, disability and the third age.' *Journal of Practical Approaches to Developmental Handicap 18*, 1.

Hogg, J. and Lambe, L. (1998) *Older People with Learning Disabilities: A Review of the Literature on Residential Services and Family Caregiving.* London: Mental Health Foundation.

Hogg, J. and Lambe, L. (2000) 'Stability and change in the later years: The impact of service provision on older people with intellectual disabilities.' In D. May (ed) *Transitions in the Lives of People with Learning Disabilities.* London: Jessica Kingsley Publishers.

Hogg, J. and Moss, S. (1993) 'The characteristics of older people with intellectual disabilities in England.' In N. Bray (ed) *International Review of Research in Mental Retardation*, vol.19. New York: Academic Press.

Hogg, J., Moss, S. and Cooke, D. (1988) *Aging and Mental Handicap.* London: Croom Helm.

Holburn, S. and Vietze, P. (2002) *Person Centred Planning, Research, Practice and Future Directions.* Baltimore: Brookes.

Hollins, S. (1995) 'Managing grief better: People with developmental disabilities.' *Habilitative Mental Healthcare Newsletter 14*, 3.

Hollins, S. (2000) 'Developmental psychiatry: Insights from learning disability.' *British Journal of Psychiatry 177*, 201–206.

Hollins, S. and Esterhuyzen, A. (1997) 'Bereavement and grief in adults with learning disabilities.' *British Journal of Psychiatry 170*, 497–501.

Hooyman, N. (1983) 'Social support networks in services to the elderly.' In J. Whittaker and J. Garbarino (eds) *Social Support Networks: Informal Helping in Human Services.* New York: Aldine.

Hooyman, N. and Kiyak, H. (1999) *Social Gerontology. A Multidisciplinary Perspective*, 5th edn. Massachusetts: Allyn and Bacon.

Howe, A. (1999) 'Where do you live? The question of aging in place.' *National Health Care Journal*, August.

Howe, A. (2001) 'Recent developments in aged care policy in Australia.' *Journal of Aging and Social Policy 13*, 2/3, 101–116.

Howells, G. (1986) 'Are the medical needs of mentally handicapped adults being met?' *Journal of the Royal College of General Practitioners 36*, 449–453.

Hughes, B. (1995) *Older People and Community Care: Critical Theory and Practice.* Buckingham: Open University Press.

Ife, J. (1997) *Rethinking Social Work: Towards Critical Practice.* Melbourne: Longman.

Jameson, C. (1998) 'Promoting long term relationships between individuals with mental retardation and people in their community.' *Mental Retardation 36*, 2, 116–127.

Janicki, M. (1990) 'Growing old with dignity: On quality of life for older persons with lifelong disability.' In R. Schalock (ed) *Quality of Life: Perspectives and Issues.* Washington: American Association on Mental Retardation.

Janicki, M. (1991) *Building the Future: Planning and Community Development in Aging and Developmental Disabilities.* Albany, NY: New York State Office of Mental Retardation and Developmental Disabilities.

Janicki, M. (1992) *Integration Experiences Casebook: Program Ideas in Aging and Developmental Disabilities.* Albany, NY: New York State Office of Mental Retardation and Developmental Disabilities.

Janicki, M. (1994) 'Policies and supports for older persons with mental retardation.' In M. Seltzer, M. Krauss and M. Janicki (eds) *Life Course Perspectives on Adulthood and Old Age.* Washington: American Association on Mental Retardation.

Janicki, M. (1996) *Help for Caring – for Older People Caring for Adults with a Developmental Disability.* Albany, NY: New York State Developmental Disabilities Planning Council.

Janicki, M. (2002) 'A dilemma in older age: Measuring self determination with parental planning.' Paper presented at the Inaugural European International Association for the Scientific Study of Intellectual Disability Conference, Dublin, Ireland.

Janicki, M. and Ansello, E. (2000) *Community Supports for Aging Adults with Lifelong Disabilities.* Baltimore: Brookes.

Janicki, M. and Dalton, A. (1999) 'Dementia in developmental disabilities.' In N. Bouras (ed) *Psychiatric and Behavioural Disorders in Developmental Disabilities and Mental Retardation.* Cambridge: Cambridge University Press.

Janicki, M. and Dalton, A. (2000) 'Prevalence of dementia and impact on intellectual disability services.' *Mental Retardation 38,* 3, 276–288.

Janicki, M., Dalton, A., Henderson, C. and Davidson, P. (1999) 'Mortality and morbidity among older adults with intellectual disability: Health services considerations.' *Disability and Rehabilitation 21,* 5/6, 284–294.

Janicki, M., Davidson, P., Henderson, C., McCallion, P., Teates, J., Force, L., Sulkes, S., Frangenberg, E. and Ladrigan, P. (2002) 'Health characteristics and health service utilisation in older adults with intellectual disability living in community residences.' *Journal of Intellectual Disability Research 46,* 4, 287–298.

Janicki, M., Heller, T., Seltzer, G. and Hogg, J. (1996) 'Practice guidelines for the clinical assessment and care management of Alzheimer disease and other dementias among adults with intellectual disability.' *Journal of Intellectual Disability Research 40,* 374–382.

Janicki, M., McCallion, P. and Dalton, A. (2000) 'Supporting people with dementia in community settings.' In M. Janicki and E. Ansello *Community Supports for Aging Adults with Lifelong Disabilities.* Baltimore: Brookes.

Janicki, M., McCallion, P., Force, L., Bishop, K. and LePore, P. (1998) 'Area agency on aging and assistance for households with older carers of adults with a developmental disability.' *Journal of Aging and Social Policy 10,* 1, 13–36.

Janicki, M., Otis, J., Puccio, P. Rettig, J. and Jacobson, J. (1985) 'Service needs among older developmentally disabled persons.' In M. Janicki and H. Wisniewski (eds) *Aging and Developmental Disabilities.* Baltimore: Brookes.

Janicki, M. and Seltzer, M. (1991) *Aging and Developmental Disabilities: Challenges for the 1990s. Proceedings of the Boston Round Table on Research Issues and Applications in Aging and Developmental Disabilities.* Washington: American Association on Mental Retardation.

Jones, E., Perry, J., Lowe, K., Felce, D., Toogood, S., Dunstan, F., Allen, D. and Pagler, J. (1999) 'Opportunity and the promotion of activity among adults with severe intellectual disability living in community residences: The impact of training and staff in active support.' *Journal of Intellectual Disability Research 43,* 3, 164–178.

Jorm, A., Christensen, H., Henderson, S., Jacomb, P., Korten, A. and Mackinnon, A. (1998) 'Factors associated with successful aging.' *Australasian Journal on Aging 17,* 1, 33–37.

Jung, C. (1959) 'Concerning the archetypes, with special reference to the anima concept.' In C. G. Jung, *Collected Works, Vol.9 Part 1.* Princeton, NJ: Princeton University Press.

Kalsy, S. (2003) 'The Birmingham Psychology Service for older adults with intellectual disability.' Paper presented at the Thirteenth Annual Roundtable of the International

Association for the Scientific Study of Intellectual Disability, Special Interest Group on Aging and Intellectual Disability, Volos, Greece.

Kapell, D., Nightingale, B., Rodriguez, A., Lee, J., Zigman, W. and Schupf, N. (1998) 'Prevalence of chronic medical conditions in adults with mental retardation: Comparison with the general population.' *Mental Retardation 36*, 4, 269–279.

Kaufman, A., Adams, J. and Campbell, V. (1991) 'Permanency planning by older parents who care for adult children with mental retardation.' *Mental Retardation 29*, 293–300.

Kaufman, A., Glicken, M. and Deweaver, K. (1989) 'The mentally retarded aged – implications for social work practice.' *Journal of Gerontological Social Work 14*, 93–110.

Kearney, G., Krishman, V. and Londhe, R. (1993) 'Characteristics of elderly people with a mental handicap living in a mental handicap hospital. A descriptive study.' *British Journal of Developmental Disabilities 39*, 31–50.

Kennedy, J. (1989) 'Bereavement and the person with a mental handicap.' *Nursing Standard 4*, 36–38.

Kennedy, J. and Minkler, M. (1998) 'Disability theory and public policy: Implications for critical gerontology.' *International Journal of Health Services 28*, 4, 757–776.

King, N. and Harker, M. (2000) 'Living alone or with others. Housing support for people with learning disabilities.' London: Foundation for People with Learning Disabilities.

Knox, M. and Hickson, F. (2001) 'The meaning of close friendships: The view of four people with intellectual disabilities.' *Journal of Applied Research in Intellectual Disabilities 14*, 3, 276–291.

Koenig, B. (1996) 'Assessing change.' *Aged and Dementia Care Issues for People with Intellectual Disability*, Vol.3. Adelaide, SA: Minda.

Krause, N. (2001) 'Social support.' In R. Binstock and L. George (eds) *Handbook of Aging and Social Sciences*, 5th edn. New York: Academic Press.

Krauss, M. (1990) 'Later life placements: Precipitating factors and family profiles.' Paper presented at the 114th Annual Meeting of the AAMR. Atlanta, GA: American Association on Mental Retardation.

Krauss, M., Seltzer, M. and Goodman, S. (1992) 'Social support networks of adults with mental retardation who live at home.' *American Journal on Mental Retardation 96*, 432–441.

Krauss, M., Seltzer, M., Gordon, R. and Friedman, D. (1996) 'Binding ties: The roles of adult siblings of persons with mental retardation.' *Mental Retardation 34*, 83–93.

Kropf, N. (1994) 'Older parents of adults with developmental disabilities: Issues for practice and service delivery.' Paper presented at the Young Adult Institute 15th Annual International Conference on Developmental Disabilities, New York.

Kübler-Ross, E. (1969) *On Death and Dying*. London: Routledge.

Kultgen, P., Harlan-Simmons, J. and Todd, J. (2000) 'Community membership.' In M. Janicki and E. Ansello (eds) *Community Supports for Aging Adults with Lifelong Disabilities*. Baltimore: Brookes.

Lagay, B. (1973) 'Mental retardation in a rural New England area: The use of gatekeepers to identify retarded persons in the community.' Unpublished PhD. School Brandeis University.

Lakin, K., Anderson, S., Hill, B., Bruininks, R. and Wright, E. (1991) 'Programs and services received by older persons with mental retardation.' *Mental Retardation 29*, 65–74.

Lambe, L. and Hogg, J. (1995) *Their Face to the Wind: Service Developments for Older People with Learning Difficulties in the Grampian Region*. Dundee: Enable.

Landesman-Dwyer, S. and Berkson, G. (1984) 'Friendship and social behaviour.' In J. Wortis (ed) *Mental Retardation and Developmental Disabilities. An Annual Review. Vol.13.* New York: Plenum.

Lantman-de Valk, H., Schupf, N. and Patja, K. (2002) 'Reproductive and physical health.' In P. Noonan Walsh and T. Heller (eds) *Health of Women with Intellectual Disabilities.* Oxford: Blackwell.

Laslett, P. (1989) *A Fresh Map of Life: The Emergence of the Third Age.* London: Weidenfeld and Nicholson.

Laughlin, C. and Cotton, P. (1994) 'Efficacy of a pre-retirement planning intervention for aging individuals with mental retardation.' *Journal of Intellectual Disability Research 38,* 317–328.

Lawton, M. and Nahemow, L. (1973) 'Ecology and the aging process.' In C. Eidsdorfer and M. Lawton. (eds) *Psychology of Adult Development and Aging.* Washington: American Psychological Association.

Lazarus, R. (1966) *Psychological Stress and the Coping Process.* New York: McGraw-Hill.

Lennox, N., Diggens, J. and Ugoni, A. (1997) 'Barriers and solutions to general practice care of people with intellectual disability.' *Journal of Intellectual Disability Research 41,* 380–390.

Lennox, N., Green, M., Diggens, J. and Ugoni, A. (2001) 'Audit and comprehensive health assessment programme in the primary health care of adults with intellectual disability. A pilot study.' *Journal of Intellectual Disability Research 45,* 3, 226–232.

LePore, P. and Janicki, M. (1997) *The Wit to Win. How To Integrate Older Persons with Developmental Disabilities into Community Aging Programs,* 3rd edn. Albany, NY: New York State Office of Aging.

Lifshitz, H. (1998) 'Instrumental enrichment: A tool for enhancement of cognitive ability in adult and elderly people with mental retardation.' *Education and Training in Mental Retardation and Developmental Disabilities 33,* 1, 34–41.

Lifshitz, H. and Rand, Y. (1999) 'Cognitive modifiability in adult and older people with mental retardation.' *Mental Retardation 37,* 2, 125–138.

Lipe-Goodson, A. and Goebel, B. (1983) 'Perceptions of age and death in mentally retarded adults.' *Mental Retardation 21,* 68–75.

Litwak, E. (1985) *Helping the Elderly.* New York: Guilford Press.

Llewellyn, G. (in press) 'Family care decision-making in later life: The future is now.' In M. Nolan, U. Lundh, G. Grant and J. Keady (eds) *Partnerships across the Caregiving Career.* Buckingham: Open University Press.

MacDonald, M. and Tyson, P. (1988) 'Decajeopardy – the aging and aged developmentally disabled.' In J. Matson and A. Marchetti (eds) *Developmental Disabilities: A Lifespan Perspective.* San Diego: Grune and Stratton.

Magrill, D., Handley, P., Gleeson, S., Charles, D. and the SCP Steering Group (1997) *The Sharing Caring Project. Developing Services for Older Carers of People with Learning Disabilities.* Sheffied: Sharing Caring Project.

Mahon, M. and Mactavish, J. (2000) 'A sense of belonging.' In M. Janicki and E. Ansello (eds) *Community Supports for Aging Adults with Lifelong Disabilities.* Baltimore: Brookes.

Mansell, J., and Beadle-Brown, J. (in press) *Person-centred Planning or Person-centred Action? Policy and Practice in Intellectual Disability Services.*

Mansell, J. and Ericsson, K. (eds) (1996) *Deinstitutionalisation and Community Living.* London: Chapman and Hall.

Martin, G. (2003) 'Annual health reviews for patients with severe learning disabilities: Five years of a combined GP/CLDN clinic.' *Journal of Learning Disabilities 7*, 1, 9–21.

McCallion, P. and Janicki, M. (2000) *Grandparents as Carers of Children with Disabilities: Facing the Challenges.* Binghamton: Haworth Press.

McCallion, P., Janicki, M. and Grant-Griffin, L. (1997) 'Exploring the impact of culture and acculturation on older families caregiving for persons with development disabilities.' *Family Relations 46*, 4, 347–358.

McCallion, P. and Tobin, S. (1995) 'Social workers' perceptions of older adults caring at home for sons and daughters with developmental disabilities.' *Mental Retardation 33*, 153–162.

McCarthy, M. (2002) 'Going through the menopause: Perceptions and experiences of women with learning disabilities.' *Journal of Intellectual and Development Disabilities 27*, 4, 281–295.

McCarthy, M. and Millard, L. (2002) *Supporting Women with Learning Disabilities through the Menopause.* Brighton: Pavilion.

McCubbin, H. and Patterson, J. (1983) 'The family stress process: The double ABCX model of adjustment and adaptation.' *Marriage and Family Review 6*, 7–37.

McDaniel, B. (1989) 'A groupwork experience with mentally retarded adults on the issues of death and dying.' *Journal of Gerontological Social Work 13*, 187–191.

McEnhill, E. and Blackman, N. (2002) 'Crossing cultures: Setting up of a national network for the palliative care of people with intellectual disabilities.' Paper presented at inaugural European conference of the International Association for the Scientific Study of Intellectual Disability, Dublin, Ireland.

McGrath, M. and Grant, G. (1993) 'The lifecycle and support networks of families with a mentally handicapped member.' *Disability Handicap and Society 8*, 25–41.

McGrother, C., Hauck, A., Bhaumik, S., Thorp, C. and Taub, N. (1996) 'Community care for adults with learning disability and their carers: Needs and outcomes from the Leicestershire register.' *Journal of Intellectual Disability Research 40*, 183–190.

Mendes de Leon, C., Glass, T., Beckett, L., Seeman, T., Evans, E. and Berkman, L. (1999) 'Social networks and transitions across eight intervals of yearly data in the New Haven ESPESE.' *Journal of Gerontology 54*, 3, 162–172.

Mengel, M., Marcus, D. and Dunkle, R. (1996) "What will happen to my child when I'm gone?" A support and education group for aging parents as caregivers.' *The Gerontologist 36*, 6, 816–820.

Messant, P., Cooke, C. and Long, J. (1999) 'Primary and secondary barriers to physically active healthy lifestyles for adults with learning disabilities.' *Disability and Rehabilitation 21*, 9, 409–419.

Minichiello, V., Browning, C. and Aroni, R. (1992) 'The challenge of the study of aging.' In V. Minichiello, L. Alexander and D. Jones *Gerontology: A Multidisciplinary Approach.* Sydney: Prentice Hall.

Missingham, D. (1999) 'Giving people with intellectual disabilities an understanding of the death of a loved one.' Paper presented at the national conference of the Australian Association for the Study of Intellectual Disability, Randwick, Sydney.

Moss, S. (1991) 'Age and functional abilities of people with mental handicap: Evidence from the Wessex Mental Handicap Register.' *Journal of Mental Deficiency Research 35*, 430–445.

Moss, S. (1993) *Aging and Developmental Disabilities: Perspectives from Nine Countries.* Durham, NH: International Exchange of Experts and Information in Rehabilitation.

Moss, S. (1994) 'Quality of life and aging.' In D. Goode (ed) *Quality of Life for Persons with Disabilities*. Cambridge, MA: Brookline Books.

Moss, S. (1999) 'Mental health issues of access and quality of life.' In S. Herr and G. Weber (eds) *Aging, Rights and Quality of Life*. Baltimore: Brookes.

Moss, S. and Hogg, J. (1989) 'A cluster analysis of support networks of older people with severe intellectual impairment.' *Australia and New Zealand Journal of Developmental Disabilities 15*, 169–188.

Moss, S., Hogg, J. and Horne, M. (1989) *Residential Provision and Service Patterns in a Population of People over the Age of 50 Years and with Severe Intellectual Impairment. A Demographic Study of Older People with Mental Handicap in Oldham Metropolitan Borough. Part 2.* Manchester: Hester Adrian Research Centre.

Moss, S., Hogg, J. and Horne, M. (1992) 'Individual characteristics and service support of older people with moderate, severe and profound learning disability with and without community mental handicap team support.' *Mental Handicap Research 6*, 3, 3–17.

Moss, S., Lambe, L. and Hogg, J. (1998) *Aging Matters: Pathways for Older People with a Learning Disability*. Kiddeminster: British Institute of Learning Disabilities.

Mount, B. (1992) *Person Centred Planning: A Source Book of Values, Ideas and Methods to Encourage Person Centred Developments*. New York: Graphic Futures.

Murray, G., McKenzie, K. and Quigley, A. (2000) 'An examination of the knowledge and understanding of health and social care staff about the grieving process in individuals with a learning disability.' *Journal of Learning Difficulties 4*, 1, 77–90.

Nahemow, L. (1990) 'The ecological theory of aging. How it has been used.' Paper presented to the American Psychological Association at the Boston Symposium on Environment and Aging.

Nolan, M., Davies, S., Grant, G. (2001) 'Integrating perspectives.' In M. Nolan, S. Davies and G. Grant *Working with Older People and Their Families*. Buckingham: Open University Press.

Noonan Walsh, P. and Heller, T. (2002) (eds) *Health of women with intellectual disabilities*. Oxford: Blackwell Science.

Oliver, M. (1996) *Understanding Disability: From Theory to Practice*. London: Macmillan.

O'Malley, P. (1996) 'Group work with older people who are developmentally disabled and their caregivers.' *Journal of Gerontological Social Work 25*, 1–2, 105–120.

Oswin, M. (1990) 'The grief that does not speak.' *Search 4*, 5–7.

Overeynder, J., Turk, M., Dalton, A. and Janicki, M. (1992) *'I'm Worried about the Future': The Aging of Adults with Cerebral Palsy*. Albany, NY: New York State Developmental Disabilities Planning Council.

Parry-Jones, B., Grant, B., McGrath, M., Caldock, K., Ramcharan, P. and Robinson, C. (1998) 'Stress and job satisfaction among social workers, community nurses and community psychiatric nurses: Implications for the care management model.' *Health and Social Care in the Community 6*, 4, 271–285.

Parsons, M., Harper, V., Jensen, J. and Reid, D. (1997) 'Assisting older adults with severe disabilities in expressing leisure preferences: A protocol for determining choice-making skills.' *Research in Developmental Disabilities 18*, 2, 113–126.

Perske, R. (1993) 'Introduction.' In A. Novak Amado (ed) *Friendships and Community Connections between People with and without Developmental Disabilities*. Baltimore: Brookes.

Pierce, G. (1993) 'Who cares for aging carers. Lifelong caring and coping has few just rewards.' Unpublished paper. Melbourne: Department of Social Work, University of Melbourne.

Prasher, V. (1995) 'Age specific prevalence of thyroid dysfunction and depressive symptomology in adults with Down syndrome and dementia.' *International Journal of Geriatric Psychiatry 10*, 25–31.

Priestley, M. (2002) 'Whose voice? Representing the claims of older disabled people under New Labour.' *Policy and Politics 30*, 3, 361–372.

Priestley, M. and Rabiee, P. (2002) 'Same difference? Older people's organizations and disability issues.' *Disability and Society 17*, 6, 597–612.

Prosser, H. (1989) *Relationships within Families and the Informal Networks of Older People with Severe Intellectual Impairment (Mental Handicap). A Demographic Study of Older People with Mental Handicap in Oldham Metropolitan Borough. Part 3.* Manchester: Hester Adrian Research Centre.

Prosser, H. (1997) 'The future care plans of older adults with intellectual disabilities living at home with family carers.' *Journal of Applied Research in Intellectual Disabilities 10*, 1, 15–32.

Prosser, H. and Moss, S. (1996) 'Informal care networks of older adults with intellectual disability.' *Journal of Applied Research in Intellectual Disabilities 9*, 1, 17–30.

Putnam, M. (2002) 'Linking disability theory and disability models: Increasing the potential to explore aging with physical impairment.' *The Gerontologist 42*, 6, 799–806.

Ramcharan, P. and Grant, G. (2001) 'Views and experiences of people with intellectual disabilities and their families. (1) The user perspective.' *Journal of Applied Research in Intellectual Disabilities 14*, 248–363.

Ramcharan, P. and Grant, G. (1997) 'Voices and choices: Mapping entitlements to friendships and community contacts.' In P. Ramcharan, G. Roberts, G. Grant and J. Borland (eds) *Empowerment in Everyday Life Learning Disabilities.* London: Jessica Kingsley Publishers.

Rapley, M. and Beyer, S. (1996) 'Daily activity, community participation and quality of life in an ordinary housing network: A two-year follow-up.' *Journal of Applied Research in Intellectual Disabilities 11*, 1, 34–43.

Read, S. (1998) 'The palliative care needs of people with learning disabilities.' *International Journal of Palliative Nursing 4*, 5, 246–251.

Read, S. (2001) 'A year in the life of a bereavement counseling and support service for people with learning disabilities.' *Journal of Learning Disabilities 5*, 1, 19–33.

Rehabilitation and Research Training Centre on Aging and Developmental Disabilities at the University of Illinois in Chicago. http://www.uic.edu/orgs/rrtcamr/ accessed 7 June 2003.

Reinders, J. (2002) 'The good life for citizens with intellectual disability.' *Journal of Intellectual Disability Research 46*, 1, 1.

Richardson, A. and Ritchie, J. (1989) *Letting Go: Dilemmas for Parents whose Son and Daughter have a Mental Handicap.* Milton Keynes: Open University Press.

Riddick, C. and Keller, M. (1990) 'Developing recreation services to assist elders who are developmentally disabled.' *Activities, Adaptation and Aging 15*, 19–34.

Rimmer, J. (1997) *Aging, Mental Retardation and Physical Fitness.* Arlington: Arc of the United States.

Rioux, M. (1994) 'Towards a concept of equality of well-being: Overcoming the social and legal construction of equality.' In M. Rioux and M. Bach (eds) *Disability is not Measles: New Research Paradigms in Disability.* Ontario: Roeher Institute.

Robertson, J., Moss, S. and Turner, S. (1996) 'Policy, service and staff training for older people with intellectual disability in the UK.' *Journal of Applied Research in Intellectual Disabilities 9*, 2, 91–100.

Rogers, N., Hawkins, B. and Eklund, S. (1998) 'The nature of leisure in the lives of older adults with intellectual disability.' *Journal of Intellectual Disability Research 42* (part 2), 122–130.

Routledge, M. and Sanderson, H. (2002) *Planning with People. Towards Person Centred Planning Approaches – Guidance for Implementation Groups.* London: Department of Health.

Rowe, J. and Kahn, R. (1998) *Successful Aging.* New York: Random House.

Royal College of General Practitioners (RCGP) (1990) 'Primary care for people with a mental handicap.' Occasional paper no.47. London: Royal College of General Practitioners.

Russell, P. (1995) 'Supporting families.' In T. Philpot and L. Ward *Values and Visions. Changing Ideas for Services for People with Learning Difficulties.* Oxford: Butterworth-Heinemann.

Sach and Associates (1991) *The Housing Needs of People with Disabilities.* Canberra: Australian Government Publishing Service.

St George's Hospital Medical School and Royal College of Psychiatrists. *Books Beyond Words.* London: St George's Hospital Medical School and Royal College of Psychiatrists.

Salvatori, P., Tramblay, M., Sandys, J. and Marcaccio, D. (1998) 'Aging with an intellectual disability – a review of Canadian literature.' *Canadian Journal on Aging 17,* 3, 249–271.

Sanderson, H. (2000) *Person Centred Planning: Key Features and Approaches.* York: Joseph Rowntree Foundation.

Sanderson, H. (2002) 'A plan is not enough: Exploring the development of person centred teams.' In S. Holburn and P. Vietze *Person Centred Planning, Research, Practice and Future Directions.* Baltimore: Brookes.

Sandvin, J. and Soder, M. (1996) 'Welfare state reconstruction.' In J. Tossebro, A. Gustavsson and G. Dyrendahl *Intellectual Disabilities in the Nordic Welfare States.* Norway: Hoyskole Forlaget.

Schalock, R. and Alonso, M. (2002) *Handbook on Quality of Life for Human Service Practitioners.* Washington: American Association on Mental Retardation.

Scholes, K. and Scholes, R. (1992) *Home of the Brave.* Videorecording. Melbourne: Edward Street Films (with the assistance of Film Victoria for Disability Services, Department of Community Services).

Scottish Executive (2002) *The Same as You? A Review of Services for People with Learning Disabilities.* Edinburgh: Scottish Executive.

Segal, R. (1990) 'Helping older mentally retarded persons expand their socialization skills through the use of expressive therapies.' *Activities, Adaptation and Aging 15,* 99–110.

Seltzer, G. (1985) 'Selected psychological processes and aging among older developmentally disabled persons.' In M. Janicki and H. Wisniewski (eds) *Aging and Developmental Disabilities. Issues and Approaches.* Baltimore: Brookes.

Seltzer, G. (1993) 'Psychological adjustment in midlife for persons with mental retardation.' In E. Sutton, A. Factor, B. Hawkins, T. Heller and G. Seltzer (eds) *Older Adults with Developmental Disabilities: Optimising Choice and Change.* Baltimore: Brookes.

Seltzer, G., Begun, A., Seltzer, M. and Krauss, M. (1991) 'Adults with mental retardation and their aging mothers: Impacts of siblings.' *Family Relations 40,* 310–317.

Seltzer, G. and Luchterhand, C. (1994) 'Health and well-being of older persons with developmental disabilities. A clinical review.' In M. Seltzer, M. Krauss and M. Janicki (eds) *Lifecourse Perspectives on Adulthood and Old Age.* Washington: American Association on Mental Retardation.

Seltzer, M. (1988) 'Structure and patterns of service utilization by elderly persons with mental retardation.' *Mental Retardation 26,* 181–185.

Seltzer, M., Greenberg, J., Krauss, M. and Hong, J. (1997) 'Predictors and outcomes of the end of co-resident caregiving in aging families of adults with mental retardation or mental illness.' *Family Relations 46*, 1, 13–23.

Seltzer, M. and Krauss, M. (1987) *Aging and Mental Retardation. Extending the Continuum.* Washington: American Association on Mental Retardation.

Seltzer, M. and Krauss, M. (1989) 'Aging parents with mentally retarded children. Family risk factors and sources of support.' *American Journal on Mental Retardation 94*, 303–312.

Seltzer, M. and Krauss, M. (1994) 'Aging parents with co resident adult children. The impact of lifelong caring.' In M. Seltzer, M. Krauss and M. Janicki (eds) *Lifecourse Perspectives on Adulthood and Old Age.* Washington: American Association on Mental Retardation.

Seltzer, M. and Krauss, M. (2001) 'Quality of life of adults with mental retardation/developmental disabilities who live with family.' *Mental Retardation and Developmental Disabilities Reviews 7*, 105–114.

Seltzer, M. and Ryff, C. (1996) 'Parenting across the lifespan. The normative and nonnormative cases.' In D. Featherman, R. Learner and M. Perlmutter (eds) *Lifespan Development and Behaviour. Vol.12.* Hillsdale, NJ: Erlbaum.

Seltzer, M. and Seltzer, G. (1985) 'The elderly mentally retarded. A group in need of service.' In G. Getzel and M. Mellor (eds) *Gerontological Social Work Practice in the Community.* New York: Haworth Press.

Shaddock, A. (2002) 'An unplanned journey into individualised planning.' *International Journal of Disability, Development and Education 49*, 2, 191–200.

Sharing Caring Project (1999) *My Life Book.* Sheffield: Sharing Caring Project.

Shearn, J. and Todd, S. (1996) 'Identities at risk: The relationships parents and their co resident adult offspring with learning disabilities have with each other and their social worlds.' *European Journal on Mental Disability 3*, 9, 47–60.

Silverstone, B. and Burack Weiss, A. (1983) *Social Work Practice with the Frail Elderly and their Families. The Auxiliary Function Model.* Springfield: Charles C. Thomas.

Simmons, K. (1998) *Living Support Networks – an Evaluation of the Services Provided by Keyring.* York: Pavilion.

Simmons, K. and Watson, D. (1999) *The View from Arthur's Seat: A Literature Review of Housing and Support Options 'Beyond Scotland'.* Edinburgh: Scottish Office Central Research Unit.

Simmons, K. and Watson, D. (1999) *New Directions: Day Services for People with Learning Disabilities in the 1990s. A Review of Research.* Exeter: University of Exeter.

Skeie, G. (1989) 'Contact between elderly people with mental retardation living in institutions and their families.' *Australia and New Zealand Journal of Developmental Disabilities 15*, 201–206.

Smith, G. (1996) 'Caregiving outcomes for older mothers of adults with mental retardation. A test of the two factor model psychological well being.' *Psychology and Aging 11*, 1–9.

Smith, G. (1997) 'Aging families of adults with mental retardation: Patterns and correlates of service use, need and knowledge.' *American Journal on Mental Retardation 102*, 1, 13–26.

Smith, G., Fullmer, E. and Tobin, S. (1994) 'Living outside the system: An exploration of older families who do not use day programmes.' In M. Seltzer, M. Krauss and M. Janicki (eds) *Lifecourse Perspectives on Adulthood and Old Age.* Washington: American Association on Mental Retardation.

Smith, G., Majeski, R. and McClenny, B. (1996) 'Psychoeducational support groups for aging parents: development and preliminary outcomes.' *Mental Retardation 34*, 3, 172–181.

Smith, G. and Tobin, S. (1989) 'Permanency planning among older parents of adults with lifelong disabilities.' *Journal of Gerontological Social Work 114*, 35–59.

Smith, G. and Tobin, S. (1993a) 'Case managers' perceptions of practice with older parents of adults with developmental disabilities.' In K. Roberto (ed) *The Elderly Caregiver: Caring for Adults with Developmental Disabilities.* Newbury Park: Sage.

Smith, G. and Tobin, S. (1993b) 'Practice with older parents of developmentally disabled adults.' In T.L. Brink (ed) *The Forgotten Aged: Ethnic, Psychiatric and Societal Minorities.* Binghampton, NY: Haworth Press.

Smith, G., Tobin, S. and Fullmer, E. (1995) 'Elderly mothers caring at home for offspring with mental retardation: A model of permanency planning.' *American Journal on Mental Retardation 99*, 5, 487–499.

Smull, M. and Burke Harrison, S. (1992) *Supporting People with Severe Reputations in the Community.* Alexandria, VA: National Association of State Mental Retardation Program Directors.

Stancliffe, R. and Keane, S. (2000) 'Outcomes and costs of community living: A matched comparison of group homes and semi independent living.' *Journal of Intellectual and Developmental Disability 25*, 4, 281–306.

Star (1987) *Retirement: Where to from What. A Study to Investigate the Leisure Needs of Older People with an Intellectual Disability.* Collingwood, Victoria: Star.

Stehlik, D. (1997) 'Learning to be "consumers" of community care: Older parents and policy discourse.' In M. Caltabiano, R. Hill and R. Frangos (eds) *Achieving Inclusion: Exploring Issues in Disability.* Queensland: Centre for Social and Welfare Research, James Cook University, North Queensland.

Strauss, D. and Eyman, R. (1996) 'Mortality of people with mental retardation in California with and without Down syndrome, 1986–1999.' *American Journal of Mental Retardation 100*, 643–653.

Sutton, E., Factor, A., Hawkins, B., Heller, T. and Seltzer, G. (1993) *Older Adults with Developmental Disabilities: Optimising Choice and Change.* Baltimore: Brookes.

Sutton, E., Heller, T., Sterns, H., Factor, A. and Miklos, S. (1993) *Person-Centred Planning in Later Life: A Curriculum for Adults with Mental Retardation.* Illinois: University of Illinois.

Sutton, E., Sterns, H. and Schwartz, L. (1991) *Realities of Retirement for Older Persons with Developmental Disabilities.* Akron, OH: Rehabilitation, Research and Training Centre Consortium on Aging and Developmental Disabilities.

Thompson, D. (2002) 'Growing older with learning disabilities: the GOLD programme.' *Tizard Learning Disability Review 7*, 2, 19–26.

Thompson, D. and Wright, S. (2001) *Misplaced and Forgotten: People with Learning Disabilities in Residential Services for Older People.* London: Mental Health Foundation.

Thorpe, L., Davison, P. and Janicki, M. (2001) 'Healthy aging – adults with intellectual disabilities. Biobehavioural issues.' *Journal of Applied Research in Intellectual Disabilities 14*, 3, 218–228.

Todd, S. (2002) 'Death does not become us: The absence of death and dying in intellectual disability research.' *Journal of Gerontological Social Work 38*, 1/2, 225–240.

Todd, S. and Shearn, J. (1996) 'Time and the person: The impact of support services on the lives of parents of adults with intellectual disabilities.' *Journal of Applied Research in Intellectual Disabilities 9*, 40–60.

Todd, S., Shearn, J., Beyer, S. and Felce, D. (1993) 'Careers in caring. The changing situation of parents caring for offspring with learning difficulties.' *Irish Journal of Psychology 14*, 130–153.

Todis, B. (1992) 'Nobody helps: Lack of perceived support in the lives of elderly people with developmental disabilities.' In P. Ferguson, D. Ferguson and S. Taylor (eds) *Interpreting Disability. A Qualitative Reader.* New York: Teachers College Press.

Tor, J. and Chiu, E. (2002) 'The elderly with intellectual disability and mental disorder: A challenge for old age psychiatry.' *Current Opinion in Psychiatry 15*, 383–386.

Treanor, B. (1997) 'Parkside leisure, a newly established day support service in Southern Tasmania.' *Network News, Australian Society of the Study of Intellectual Disability 2*, 3–4.

Tremblay, M., Tryssenaar, J., Clark, K., Richardson, J., Watt, S., Rosenthal, C., Tompkins, C., Turpie, I., McColl, M. and Pentland, W. (1997) 'Aging with a pre existing disability: developing a bibliography and curriculum guide for health and social science educators.' *Educational Gerontology 23*, 6, 567–579.

United Nations (1994) *The Standard Rules on the Equalisation of Opportunities for Persons with Disabilities.* New York: United Nations.

Valliant, G. and Valliant, C. (1990) 'Natural history of male psychological health: A 45 years study of predictors of successful aging.' *American Journal of Psychiatry 147*, 31–37.

Wadsworth, J. and Harper, D. (1991) 'Grief and bereavement in mental retardation. A need for a new understanding.' *Death Studies 15*, 281–292.

Walden, S., Pistrang, N. and Joyce, T. (2000) 'Parents of adults with intellectual disabilities: Quality of life and experiences of caring.' *Journal of Applied Research in Intellectual Disabilities 13*, 2, 62–76.

Walker, A. and Walker, C. (1998) 'Normalisation and "normal" aging: The social construction of dependency among older people with learning difficulties.' *Disability and Society 13*, 1, 125–142.

Walker, C., Walker, A. and Ryan, T. (1995) 'What kind of future: Opportunities for older people with a learning difficulty.' In T. Philpott and L. Ward (eds) *Values and Visions. Changing Ideas in Services for People with Learning Difficulties.* Oxford: Butterworth Heinemann.

Walker, A., Walker, C. and Ryan, T. (1996) 'Older people with learning difficulties leaving institutional care – a case of double jeopardy.' *Aging and Society 16*, 125–150.

Walker, P. (1995) 'Community based is not community: The social geography of disability.' In S. Taylor, R. Bogdan, Z. Lukfiyya *The Variety of Community Experiences.* Brookes: Baltimore.

Walmsley, J. (1996) 'Doing what mum wants me to do: Looking at family relationships from the point of view of adults with learning disabilities.' *Journal of Applied Research in Intellectual Disabilities 9*, 4, 324–341.

Walsh, P., Conliffe, C. and Birbeck, G. (1993) 'Permanency planning and maternal well-being: A study of caregivers of people with intellectual disability in Ireland and Northern Ireland.' *Irish Journal of Psychology 14*, 176–188.

Wen, X. (1997) *The Definition and Prevalence of Intellectual Disability in Australia.* Canberra: Australian Institute of Health and Welfare.

Wenger, C. (1994) *Understanding Support Networks and Community Care. Network Assessment for Elderly People.* Aldershot: Avebury.

Wilkinson, H. and Janicki, M. (2002) 'The Edinburgh Principles with accompanying guidelines and recommendations.' *Journal of Intellectual Disability Research 46*, 3, 279–284.

Williams, V. and Robinson, C. (2001) 'More than one wavelength: Identifying, understanding and resolving conflicts of interest between people with intellectual disabilities and their cares.' *Journal of Applied Research in Intellectual Disabilities 14*, 1, 30–46.

Wilson, C. (1998) 'Providing quality services for individuals who are aging in community based support settings: What are the issues for service providers?' Paper presented at the 34th Annual Conference of the Australian Society for the Study of Intellectual Disability, Adelaide, SA.

Wilson, C., Angelo-Forrest, S. and Janes, R. (1997) 'Comparative report by standards and monitoring services (SAMS) on three different agencies that provide residential services for older people who have intellectual disabilities.' Unpublished paper. New Zealand: Standards and Monitoring Services.

Wilson, D. and Haire, A. (1990) 'Health screening for people with mental handicap living in the community.' *British Medical Journal 301*, 1, 379–380.

Wolfensberger, W. (1985) 'An overview of social role valorisation and some reflections on elderly mentally retarded persons.' In M. Janicki and H. Wisniewski (eds) *Aging and Developmental Disabilities: Issues and Approaches.* Baltimore: Brookes.

Wood, B. (1993) 'Planning for the transfer of care: Social and psychological issues.' In K. Roberto (ed) *The Elderly Caregiver: Caring for Adults with Developmental Disabilities.* Newbury Park: Sage.

Wood, J. and Skiles, L. (1992) 'Planning for the transfer of care.' *Generations*, winter, 61–63.

World Health organization (WHO) (2001) 'Healthy aging – adults with intellectual disabilities. Summative report.' *Journal of Applied Research in Intellectual Disabilities 14*, 3, 256–275.

www.statistics.gov.uk. Accessed June 2003.

Yang, Q., Rasmussen, S. and Friedman, J. (2002) 'Mortality associated with Down syndrome in the USA from 1983 to 1997: A population based study.' *The Lancet 359*, 9311, 1019–1025.

Zigman, W. (1997) 'The epidemiology of Alzheimer disease in intellectual disability: Results and recommendations from an international conference.' *Journal of Intellectual Disability Research 41*, 1, 76–80.

Zigman, W., Seltzer, G. and Silverman, W. (1994) 'Behavioral and mental health changes associated with aging in adults with mental retardation.' In M. Seltzer, M. Krauss and M. Janicki (eds) *Lifecourse perspectives on adulthood and old age.* Washington: AAMR.

Subject Index

Author Index